PORTRAIT

of a Border City
BROWNSVILLE, TEXAS

By
William L. Adams
and
Anthony K. Knopp

EAKIN PRESS ★ Austin, Texas

FIRST EDITION

Copyright © 1997
By William L. Adams and
Anthony K. Knopp

Published in the United States of America
By Eakin Press
An Imprint of Sunbelt Media, Inc.
P.O. Drawer 90159   ★   Austin, TX 78709-0159

ALL RIGHTS RESERVED. No part of this book may be reproduced in any form without written permission from the publisher, except for brief passages included in a review appearing in a newspaper or magazine.

ISBN 1-57168-174-4

Library of Congress Cataloging-in-Publication Data

Adams, William L., 1946–
    Portrait of a border city : Brownsville, Texas / by William L. Adams and Anthony K. Knopp.
        p.   cm.
    Includes bibliographical references and index.
    ISBN 1-57168-174-4
    1. Brownsville (Tex.) — History. 2. Brownsville (Tex.) — Description and travel. 3. Brownsville (Tex.) — Biography. I. Knopp, Anthony K., 1940–. II. Title.
F394.B88A32 1997
976.4'495--dc21 97-15371
                                        CIP

To

Roselyn, Alma and Bennie

Resacas or ox-bow lakes are ancient meanders of the Rio Grande that became cut-off from the river's main channel. "Approximately two dozen of these resacas grace Brownsville, and lots with resaca frontages are Brownsville's most sought after real estate." Shown here is the Fort Brown Resaca. The Fort Brown Hotel is in mid-photo and a small portion of the UT-Brownsville campus appears to the left. The metal warehouses of the old Brownsville Cotton Compress at top left were torn down in January 1996 to make room for university expansion.

Contents

Preface

This project originated as an effort to update former colleague Russell Richardson's *A Citizen's Guide to Government and Politics in Brownsville*, but soon took on a life of its own. We wanted our fellow "Brownsvillains" or "Brownsvillites" to see our city the way we saw it . . . and to try to explain the unique features of our community to those who have preconceived notions about "dusty little border towns." Neither of us are Brownsville natives, but while that can be a limiting factor in the temporal sense of the community, it can also provide a degree of external perspective. Certainly, we did not attempt to write an exposé; we have made an honest attempt to report and analyze. We did not seek to offend anyone, and those who disagree with our views are free to provide their own version. We hope that readers will gain an appreciation for Brownsville, warts and all, and understand our affection for and enjoyment of our city.

There are a number of people we want to thank for their help. Foremost of these is Dr. Bennie Walthall, a petroleum geologist who retired to Brownsville and who, when he learned of the project, volunteered to financially underwrite it to whatever extent necessary for us to "do it right." We hope we have done so, and that this book at least partially justifies Bennie's generosity. Limited financial support (but unlimited moral support) was also provided by our mother institution, the University of Texas at Brownsville, and for this we thank Department Chairman Robert Angell, Graduate Studies Director Chuck Comeaux, Dean Tony Zavaleta, Vice President Phillip Kendall, and President Juliet Garcia.

As neither of us authors is computer literate, and this may very well be the last book in America written entirely in longhand, we owe a special debt to the Social Science Department's office staff who had to decipher our scribblings and make the computer entries. Our principal thanks go to our department's delightful secretary, Carmen Gonzalez, but also to Work Studies Edgar Cerda, Georgina Gonzalez, Carlos Jaramillo, Richard Martinez, and Emilia Taylor.

Russell Adams, Fred Garza, and Joel Tovar assisted us in preparing and conducting the various surveys, while Roselyn Adams and Alma Knopp proofread large sections of the manuscript and offered useful criticism. The book's lovely photographs were shot by Annette and Bill Landry of Landry Studio, and by Jose Duarte of the University's media center. The book's superb cover was a gift from our friend — Brownsville's foremost artist — Don Breeden.

Finally, we have to thank a number of Brownsvillites for their time and interest in furthering our project. Nearly a hundred of our fellow residents agreed to be interviewed over the course of the past two years, and preparing the first-person vignettes that introduce each of our chapters required us to cling like limpets to our subjects and follow them around, sometimes for hours on end. For cheerfully subjecting themselves to our observation — for sharing their work lives with us — we are heartily grateful to our friend Manuel Alcocer of Eaton Corporation, shrimper Dolores Dominguez, Capt. Jim Franceschi of the Brazos Santiago Pass Pilots Association, officers Arturo Mena and Robert Nieto of the Brownsville Police Department, and engineer Pat Metzler of Union Pacific Railways.

WILLIAM L. ADAMS AND ANTHONY K. KNOPP
May 1997

CHAPTER 1

Over Brownsville

I have just driven up to the old Pan Am building at the air-port. I crunch across the gravel of the parking lot, pick my way through a dozen Asian males milling about at the foot of the external stairway, and walk up to the second floor offices of Southwind Aviation where I pay down $46.65 for a flight over Brownsville I had booked two hours previously. I was supposed to have paid $60.18 for two persons, but my partner, Tony Knopp, who had been acting "funny" ever since I suggested the flight, backed out at the last minute. So, instead of requiring a four-seater, a cheaper two-seater will do. There will be just the pilot-instructor and myself. Money paid, the secretary introduces me to my pilot — 23-year-old Ohioan Paul Selby, one of those clean-cut, medium-built, competent-looking types. He is neatly dressed, even to the point of a tie — a nice touch, no doubt intended to inspire confidence in skittish passengers. He speaks with a soft Midwestern drawl.

He hands me a headset, and we walk out to the tarmac. By way of conversation I ask him if he ever worries that the pilots he trains are "aspiring drug runners." No, Southwind has a contract with the Indonesian government to conduct initial flight training for young men destined for Indonesia's national airline (Garuda), which, of course, accounts for the Asians at the stair-

way. They make up the bulk of the trainees. As for the Mexicans he trains: "I don't know what they do when they leave here."

We arrive at our plane, a discouragingly dinky affair — a Piper Tomahawk. We scramble up the wings and crawl in. We both have a steering wheel and right and left brake pedals before us. We put on our headsets to insure we can hear each other and the control tower. The last thing he says before starting the plane is that he doesn't expect any trouble, but should we go down, "if either one of us is conscious, he'll drag the other one out. Right?" I have no reply.

We hurtle down the runway and at 70 mph lift off, soar. In moments the horizon recedes dramatically to twenty miles' distance or more. And the land is so green! The effect of Tropical Storm "Gabriel" that dumped five inches of rain on our drought-ridden area just a few days before. "Where to?" Paul asks, and I tell him to head for the Rio Grande and follow it upriver so that we pass directly between Brownsville and Matamoros. I want to get a bird's eye view of the two cities — an impression of the physical differences of the two cities.

As we approach the river, Paul says, "You can see the wetbacks coming across right now." Sure enough, far below us in the farm land east of Brownsville, a drama in miniature is being played out. A lone male is in mid-river. You can tell the crossing isn't an easy one. He's waist deep in the swift, rain-swollen river, and he's sort of hunched over with his arms outstretched for balance — like a tight-rope walker carefully feeling out each step. He's wearing a black T-shirt and carrying nothing. He must hear the drone of the plane, but I don't see him look up. His whole attention is devoted to the river that's trying to pull him down. I hear Paul's voice in my headset: "Sometimes you see a whole crap load of 'em coming across together." I say nothing, but I'm immediately aware of a gulf between Paul, a Midwesterner, and myself, a Brownsvillite of ten-years' standing. I've never heard any Brownsvillite — or any Texan for that matter — whatever his views on illegals, dismiss these people in such pejorative terms.

We continue upriver towards the twin cities, flying right above the border and sometimes nicking Mexican air space as we fly as the crow flies and cut across the meanders of the river. Paul says the Mexican air controllers at Matamoros airport will have us on their radar screens and will "squawk" if we infringe too deeply. We bisect the two cities. Matamoros hulks large on our left — far, far and away the larger city. Dense block after dense block, a nearly unrelieved grid of gray-brown city blocks. Almost no green areas. We fly high over Gateway International Bridge, clogged with toy trucks and cars that are backed up for blocks into Matamoros. Snaking through the western side of the city is a toy train pulled by a blue locomotive. At the western edge of the city, the silver-gray slabs of factory roofs at the General Motors complex and FINSA industrial park.

We bank hard right and are over Brownsville, almost insignificant compared to its twin. It's a much more scattered city with sporadic clumps of housing, factories, stores. The bulk of the city area is taken up with green, big green yards, green parks. Even the water of the resacas is green. We fly down Boca Chica Boulevard from end to end. We fly to the zoo and then spiral down to it in a tight, right-hand turn. It's strikingly pretty, perhaps the prettiest site in the city. Dense foliage, intricate pathways and bridges, its many tiny islands marooning different species: monkeys, elephants, bears.

We set off for the Port of Brownsville and Paul asks if I want to fly. I start by getting a feel for the controls: right, left, up, and down. At first, the controls seem to over-respond. I pull back on the steering wheel and we climb much too steeply — if I keep it up, we'll loop right over. At the edge of panic, I push the column back and now, of course, we are plunged into a steep dive. Brownsville seems to be hurtling up at me. Once again, I jerk back and up we go. Finally, I coax the plane into level flight. The Port of Brownsville is five miles dead ahead. We proceed. I begin to relax a bit. Paul says — God knows what standard he employs — that I'm doing "good." This is fun. At the port I fly down the north side of the basin, over the tank farms, over the cranes of AMFELS, over the shrimp basin. Not a single shrimp boat is in harbor. Three hundred shrimp boats, and not a single one held back by mechanical difficulties during this, the height of the shrimping season. All are out on the Gulf, which is now well within the horizon being sliced by our propeller. Slowly, slowly, I bank right and fly back up the south side of the Port of Brownsville. A dredging vessel is at work in the lower basin, a tugboat is puttering about, only one large ship is in — a blue and white cargo vessel — discharging or loading, I can't tell which, at the far end of the turning basin.

And so, we head back towards Brownsville. Just before our forty-minute flight ends, Paul takes the controls, and we traverse the sky in a high, bold arc above the urban area. Looking down on Brownsville-Matamoros from this God-like height, it is difficult not to wax philosophic. Seeing the two cities lying there below, the viewer really does come to appreciate we are but a single community; our fates but one.

W.L.A.

The Geographic Setting

Brownsville is poorly named. The name is doubly misleading. Visitors and newcomers to the area regularly remark that they arrive expecting to find a drab, dusty, pokey little border village — a vision inevitably evoked by the "Brown" and "ville" in the name. What they are surprised to discover, of course, is a rather lush, green, semi-tropical city that is home to more than 100,000 "official residents" and an estimated 25,000 "unofficial" illegal aliens. Hardly a village. In fact, Brownsville is but the smaller part of a twin-city. Its much heftier sibling is Matamoros, a Mexican city of half a million residents, literally a stone's throw away on the southern bank of the Rio Grande, which laces its way between the two cities.

It is the legendary Rio Grande that has shaped the topography of Brownsville and its environs. The river originates in the San Juan Mountains of southern Colorado, flows south through New Mexico, and then trends generally southeastward in its long journey to the Gulf of Mexico. During the 2,200 miles of its course, its character changes dramatically. First, it is a typically vigorous, rapid Rocky Mountain river, then a river of the interior deserts, and, finally, as it reaches the flat Gulf coastal plain, it slows and begins to meander greatly as it seeks out minuscule variations in elevation that will take it to the Gulf and sea level. So distinctive are the physiographic features of the river in its three states that the Mexicans assign the river three names. They call its upper course the Rio del Norte, its middle course the Rio Bravo, and reserve the name Rio Grande only for its lower course where it broadens out and makes its final trek across the coastal plain.

It is, of course, the river's behavior in its lower course that has formed the local area's particular topography. For millennia, the mouth of the Rio Grande has been creeping all over the delta land that appears on maps like a swollen boil on the largely smooth coastal skin of South Texas and northern Mexico. This delta area is dotted with curiously shaped lakes. In the past, the great looping meanders of the river, characteristic of any water flowing over a nearly perfectly flat surface, would occasionally become cut off during periods of flood. The engorged, racing river, like a speeding car failing to make a bend, would fail to turn into a meander and, instead, burst through its bank and foreshorten the channel. The cut off meander would then dry up or, if rainfall and ground seepage were sufficient, remain as an ox-bow lake. These crescent-shaped ox-bow lakes are termed *"resacas"* in Spanish, and so are they called locally. Approximately two dozen of these *resacas* grace Brownsville, and lots with *resaca* frontages are Brownsville's most sought after (and expensive) residential real estate. But, whereas Matamoros and the Mexican side of the delta area have few *resacas*, most having been drained and built upon or farmed over, *resacas* dot the landscape north of Brownville for twenty-five miles — all the way up to the most ancient mouth of the river in the vicinity of the present-day Laguna Atascosa National Wildlife Refuge. Flying between Brownsville and that area, one sees scores of *resacas* or, where they have dried up, dark-green, crescent-shaped smudges on the landscape where trees have clustered to subsist on the run-off water and ground water that collects just below the surface depression of the dried-up bed.

Nowadays, if you were to go to Gateway International Bridge — the main bridge linking Brownsville and Matamoros — and you were to look down at the river, you would not find the Rio Grande all that "grand." The river is damned far upstream by the Amistad and Falcon dams to create irrigation reservoirs and to provide flood control and hydroelectric power, so the river is reduced to a meager forty-foot width for its passage through Brownsville. Nor is the river deep. During most of the year it is no more than knee to waist deep, and there is no need for the illegal "wetbacks" to actually get their backs wet. They haul up in downtown Brownsville and walk around in damp pants and squishy sneakers or, if prudent, wade across in their underwear with their clothes in a plastic bag and redress on the American bank. The river has a coffee-with-cream color, and not too much cream at that. The river is hauling a lot of mud and the raw sewage of dozens of Mexican border towns in the 1,300-mile segment of its journey along the U.S.-Mexican border between Ciudad Juarez and the Gulf. Twenty-two miles east of Brownsville, the Rio Grande dumps its unsavory load into the Gulf of Mexico.

Brownsville itself is connected to the Gulf by a nearly arrow-straight, seventeen-mile-long shipping channel that runs roughly parallel to the meandering and unnavigable river. This shipping channel allows Brownsville to serve not only as home to America's largest shrimping fleet, but also as an important deep water harbor for southern Texas and northern Mexico. The largest source and destination for cargo handled at the Port of Brownsville is Monterrey, Mexico, which lies 215 road miles due west. This inland industrial giant of 3.5 million must rely in part on the Port of Brownsville in the absence of any suitable, comparably-distanced Mexican sea outlet. As a result, Brownsville's streets and highways are daily clogged by scores and even hundreds of 18- and 22-wheelers rumbling to and from the international bridges and border crossings.

Just as the Brownsville ship channel runs parallel to the Rio Grande in the final stage of its journey to the Gulf, a state highway, in turn, runs alongside the channel. The highway and channel pass through usually bone-dry salt pans and tidal flats until they reach the small coastal town of Port Isabel. Here, the highway is lifted over the Laguna Madre ("Mother Lagoon") by a two-mile long bridge/causeway to reach South Padre Island ("Father Island"). This nice symmetry of names is a mere coincidence. Padre Island is named after Father Balli who was granted proprietorship of the island by the Spanish. South Padre is a thin, sandy barrier island that arcs along the Texas Coastal Bend towards Corpus Christi. The island resort community of South Padre Island at its southern tip has gained justifiable fame for its beaches, hotels, fishing and sporting activities, and provides year-round weekend recreational activities for Brownsville and Matamoros residents. However, most Brownsville and Matamoros residents shun the Island in March and April during the notorious "Spring Break" when thousands of obstreperous college students descend on the island to booze, fornicate, and take over the beaches.

Whereas, Mexico lies to the south of Brownsville and the Gulf and barrier island to the east, to the west and northwest lies the region known as the Lower Rio Grande Valley. This is a rich agricultural area that relies upon the irrigation potential of the Rio Grande and the warm climate to assist Florida and southern California in serving as a "winter garden" for the American food industry. Vegetables, citrus fruit, sugar cane, and cotton are produced on the farms and groves of the Lower Valley, and a nearly unbroken chain of cities and towns runs from Brownsville to McAllen, a distance of sixty miles. Running westward and upriver, the sequence is: Brownsville-San Benito-Harlingen-La Feria-Mercedes-Weslaco-Donna-Alamo-San Juan-Pharr-McAllen. Brownsville and McAllen anchor the chain at either end, while Harlingen forms the main link in the middle. This linear conurbation is home to more than a million people (overwhelmingly Hispanic), and is the region which Johnny Carson used to jokingly refer to as "Occupied America."

The climate in Brownsville is semi-tropical. Located near the warm, moderating waters of the Gulf at a mere twenty to forty feet of elevation, and at Latitude 25° 54' North and Longitude 97° 30' West (less than two hundred miles north of the Tropic of Capricorn and the true tropics), Brownsville enjoys a warm climate and a 365-day growing season. No measurable snow has fallen on the city for more than a hundred years, since 1895, to be exact, when an amazing six inches fell on the city. The only other recorded fall was in 1866 when four inches blanketed the area. The mean annual temperature is a room-like 74°. Of course, that's just an average — the historical extremes range from an all-time low of 12° (February 13, 1899) to an all-time high of 106° (March 27, 1984). Generally, spring and fall provide the most pleasant months, months when many Brownsvillites throw open their windows and get by without any heating or air-conditioning, and have delightfully small utility bills. Winter days are also usually pleasant, but occasionally, the warm prevailing south, southeasterly winds off the Gulf will be overpowered by very high pressure cold air masses coming down from the north. These occurrences are known locally as "northers," and they can, on occasion, not often, but every few years or so, drop the temperature to freezing or even below. As a result, citrus farming is "iffy" in the area. Most plants and trees in the area can withstand 30°, most can withstand even 29°, but once temperatures drop to the 26°-28° range and stay there for a few hours, the area's citrus groves and the city's tropical foliage — the banana trees, the papayas, even the palm trees — begin to die. When this happens, a few days later residents will be seen chopping down their dead trees and ripping out their rotting plants and dragging the whole mess out to their roadsides for the city's workers to haul off. And always these residents claim they'll never plant tropicals again — but usually do that very thing.

If there is one "bad" season in Brownsville, that would be summer. Most residents and visitors find it too hot and humid to be comfortable out-of-doors in the daytime. Only the night brings some relief. The summer days usually begin with morning humidity readings right around ninety percent; this trails off to about sixty percent by mid-afternoon. Anyone exerting himself out-of-doors will sweat buckets and need to take liquids frequently. However, Don Ocker, a meteorologist representing the National Weather Bureau in Brownsville, believes the bad reputation of Brownsville's summers is largely undeserved. He says that the summers are worse (hotter and stickier) in other southern cities in which he has served, like Houston, Galveston, New Orleans, Jackson, and Key West, Florida. In fact, Ocker claims, "Summers in Brownsville are more comfortable than almost anywhere else in the Southeast." Well, maybe.

As for rainfall, Brownsville's annual average is 27 inches. September is the wettest month with a 6.0 inch average, while March is the driest with 0.53 inches. The 27-inch average total would seem quite adequate to sustain healthy vegetation, but it must be remembered that Brownsville's hot climate and pervasive sunshine (220 days average per year) result in very high evaporation rates. Twenty-seven inches of rainfall would be quite ample to sustain crops and plants in cooler, cloudier regions, but in South Texas, this is not sufficient to sustain anything more than drought-tolerant cacti, mesquite, and brush — a native vegetation known as "chaparral savanna." It is only by tapping the Rio Grande for field irrigation and lawn watering that Brownsville and the Lower Rio Grande Valley maintain their lush appearance.   W.L.A.

CHAPTER 2

Historian's Catnip: At the Battle of Palo Alto

I knew that local historians would be excited. I was excited! The re-enactors were coming to town, but we weren't supposed to call them that. The event could be the culmination of a lengthy effort to raise community awareness of the origin of the U.S.-Mexican War of 1846 in the Brownsville area. More than a dozen years ago, two local businessmen, Walter Plitt and Joseph O'Bell, began their quest to have Palo Alto, site of the first major battle of the war, established as a national park. Their efforts came to fruition in 1992, and National Park Service personnel took up residence, but the actual battlefield site has yet to be acquired from the private owner, and there has been little physical evidence of the existence of the park.

Walter Plitt, National Park Service professionals, and local historians had begun to see Palo Alto, the Fort Brown earthworks at the golf course, and the Resaca de la Palma battlefield as parts of an integrated story of the beginning of the war. With the sesquicentennial of the war at hand in 1996, interested parties sought an appropriate means of commemorating those events which had occurred locally. Thanks to Steven Butler and the Descendants of Mexican War Veterans, we had become acquainted with Steve Abolt, a Fort Worth tailor and actor, who was the organizer (and "commander") of the Seventh Infantry Regiment of re-enactors. The original "7th" was one of the units that fought at Palo Alto and Resaca de la Palma. Kevin Young, who I knew from academic conferences on the war, would serve as coordinator for the several re-enactor units. Several of us thought that a re-enactor encampment would draw attention to the sesquicentennial.

Although I was involved with several of the groups engaged in organizing the event, my participation in the planning and organizing was peripheral. Michael Garza, the youthful Brownsville City Heritage officer, had taken responsibility for local arrangements. Since most Brownsville citizens seemed to know little of re-enactors, Garza showed a ten-minute video clip to several of the groups involved. A basic purpose of the project was to include school children, and I helped Walter Plitt's group write a grant proposal for a curriculum development plan for the public schools.

Trouble soon appeared. The U.S.-Mexican War had been a disaster for Mexico, so U.S. organizers of events related to the local aspects of the war had made every effort to accommodate Mexican sensitivities. Despite the passage of 150 years, many Mexicans still saw the war as an example of on-going attempts by the "gringos" to dominate Mexico. Local American organizers emphasized the commemoration aspect of the event — we would not be celebrating American victories over Mexicans. And there would be participants representing the Mexican soldiers. The event was billed as "Soldados and Doughboys: A Sesquicentennial Living History Program." The term "re-enactment" was to be avoided since it implied mock battles (and Mexican defeats).

Despite the efforts to avoid "stepping on toes," some local people remained skeptical. More than one told me that we shouldn't "stir-up the past" here on the border, because it would only remind Mexicans and some Mexican-Americans of the humiliation of the defeat and the ensuing loss of land and status north of the river. Some were hostile to an image of "a bunch of rednecks" pretending to kill Mexicans. Michael Garza began to encounter resistance in a few offices, and there was a momentary concern that public school children would not be able to attend. I put in my "two cents worth," along with more influential types, and the project got back on track. I was convinced that once the re-enactors put on their show, it would raise local consciousness of Brownsville's place in history and alleviate the concerns of some opponents.

And so it came to pass. Fausto Yturria, descendant of a pioneer family, offered his family's old polo field on the Resaca de la Palma battlefield for the encampment. On Friday morning I drove by the site, spotted some tents in the distance, and entered through the open gate. A "cook" bent over an open fire informed me that neither Abolt nor Young were on site, but that they would probably have some free time after the busloads of kids departed in mid-afternoon. When I returned, the camp was in full operation. Snapping away furiously with my camera, I attempted to capture an image of the site 150 years ago.

Walking in from a parking area near the gate, I first encountered "O'Doole's Saloon and Bath House," consisting of a couple of tents, a rough-hewn bar with kegs and bottles, an enormous sheet (buffeted by the wind) bearing the image of two very scantily-clad Rubenesque females advertising the establishment. Soft drinks were available. Straight ahead were the officers' tents, and here I found Cynda Carpenter, a seasonal park ranger at Appomattox, Virginia, preparing the evening meal. In her role as "Major Gatlin's cook," she informed me that she was a former laundress whose soldier-husband had died in "the Floridas," and took umbrage when I asked if she shared Major Gatlin's tent. Cordiality restored, I inquired about the meal she was preparing. The menu consisted of spinach salad, sweet potatoes, snap beans, roasted game hen, smoked oysters "from the Laguna Madre," "a new dish called pico de gallo*," and bread pudding with whiskey sauce. I had a hunch that the re-enactors were eating quite a bit better than the originals did 150 years ago, especially if this were the night before the battle. The cook informed me that she and the other women would be "sent back" if it looked like there would be a battle.*

Steve Abolt and Kevin Young were there now, both in 1840s casual attire. Kevin, portraying future Confederate General James Longstreet, explained that he became attracted to re-enactments when he first saw a Civil War version twenty years ago. Steve got the "bug" from his love of history and fascination with the U.S.-Mexican War, especially the role of the "regular" army. The re-enactors are real fanatics for authenticity, from food and clothing (usually wool), to the sparse accommodations in cotton tents with straw for mattresses.

Passing by other tents, I came upon the sutler, who sells provisions to the soldiers. Actually available for sale to visitors were Bowie knives and army uniforms (reproductions). Behind me was a double row of tents for enlisted men, another cook/laundress, and a cannon. The artillery men told me that on their way down towing the cannon in a trailer, they had been amazed to see one of their trailer wheels passing them on the highway. Obviously, this had delayed their arrival

A short distance apart from the general encampment a Mexican flag fluttered in the wind over the two tents representing General Mariano Arista's army. In fact, General Arista himself was there in the person of Rudy Elizondo, a San Antonio accountant.

Covered with dust from the dry campground, I hurried home to prepare for the evening reception at the Historic Brownsville Museum, a refurbished Southern Pacific Railroad depot. My next-door neighbors, John and Louise Chosy, were handling the reception. The U.S. and Mexican re-enactors were in attendance in full dress uniforms. Awards, plaques, and recognitions were widely distributed, as was the "border buttermilk" (tequila and lemonade).

The next morning I followed my usual route to the university, then turned up an obscure road to the golf course. Alongside the first tee, bewildered golfers observed the Hanna High School Golden Eagle Band strike up a John Philip Sousa march. Folding chairs were arranged before a newly erected flagpole and three markers commemorating the original Fort Brown and the siege that occurred the first week of May in 1846. I took pride in having provided one of the descriptive markers myself. Michael Garza introduced Congressman Solomon Ortiz, Mayor Henry Gonzalez, and other dignitaries, and Steve Butler, president of the Descendants of Mexican War Veterans, gave a brief address in dedicating the flagpole our organization had provided. The re-enactors marched in to raise a giant hand-sewn 1846 flag of their own manufacture. The cannon fired a salute, and the band played both the American and Mexican national anthems. National Park Service ranger-historians and Steve Abolt led attendees on a trek across the golf practice range to the still-visible remnants of the earthworks fort.

The encampment continued through Saturday and Sunday morning to the enjoyment of a steady trickle of visitors. The high point of the whole experience for Steve Abolt came on Saturday when he and some others were brought to the Casa Mata Museum in Matamoros in their uniforms and were invited by the Mexicans to raise their giant flag on the museum flagpole. It had been a great weekend for local history, and I had a feeling that the re-enactors would be coming back soon.

A. K. K.

The Historical Development of Brownsville

The story of Brownsville begins with Matamoros and the Spanish settlement of northeastern Mexico. The story of the discovery of the Lower Rio Grande Valley, however, has been clouded by controversy. For many years, local historians and tourism officials proclaimed the Rio Grande to be the Rio de Las Palmas discovered by Alonso Alvarez de Pineda in 1519. A tablet found near the mouth of the river in modern times seemed to confirm the discovery. Recently, Brownsville's connection to the era of Spanish exploration and *conquistadores* came under the scrutiny of the historian Don Chipman, whose research demonstrated that the Rio de Las Palmas was actually located many miles south in Mexico. *Sic transit gloria* Brownsville. Of course, historian Chipman is *persona non grata* to the local tourism establishment.

In any case, the Rio Grande region was bypassed by the Spanish, who crossed through the area to settle portions of Texas first. Not until 1746 did Spanish officials authorize Jose de Escandon, commander of the military garrison at Queretaro, to begin exploration and settlement of what became known as Nuevo Santander. Escandon was responsible for the establishment of Rio Grande towns such as Laredo, Camargo, and Reynosa. In 1774 (two years before the American Revolution) ten families from Camargo began the purchase of cattle ranches and agreed to establish a town at present-day Matamoros. First named San Juan de los Esteros Hermosos (St. John of the Beautiful Lakes), the new settlement prospered from ranching and the beginnings of an illegal trade with New Orleans, which involved visits from pirate Jean Lafitte. Thus, the earliest epoch of the Lower Rio Grande Valley saw the development of two of the major economic factors for the next two centuries — ranching and smuggling.

Commerce, whether legal or illegal, provided the attraction for foreigners, including Americans, to migrate to the river settlement. Among the most prosperous of the foreign merchants who dominated local commerce was Charles Stillman, future founder of Brownsville. Mexican independence in 1821 resulted in the renaming of the town in honor of independence hero Mariano Matamoros.

The cosmopolitan prosperity of early Matamoros was threatened by the disruptive influence of military conflict during the war for Texas independence and the war between the United States and Mexico that followed. This war, which resulted in the creation of Brownsville, exploded into violence on the north bank of the Rio Grande. In 1846 Gen. Zachary Taylor, acting under orders from President James K. Polk, brought an army into the (South Texas) territory disputed between Mexico and the United States. Arriving on the Rio Grande opposite Matamoros, Taylor began construction of an earthworks fort, portions of which can still be seen today near the Fort Brown golf course. Mexican Gen. Mariano Arista sent a force across the river to intercept an American patrol, and "American blood had been shed on American soil." This incident provided President Polk with his justification for a declaration of war.

The opening of hostilities prompted General Taylor to look to the security of his supply line to the coast. Leaving a small force under the command of Maj. Jacob Brown to hold the uncompleted fort, Taylor departed for the coast. The Mexicans soon began shelling the fort, and Major Brown was mortally wounded. Both the fort and the nearby town were later named in honor of the fort commander who lost his life in service to his country. General Taylor, who could hear the cannonading, began his return to the fort, but General Arista's larger Mexican force obstructed the Americans at Palo Alto. Utilizing a mobile "flying" artillery, the Americans fought off a Mexican attack, and the Mexicans withdrew to a stronger defensive position at Resaca de la Palma. The next day advancing American forces broke through the extended Mexican lines, forcing a Mexican retreat to Matamoros. Both the Palo Alto and Resaca de la Palma battle sites are memorialized along Paredes Line Road. A few years ago, Palo Alto was named a National Historic Battlefield Site under the auspices of the National Park Service.

Mexican forces soon abandoned Matamoros, and General Taylor occupied the city as he began preparations for his advance on Monterrey. Taylor extended his control along the Rio Grande as far as Camargo (some eighty miles) since river transportation could facilitate the movement of supplies. Merchants in Matamoros soon discovered large profits could be made by providing supplies to the army and by importing untaxed American goods. The advantage to the south side of the river ended, however, when a new American tariff was applied to occupied Matamoros. The foreign merchants sought new opportunities on the north bank, especially after the war concluded with an international boundary at the river.

Despite several rival attempts at founding a new town north of Matamoros, Charles Stillman succeeded by obtaining title (later disputed) to several thousand acres adjacent to the site selected for the relocation of Fort Brown. Stillman and two partners established the Brownsville Town Company to subdivide and sell lots. Within two years, the town had acquired a population of 3,000 and was serving as an entrepot for the trade of northeastern Mexico through the Brazos de Santiago port on the Gulf of Mexico (near present-day Port Isabel). Many of the leading citizens of the new town were merchants who had spent years in Matamoros and shrewdly retained operations in that city. In this manner, they could take advantage of the rise or fall in economic conditions on either side of the new border. Not surprisingly, smuggling continued as a major economic activity for the border towns.

A new source of wealth resulting from the Mexican-American War was the steamboat traffic which continued to grow during the 1850s. Richard King and Mifflin Kenedy, riverboat captains who arrived with General Taylor, formed a partnership with Charles Stillman and established a virtual monopoly of traffic on the Rio Grande. All three partners soon turned their attention to the acquisition of ranch lands, with King and Kenedy founding what became the largest ranch in the U.S.—the King Ranch.

Brownsville's early prosperity was threatened from several directions: Indian raids, yellow fever and cholera epidemics, fire, and disputes over land ownership. The depredations of Juan N. Cortina also played a major role in the disruptions of the 1850s. The legendary Cortina, controversial then as now, was denounced as a cattle rustler and bandit by Brownsville's leaders. To some Mexican-Americans, however, Cortina was a charismatic firebrand who stood up for them against an oppressive Anglo establishment. In any case, Cortina led a violent raid on Brownsville in 1859 and then laid siege to the town. Returning army troops and Texas Rangers pursued Cortina upriver inconclusively. Thereafter, Cortina turned his attentions south, became a Mexican general and military governor of Tamaulipas, and later mayor of Matamoros.

Cortina's American nemisis was John "Rip" Ford, Texas Ranger captain and future mayor of Brownsville. Ford was a veteran of the war with Mexico as well as other south-of-the border military activities. At the conclusion of the Cortina episode, Ford became a major player in the next struggle for Brownsville — the Civil War. He was elected to the Texas secession convention and commanded the Confederate forces that occupied Fort Brown as Union forces withdrew.

Control of Fort Brown and Brownsville proved to be critical as the Civil War progressed. The Confederacy depended on trading cotton for the industrial goods necessary to pursue the quest for independence. By late 1861 a Union blockade threatened to disrupt that trade, but the blockade could not extend into Mexican waters south of the Rio Grande. Cotton shippers soon discovered that they could move their goods through Brownsville to Matamoros and the port of Bagdad and on to waiting ships offshore without interference from the Union navy.

In an effort to plug the hole in the blockade six thousand Union forces arrived at Brazos de Santiago and advanced on Brownsville. As the outnumbered Confederates evacuated Fort Brown, the fort itself caught fire and the conflagration consumed several blocks of the city as well. The cotton trade was not halted, however, as goods were moved to crossings upriver. In 1864 Union forces again evacuated Fort Brown and Col. Rip Ford's Confederates resumed occupancy. Ford led his men in a successful attack that marked the last battle of the Civil War, Palmito Hill, fought over a month after Lee's surrender at Appomattox.

Brownsville and Fort Brown continued to be of military significance as the United States applied pressure to end the French occupation of Mexico. Gen. Philip Sheridan and a large force of veteran Union soldiers moved into Fort Brown, serving to intimidate Mexican forces supporting the Emperor Maximillian. General Sheridan's Brownsville experience prompted him to write, "If I owned Texas and all Hell, I would rent out Texas and live in Hell."

The end of the Civil War saw the beginning of a long economic decline for Brownsville. Charles Stillman left town in 1866 to settle in New York, although he maintained his local business interests through agents. In 1874 Kenedy and King sold their steamboat business to concentrate on ranching interests, but ranchers suffered from extensive rustling to Mexico, much of it apparently organized by Juan Cortina, who became mayor of Matamoros in 1874. Brownsville also was subjected to a variety of natural disasters ranging from a devastating hurricane in 1867 to yellow fever epidemics.

The single greatest blow to Brownsville's economic well-being came with the U.S. - Mexico railroad connection through Laredo in the early 1880s. Bypassed for all significant trade, Brownsville declined into a sleepy border town with a daily *siesta* lasting from 11:00 to 5:00 due to lack of business activity. Ironically, it was during this era of stagnation that U.S. Army Lieutenant W. H. Chatfield produced *The Twin Cities of the Border,* which portrayed a vibrant and prosperous border community.

Chatfield's public relations effort had little impact on Brownsville development. Economic resuscitation finally occurred in the very early years of the new century due to the convergence of two factors: extensive irrigation and the arrival of the railroad. The irrigation permitted the production of citrus and vegetables, and the railroad enabled the shipment of such produce to distant markets. The combination attracted Midwesterners who invested in Valley real estate. Complementing Brownsville's railroad link to Houston was Matamoros' rail connection to Monterrey in the same year (1905). The two border towns were linked by the first international bridge over the Rio Grande in 1910.

Brownsville's return to prosperity was accompanied by an episode which provoked a national furor. In 1906 three companies of black troops ("buffalo soldiers") arrived at Fort Brown. Segregationist attitudes resulted in incidents of ethnic friction and ill-feelings between townspeople and black soldiers. On the night of August 13 shots were fired into the homes and businesses adjacent to Fort Brown. A police lieutenant was seriously wounded and a bartender killed during what became known as the Brownsville Raid. *The Brownsville Herald* denounced the "Dastardly Outrage by Negro Soldiers," and the government removed and later discharged all the black soldiers. The whole episode erupted into a national controversy involving President Theodore Roosevelt and a senate hearing. Many years later, the soldiers were awarded honorable discharges, but their guilt or innocence has never been clearly established.

The Brownsville Raid had little impact on the resurgent growth of Brownsville, but wars did—both the Mexican Revolution and World War I. Although Matamoros was attacked twice (once successfully) by rebel armies, the impact on Brownsville of these battles came in the form of refugees and the occasional stray bullet. Much more significant was the breakdown in law and order on the Mexican side which resulted in bandit depredations on the U.S. side. The Texas Rangers were called in to restore order, shooting first and asking questions later.

Revolutionary violence and uncertainty during World War I had stifled a land boom which returned with renewed vigor during the twenties. Trainloads of prospective buyers were housed in luxurious club houses while agents plied their sales pitches. Brownsville's economy grew so fast that the city's population nearly doubled during the decade.

The land boom fizzled out with the beginning of the Depression, but Brownsville did not experience the full impact of the economic collapse. Shipments of fruits and vegetables continued to rise during the thirties, and the opening of the new Port of Brownsville in 1936 stimulated commerce. The first Charro Days in 1937 marked the beginning of a serious effort to attract tourists.

The agricultural boom continued after World War II but began to level off by the sixties. Fortunately, the Mexican government chose this period to institute a new plan to stimulate economic growth in Mexican border cities. The Border Industrial Program permitted tax-free importation of machinery and raw materials, enabling foreign-owned *maquiladora* plants to take advantage of cheap Mexican labor in Matamoros. Factories and other businesses rapidly developed in Brownsville to supply and support the Matamoros *maquiladoras.*

Accompanying the industrial-related growth was the expansion of tourism focused on Mexico and South Padre Island. The great Brownsville smuggling tradition continued as electronic appliances moved south while illicit drugs headed north.

Massive peso devaluations brought an economic depression to the border in the early eighties. The downtown retail trade, heavily dependent on Mexican customers, was particularly devastated by the devaluations. The recovery of the Mexican economy in the late eighties was accompanied by the symbiotic recovery of Brownsville. Approval of the North American Free Trade Agreement in the early nineties held promise of significant economic growth for the border and Brownsville. A new devaluation just in time for Christmas in 1994 again raised the spectre of economic collapse, but it appeared that Brownsville's economy may have diversified sufficiently to weather the latest storm.

A.K.K.

CHAPTER 3

The Arrival of "God Neptune"

It's late on the Tuesday night of March 5, 1996, when we back our craft, Pilot-V, out of the wharf shed on South Padre Island. In the distance we can hear a muffled roar coming from one of the largest nightclubs in Texas: semi-open air Charlie's Paradise Bar. Thousands of raucous Spring Breakers shout and clap with the band. Drunken hoots are carried over the water on the night air. But there is no merriment among the three gray-haired, middle-aged men on board: Pilot-V captain Charles Sheldon, pilot Jim Franceschi, and myself; we know the open waters beyond the jetties are rough. We round the southern tip of the island, line ourselves up with the navigation markers and head between the jetties towards the Gulf and what promises to be a difficult midnight rendezvous with the Hai Wang Xing — a colossal, 37,000 ton cruiser out of Dalian in the People's Republic inbound with a load of crushed Nova Scotian granite.

Once beyond the protective barrier of the jetties, the craft starts to buck the six- to eight-foot waves, and the three of us get up out of our seats in the blackened cabin and find handholds to brace ourselves. Charles turns the windshield wipers on to combat the spray; dark clouds scud across the face of the full moon. With each rise of the boat, we can now make out the sea buoy at the ten-fathom line two miles ahead as its light perpetually blinks a "short" and a "long," a "short" and a "long"—Morse code for the letter

"A"—international symbol for a port's channel entrance. Hopefully, the Hai Wang Xing *lies somewhere beyond. Charles flips on the radar, and an anchored tanker shows on the scope to starboard, but nothing else. However, just a few sweeps later, and a second, much larger, blip appears; this one at the very top of the scope. This will be our ship:* Hai Wang Xing *("God Neptune") is six miles dead ahead. Moments later, our radio crackles: "Hai Wang Xing, Hai Wang Xing calling pilot boat, calling pilot boat. Are you there?" Jim replies for us, and we begin our convergence. Now we can make out their fore and aft navigation lights and line up for a bow to bow approach. As we draw near, the* Hai Wang Xing *puts herself about, doing her best to use her vast bulk to shield us from the winds and heavy seas. A rope "Jacob's ladder" is dropped over the ship's side and a search light is trained on it. Charles begins to close while Jim and I prepare to go out on the open deck. Jim warns me twice to hold tight to the deck railings and jump for the ladder when our boat's at the top of a rise, and once on the ladder to climb rapidly before the next wave hits. Once that's all clear, Jim says, "Okay. Let's give it a try." We go out onto the open deck and work ourselves towards the pilot boat's heaving bow, gripping tightly to the hand rails. But in the final few feet of our approach, things go badly. We are closing the ship's hull too rapidly, and, at the worst possible moment, the critical moment, an unusually high swell, a ten footer, propels us towards the hull. Jim just has time to shout, "HOLD ON!" I, too, can see in that final instant that we are in for a terrific jolt, could be knocked into the water, and grip the rail with all my might. The pilot boat is lifted and slammed against the wall of the ship's hull. I'm thrown against the rail so hard it knocks the wind from me, but both of us manage to hang on. Now we scramble for the ladder. We've got to get clear before the next wave hits. I jump for the ladder and move up —Jim is right behind. We climb. A crew member waits for us at the top of the ladder and helps us over the side. Once aboard and standing, we shake hands and start walking towards the towering superstructure at the vessel's stern. This huge vessel — the fourth largest ship in China's merchant fleet — with its 30,000 metric ton cargo of granite — is literally rock solid and impervious to measely six-, eight- or even ten-foot waves.*

Once inside the island superstructure, we climb up through six decks until we reach the ultimate level — the bridge. This bridge could serve as a worthy illustration of what the frequently heard term "resurgent China" is all about. All my life I've used the expression "Chinese fire drill" as a metaphor to evoke a scene of utter confusion — near lunatic chaos. And while, in reality, I do not actually expect the control center of a Chinese vessel to be chaotic, with gibbering ninnies rushing about willy-nilly, neither do I quite expect what I find on the bridge of the Hai Wang Xing. *Perfect order. Utter serenity. A vast sweep of darkened bridge sixty feet in width. Uncluttered and immaculate. The thirty-foot long control panel — the ship's equivalent of an automobile dashboard — the ultimate in marine high technology. GPS (Global Positioning System) satellite navigation; continuous display radar scopes with a liquid, flowing effect as imaging is continuously updated; computers and other instruments glow in muted blues, greens and reds, to preserve night vision. Silence, except for the soft hum of machinery and air conditioning. As our eyes adjust to the dark, we can see that only four men are working on this vast bridge: the helmsman standing at the tiny ten-inch diameter steering wheel, an instrument monitor, the second officer and Captain Wang Yu. All four wear cotton jeans or cotton trousers, T-shirts stencilled with the ship's name and corporate logo (DMTGC—Dalian Marine Transport Group Company), and pad about in tennis shoes or those distinctive, cheap-looking, Chinese rope-soled canvas loafers.*

The captain, who speaks very reasonable English, introduces himself and his second officer to Jim and me, and immediately sends a sailor to bring us tea. While we stand and sip the tea, Jim and the captain discuss the vessel's vital statistics: length 611 feet (longer than two football fields); her displacement is 37,500 tons, and she has 30,000 tons of rock on board; her current draft is 36 feet (and since the Brownsville Ship Channel ranges from 41 to 44 feet in depth she will, relatively speaking, just scrape in); her maximum loaded speed is 14 knots (about 17 miles per hour); large rudder; single-screw propulsion; bow thruster. Due to her automated nature, her crew numbers just thirty-one. The vessel is officially designated as a "Self-Unloading Bulk Carrier." She's Bremen-built and just seven months old. She left Nova Scotia eight days ago and has traveled at full speed to Brownsville with no intervening stops. The crushed granite is to be used as the roadbed for the next phase of Brownsville's railroad relocation project. Captain Wang says his ship's self-unloading qualities — principally a gigantic 300-foot long conveyor boom — will allow him to completely unload in twenty hours. He wants to get underway immediately, and afterwards steam for Colombia, where he'll pick up coal and carry it to Boston for the New England Power and Light Company.

Once this information is exchanged, Jim takes control. For the next four hours, he will issue the commands; he will pilot the ship into the Port of Brownsville and berth it. Any mishap, of course, is his responsibility. For his services, Jim's organization, The Brazos Santiago Pass Pilots, will receive a check calculated on the basis of the ship's tonnage. In this instance, the fee will be a hefty $1,600. Jim begins giving orders.

He heads the ship for the sea buoy. He issues a variety of helm and speed alterations in order to get a "feel" for this leviathan before he enters the more confined waters of the channel. Slowly, we approach the jetties, the first of many critical points in the passage. A strong current runs parallel to the coast just beyond the jetties. Once inside the jetties, a ship is protected from this current. The problem is that with a ship of this great length once the forward part of the ship is inside the jetties and screened from the current, the aft portion of the ship will still be exposed and have the current pushing on it. The effect, naturally, will be to turn the ship sideways. Jim has to order constant rudder corrections to counter this effect until he has the whole of the ship safely inside the jetties.

We then make a number of partial turns as we move past South Padre Island, Long Island, and Port Isabel to the Brownsville Ship Channel's entrance. Jim shows me how the navigation lights in the area are assisting him. At each bend and each straightaway, there is a pair of lights set apart from each other. One is on a low platform; the other on a higher platform. Whenever Jim has them perfectly lined up one exactly above the other, the ship is aligned on the correct bearing and the ship advances in mid-channel. Once past that pair of lights, a new pair will pre-

sent themselves to align upon, and so on in our progress up the channel.

Another problem that requires frequent attention is the presence of bays, inlets, and creeks that lie adjacent to the ship channel and feed into the channel. As Jim explains, the ship's bow heading is held in the proper position, in part, by the pressure of the water we displace as we advance. This displaced water is pressed forward and out from the sides of the ship, most noticeably in our bow wave, towards the banks of the channel, where it is then checked and deflected back towards the ship. So long as we are in mid-channel and the banks are equidistant from the ship, the pressure exerted by the rebounding water is equal and the ship proceeds properly. But whenever we encounter a bay or inlet, there is no bank to deflect the bow wave on that side of the ship. This disequilibrium of pressures will cause the ship's bow to nose into these bays and inlets unless Jim makes compensating rudder adjustments.

The passage up the seventeen-mile long channel is exceedingly slow, even though Jim has the ship at full speed most of the time. The reason is, that although the vessel's maximum loaded speed is 14 knots, that speed can only be attained in open waters. In the narrow channel, the rebounding pressure from the channel banks slows us down, as does friction with the highly agitated water molecules in the very thin layer of water between the bottom of our hull and the channel bed. These twin effects exert a gigantic "drag" on the ship, and at full speed we can only make slightly more than 6 knots (7½ miles per hour).

So, while we make our slow, stately advance up channel, I pass some of the time with the unoccupied captain on the open "flying" bridge. Leaning over a railing from our magnificent eighty-foot-high perch atop the superstructure of "God Neptune," we look forward and down at the mammoth, moonlit hull being pushed before us . . . and we talk.

Wang Yu is thirty-three years old, very young to captain such a large and important vessel of China's merchant fleet. Part of the reason for his rapid rise is his excellent command of English, an attribute which many of China's older, more experienced sea captains lack and which limits their utility outside of Asian waters. Yu began his study of English at age six, at the time of Chairman Mao's Great Proletarian Cultural Revolution. As with so many other families of the middle and intellectual classes, Yu's family was punished during this Revolution for real or imagined "capitalist" tendencies and exiled to rural China to work as "coolies" on agricultural communes in order to "get their minds right." On such a commune, Yu began to learn English by a similarly exiled intellectual. Yu continued his study of English when his family was finally allowed to return to home (the city of Dalian on the Liaotung Peninsula in northern China) where Yu eventually entered Dalian Maritime University. He graduated at age twenty and has spent the past thirteen years at sea — the last five years captaining progressively larger vessels. Seven months ago, he and his crew were flown from China to Bremen, Germany, to take possession of the brand new Hai Wang Xing *for their government-owned company.*

Despite its huge size, state of the art equipment, and vaunted title, "God Neptune" is what is known in the maritime business as a "tramp." It's on no regulary-scheduled run and will go anywhere and everywhere its shipping agents can find it cargoes to haul for a fee. Yu has traveled to over 40 nations in the service of his state-owned company and spends very little time at Dalian, his home and his ship's homeport. His long service and heavy responsibilities earn him a $400 monthly salary. He does not own a car; he does, however, own a television.

I ask if he is married, if he has any children. Yes, he is married and has a five-year-old son who he has only seen for a few months of the boy's life. Yu and his wife would like also to have a daughter, but they are prevented from doing so by the Chinese government's famous (some would say infamous) "one child policy." Yu says he would lose his job if he and his wife were to have a second child. It is soon obvious this talk of family is doing Yu no good at all; his Oriental stoicism is beginning to fray. His voice betrays him. We stand silent for awhile looking out at the moonlit hull plowing its way up the channel towards another port, another city that can mean nothing, nothing at all, to Yu. Then he says, "My wife loves me very much." There is a long pause and then, still looking straight ahead, he adds, "But I love her more." I can think of no suitable reply, and his words are allowed just to drift away on the night air.

At 2:00 A.M. we begin to draw near the highly illuminated Port of Brownsville. Deck lights are switched on, and off-duty crew members are roused from their bunks. These hands begin to assemble on deck at the bow, the stern, and along the deck rails. They start laying out the lines — in this case 5-inch thick nylon hawsers — that will be used to moor the ship. To a Caucasian eye, these sailors are nearly indistinguishable. They are, like Captain Wang and the bridge crew, of the northern branch of the Chinese family, and, as such, big for Orientals — taller and heavier than their southern brethren with whom most Americans are more familiar — America's Chinatowns having been populated by South China immigrants. They, of course, have the big, tubular abdomens and stocky arms and legs characteristic of their race. They are young men — the captain says the oldest man on board is forty-five, and that the crew's average age is about thirty. But with their unlined boyish faces and identical, unsophisticated bowl-shaped haircuts, they look even younger. They go methodically about their tasks, pleasant, serious faces when seen from the front, bowl-shaped hair spiraling out from prominent helixes when seen from the back.

By 2:30 we are within a hundred yards of the berthing space the harbor master has designated for us: near the grain terminal on our port side. The fore part of the ship will lie along the grain terminal's pier while our port beam will lie abreast a moored barge. Just beyond the barge is a large barren field upon which our self-unloading conveyor boom can spew out the 30,000 tons of rock — what will be a mountain of rock. On the grain pier about a dozen people wait in the night for us — these are customs inspectors, immigration agents, shipping agent representatives, and half a dozen line handlers.

But we still have another hundred yards to go, and covering that distance will be the most delicate part of the whole operation. The average land-lubber might find it difficult to imagine any maneuvering of a 600-foot ship and a cargo of crushed rock could in any manner be "delicate," but, indeed, it is. The tremendous size, weight, and momentum inherent in such a vessel means the smallest miscalculation could do great damage. If our ship so much as "kisses" the pier, it will likely tear it away or crush it. Fortunately, tall, rangy, fifty-one-year-old Jim Franceschi is just the sort of experienced perfectionist needed for the task. Beginning as a crewman on a New York harbor tugboat, this Italian-American has (except for a stint in Vietnam) spent all his adult life handling and piloting ships. He has an intense, intelligent-looking face that views the world from behind steel-rimmed glasses. He is invariably polite, but it is also quite obvious that he is demanding, not only of himself, but also of those whom he directs.

For the final hundred yards we must cover, he has called up a tugboat, an ancient tugboat as it turns out: the eighty-one-year-old, under-powered Warsaw. *With some disgust, Jim informs me, "The tugboats are the weak link in the whole operation of this port." Jim has also decided to transfer control to the port flying bridge where he can better see the pier and barge he's going to lie the ship alongside. On the flying bridge, a sailor removes a canopy, exposing a remote panel for engine and rudder controls.*

With a hand-held radio, Jim is in communication with the tugboat captain and the shoreline handlers. He has Captain Wang stand at his side to relay orders in Chinese to the ship's crewmen. He begins issuing commands that will go on almost unremittingly for the next thirty minutes.

He has the Warsaw *shoulder in and push on the ship's starboard quarter while simultaneously employing the bow thruster to move the ship sideways towards its berth. This operation is exceedingly slow, but we grow gradually closer and closer to pier and barge. When within twenty feet of the berth, commands become even more frequent. He will order the tugboat to push for ten seconds and then back off. Order the bow thruster on for a few seconds and then order it stopped. After each of these actions, he observes the effect: watches the almost imperceptible drift of the ship. Leaning over the flying bridge rail, totally absorbed (no one dares speak to him), he studies the situation as intently as a chess master studies an end-game move.*

With excruciating care, Jim finally coaxes the ship to within a few feet of the pier, and at that point, begins ordering lines out. The crew members throw thin ropes down to the shoreline handlers. The handlers pull on these small ropes, which are in turn attached to thicker ropes, which finally are attached to the 5-inch hawsers. The teams of shorelinesmen eventually wrestle the hawsers to the big shore bollards and loop them over. Shipboard winches then pull the slack out of the hawsers and the Hai Wang Xing *is secure, at last, to its berth.*

At 3:40 A.M. *the ship's gangway is lowered to the pier, and the shore officials start coming aboard.*

"God Neptune" has arrived.

W.L.A.

Economic Overview

The distinctive nature of Brownsville's economy directly derives from the city's geographical setting, historical background, and population characteristics. The mainstays of the Brownsville economy are welfare, education, law enforcement, tourism, shrimping, transportation, commerce, and the assembly industries of the *maquiladora* (twin plant) program.

The last official U.S. census taken in 1990 revealed Brownsville to be 90% Hispanic and the poorest metropolitan region in America — its only close rivals being the Tex-Mex border cities of Laredo and McAllen further upriver. Per capita income in Brownsville was a mere one-third of the national average. With poverty of that scale, federal and state welfare assistance is naturally a critical factor in the Brownsville economy. A staggering 60,000 Brownsville residents, half the city's population, are supported wholly or, more usually, in part by food stamps (i.e., Lone Star cards), Aid to Families with Dependent Children (AFDC) or other federal/state welfare benefits. Current state and national plans to curtail or eliminate these benefits will have a large impact on the city's economy, at least in the short term.

With nearly 6,000 employees and forty-two schools, the Brownsville Independent School District (BISD) is the city's largest single employer. In addition, the city has ten private and parochial schools and the rapidly growing University of Texas at Brownsville. Together, they make education a bulwark, perhaps the one least effected by the vagaries of the economic climate, to the Brownsville economy. The extraordinary size and importance of the educational establishment in Brownsville is due largely to the unusual demographic makeup of the city. Brownsville's families, which are by and large Hispanic and Catholic, are larger than the national norm. This has led to a remarkably youthful local population. Indeed, over 35% of Cameron County's population, of which Brownsville is the county seat, is under eighteen years of age as opposed to twenty-six percent under eighteen in the nation as a whole. That, according to the 1990 national census, makes Cameron County the forty-fourth most youthful county in the entire nation. When it is also considered that Brownsville's population is increasing rapidly (ranking as the nation's forty-eighth fastest growing urban area in the 1990 census), it is evident that education will remain one of the most important segments of the city economy, and that new schools will need to be added to the system at the current rate of one or two per year.

Because of its twin status as both a county seat and a border city with Mexico, Brownsville maintains a large law enforcement/ criminal justice establishment. It is home to municipal, county, state, and federal courts. It has a host of jails, halfway houses, and detention centers tucked away here and there in and around the city. It supports lawyers, prosecutors, judges, bail bondsmen, correctional officers, policemen, sheriff's deputies, U.S. marshals, private security guards, probation and parole officers, and officers of the Department of Public Safety. It has U.S. customs officials, U.S. agricultural inspectors, officers of the Immigration and Naturalization Service, and Border Patrol. And, because of its key location along the so-called "Gulf Drug Pipeline," a main conduit for funneling Colombian cocaine and Mexican marijuana into the American market, Brownsville has agents of the Drug Enforcement Agency (DEA) and Federal Bureau of Investigation (FBI). With increasing national attention being paid to fighting crime and curtailing illegal immigration while simultaneously trying to expand trade with Mexico in the wake of the North American Free Trade Agreement (NAFTA), it seems likely that the law enforcement establishment in Brownsville, a city where virtually every home and store wears security bars, is assured a healthy future.

Tourism has blossomed in Brownsville and, according to the Texas Tourist Bureau, Brownsville is, next to San Antonio, the most frequently cited destination of tourists entering the state. The

Brownsville Economic Development Council has adopted as its new logo for Brownsville, "On the Border By the Sea," and obviously the city's main offerings as a tourist attraction are the nearby beaches of South Padre Island and ready access to Mexico. And, of course, there is the climate. Brownsville, at 25° 56' N, is the southernmost city in Texas and at about the same latitude as Miami (25° 52' N). As the Brownsville Economic Development Council likes to boast, Brownsville averages 220 days of sunshine a year, and even in December, the daytime average temperature is 63°F. What the BEDC does not mention is that the summers are quite oppressive, far too hot and humid for daytime comfort out-of-doors.

The three main categories of tourists are the woefully behaved American college students who infest the area during Spring Break; the well-behaved, mainly middle-class Mexicans who come for shopping and a cheap "foreign" vacation (and, because of the deep southerly plunge of the tip of Texas, Brownsville is the closest U.S. city to Mexico City and the densely-populated central plateau of Mexico), and, finally, the delightful "Winter Texans." The "Winter Texans," the equivalent of what are termed "snow birds" in much of the rest of the nation, are composed mainly of retirees and farming couples from the Midwest and northern plains states seeking to escape the northern winter. They arrive in the fall to fill up the camper sites and trailer parks, enjoy the mild winter, and head back north in springtime before Brownsville begins to really bake. All three of these groups contribute to the Brownsville economy, especially the last two. However, with the disastrous plunge of the peso which began in December 1994, certainly fewer Mexican visitors will be able to afford Brownsville vacations and shopping excursions.

Shrimping and seafood packing are of declining relative importance to the Brownsville economy. However, the Port of Brownsville's shrimp boat basin is still home to more than two hundred shrimp boats, and scores more dock at nearby Port Isabel. Together, they comprise 360 vessels, and are the largest shrimping fleet in the world. Nevertheless, even though the number of shrimp boats has not declined drastically, the long-term prospects of this industry are somewhat clouded. Despite restrictions on the shrimping season, and although the 1995 catch was very good, there is the specter of declining yields in the future. Shrimpers are also hampered by environmental laws requiring them to use Turtle Extruder

Devices (TEDs) under threat of heavy fines and having their catches confiscated. The trouble is the TED, which is basically a trap door in the net that theoretically allows any ensnared, air-breathing turtle to escape the net before it drowns, also allows many shrimp to escape and reduces the catch. Moreover, since the law also requires the nets to be hauled in at frequent intervals to check for trapped turtles, the whole shrimping operation becomes more complicated, more time consuming, and less profitable. Meanwhile, a coalition of environmental groups keeps pressuring Washington and the ostensibly pro-environment Clinton administration to close down the shrimping industry altogether in the interests of the endangered turtles.

Transportation and trade account for one-fourth of Brownsville's jobs, and Brownsville does have a strong transportation infrastructure. So strong, in fact, is that infrastructure that back in the seventies and eighties, the city fathers took to calling Brownsville "the Crossroads of the Americas." While that label might seem dubiously grandiose and more fittingly applied to, say, Panama City or Miami, there is at least some substance to the claim. A number of transport routes do converge or terminate at Brownsville.

Of greatest importance in Brownsville's transportation network is the Port of Brownsville. Completed in 1936 during the depths of the Depression, the Port of Brownsville was a project intended to attract trade and industry to one of the nation's economic backwaters. The port occupies a large tract on the eastern outskirts of the city and has a seventeen-mile dredged channel providing access to the Gulf of Mexico. The channel is wide enough to permit two-way traffic for ships up to 138 feet in beam (width), and deep enough at forty-two-feet to accommodate most ships, dependent on hull configuration, of up to 40,000 tons. The port's turning basin at the channel's terminus can currently turn ships up to 875 feet in length, and work is underway to extend this to permit 1,000-foot vessels to use the port. Over the years, the principal cargoes handled at the port have varied from everything from cotton to bananas and pineapples, but today the primary cargoes are petroleum products and steel.

Another attribute of the Port of Brownsville is its status as the westernmost terminus of the U.S. Inland Waterway System and the Gulf Intercoastal Waterway. These systems make use of the Army

Corps of Engineers' dredged channels that lie behind the sandy barriers islands, similar to Padre Island, that lie just off shore the U.S. mainland along most of the Gulf and Atlantic coasts. Accordingly, barge traffic from Brownsville can make use of these protected waterways to reach Houston, New Orleans, and thus, the Mississippi basin network, with minimal exposure to the open seas. Fully 60% of the U.S. market is accessible to Brownsville by barges, the cheapest of all forms of transport.

The city's airport, formally known as Brownsville-South Padre Island International Airport, also lies on the city's eastern outskirts, a little south of the seaport. It, too, was constructed during the Great Depression and served as a hub for Pan American Airlines' mail and passenger service into Mexico and other locations in Latin America. Unfortunately, in recent years air passenger service to Brownsville has been greatly curtailed or, at times, nonexistent. The trouble has been that the three main cities in the Lower Rio Grande Valley (McAllen, Harlingen and Brownsville) all have airports while the conurbation's population of one million really justifies only one. Logically, as the middle city in the linear conurbation and within thirty miles of both McAllen and Brownsville, Harlingen is best situated to serve as the region's air terminus. And this, in fact, is what has happened. It is Harlingen's Valley Regional International Airport (note the subtle diplomatic title intended to downplay inter-city rivalry) that has grown into a respectably-sized airport with a fine new terminal served by several major commercial airlines. Brownsville and McAllen, meanwhile, have been left in the dust. But Brownsville's political and economic leaders have not been gracious losers. They have fought back. Despite considerable criticism, the Brownsville City Commission, at city taxpayers' expense, is paying Continental Airlines to offer otherwise unprofitable passenger service to and from Houston. How long the city can continue a costly subsidized service by a single airline to a single destination is anyone's guess, but many Brownsvillites believe that eventually the city will have to bow to the inevitable and accept the fact that Harlingen's Valley Regional is our passenger airport too. Brownsville's airport could continue to serve, as it does already, as the region's primary cargo handling airport.

Due to its location at the very tip of the geographical extremity of South Texas, Brownsville serves as a natural terminus for several state highways and no less than three national highways. The three national highways — all ending in odd numbers which indicate they run vertically (north-south) across the nation — are: U.S. 77 with its northern terminus in South Sioux City on the Nebraska-Iowa border; and U.S. 83 and U.S. 281 with terminal points within seventy miles of each other on the U.S.-Canadian border in North Dakota. Unfortunately, neither Brownsville nor the other cities of the Lower Rio Grande Valley are serviced by the Interstate Highway System. This system, begun back in 1956 during the Eisenhower administration, was intended to connect all U.S. cities with over 50,000 population with the primary purpose (there were several others) of facilitating truck transportation and allowing all American cities easy access to a truly national market. However, since neither Brownsville nor Harlingen nor McAllen reached the 50,000 threshold population at the time, the whole Lower Valley was left unserved by the system— "the largest metropolitan area in the country without an interstate highway," according to Alan Johnson, executive vice president of Texas State Bank in Harlingen, as reported in a *Brownsville Herald* story on May 23, 1994. Valley leaders are hoping to correct this and may soon do so. In the wake of NAFTA, the U.S. Transportation Department is planning a new interstate to more directly connect the U.S. heartland to Mexico. Preliminary planning calls for an I-69 originating in Indianapolis and running from Memphis to Houston and finally Laredo, where it would then link up with the Mexican system. But Valley leaders rightly argue that Laredo already has I-35 and that I-69 should terminate at one (or more) of the Lower Valley cities where it could just as easily feed into the Mexican highway system. This would give the Valley, according to Bill Luker of Texas A&M's Texas Transportation Institute, "a sense of importance and linkage to the rest of the world which would help them overcome a collective regional inferiority complex."

The final component of Brownsville's transportation network is the railroad. Brownsville was first linked to the national rail grid in 1904, and is today served by both the Southern Pacific Railroad and Union Pacific Railroad. The B&M (Brownsville and Matamoros) International Bridge handles both road and rail traffic and allows interfacing with the government-owned National Railroads of Mexico which operates on an identical gauge. It is likely the community will get a second international rail/road bridge by 1998 as the Port of Brownsville is deep in the planning and permit seeking stage with both the U.S. government and Mexican officials.

As with virtually all cities, the real core of Brownsville's economy is its commercial life, its retail and wholesale trade. The city has over three thousand stores to serve area shoppers. Among the city's four most important clusters of stores would be Sunrise Mall on the city's northern side. This enclosed, air-conditioned mall has about sixty-five stores adjacent to U.S. 77/83. To the southwest of the city is the quaintly named Amigoland Mall which musters seventy stores within a few blocks of the B&M Bridge and which is well-situated to serve its mainly Mexican clientele. Running on a east-west axis through the center of the city is Boca Chica Boulevard. This seven-lane monstrosity is your usual urban stretch of burger joints, pizza franchises, Jiffy Lubes, Wal-marts, and strip malls. Hideous, of course, but apparently essential and inevitable. A completely different shopping experience can be found in the old downtown. Situated hard up on the banks of the Rio Grande directly opposite Matamoros, this twenty to thirty city block area is the historic core of Brownsville and has to be one of the more unique downtowns in America. It is mainly geared to serving Mexican shoppers from "across" who daily stream over nearby Gateway International Bridge by foot, car, or taxi, with string bags in hand, to buy groceries, clothes, household items, appliances, and whatever else Mexican buyers perceive to be better bargains or better quality American wares.

Stepping into downtown Brownsville is, in many ways, like stepping into the past. Small stores with narrow frontages run back into old brick buildings. Shops downstairs; storage rooms, offices, tiny apartments for the poor or elderly upstairs. Often the stores have old hardwood floors that creak as you walk across them. Goods in abundance set out on wooden tables. Few chains or franchises here with marketing experts to lay out goods in a sleek professional style. Instead, individual merchants with individual tastes on how to display merchandise — some good, but far more marvelously tacky. Store with a twelve-foot frontage. Store window: bridal gown on a blue-eyed mannequin with a chipped nose; children's clothes attached on a wire with wooden clothes pins; Hong Kong toys — plastic pail and spade, a tin jet, police car with star on top, a Barbie doll knock off — perfectly laid out in a perfectly straight line; next, another perfect line of men's watches, ladies watches, children's watches and hunting knives with bone handles. Next door, used clothes. A table of girls' shorts piled high, some dribbling off onto the floor. A table of dresses. A bin of jeans. On the floor a two-foot-high pile of women's sandals — all sizes, all styles — with a woman and child picking through them trying to find a match. To her right, another volcanic cone of sneakers — all sizes, all styles, all degrees of wear. But make no mistake, shopping in downtown Brownsville is fun. It is an experience. Virtually any item wished for, of any quality, can be obtained, and the prices are usually right. Best of all, every store has its own ambiance.

As recently as 1994, the downtown retail area was thriving. The main streets (Elizabeth, Washington, Adams) were chock-a-block with shoppers from morning to night, but the great peso devaluation of December 1994 which saw the peso plunge from three new pesos to the dollar to six to the dollar in a matter of days suddenly made U.S. goods twice as expensive and robbed Mexican buyers of half of their purchasing power. Since then, the downtown crowds have thinned and the merchants are hurting. Between December 1994 and December 1995, twenty-three downtown shops went out of business. This is a shame and should be of concern to every loyal Brownsvillite. The downtown area has real character and its preservation is essential if Brownsville is to escape becoming just another sterile blip on the increasingly pallid map of franchise America.

A final, very important sector of Brownsville's economy and the one the city is heavily banking on to serve as the locomotive of growth and prosperity is the city's manufacturing industry, especially the *maquiladora* or, literally, "twin plant" program. Brownsville, on its own and without regard to its location adjacent to Mexico, has certain advantages as a manufacturing site. Most important here would be its status as America's poorest city. Companies can get away with paying as low or lower wages than would be demanded anywhere else in the country. What is more, companies can avoid what they see (but rarely admit) as "troublesome" union and/or black employees, neither of which constitute even one percent of the Brownsville work force. For labor intensive industries, as assembly industries are, these factors argue well for a Brownsville site, even though Brownsville is of considerable distance from the main U.S. markets and population centers. However, recent developments have even enhanced Brownsville's advantages for manufacturers. These developments are the initiation of the *maquiladora* program and the creation of the North American Free Trade Association (NAFTA).

The *maquiladora* program was begun in the 1960s and has grown exponentially since then. What this Mexican-American program allows is for U.S. companies to locate on the border with twin plants: one on the U.S. side (say in Brownsville); one on the Mexican side (say in Matamoros). The U.S. plant, usually the much smaller of the two, musters the various raw materials, components and packaging materials needed for the product and sends them across to its Mexican twin where the product is assembled and packaged (using even cheaper Mexican labor) and then returned to the U.S. side for distribution. At the heart of the program is the two nations' willingness to accept the concept that the parts sent to the Mexican side are held "in bond" on a temporary basis and therefore not liable for paying the usual customs duties when crossing into Mexico for assembly or returning to the U.S. as a finished product. The only duty paid is for "value added," which mainly constitutes labor costs, and since these costs are so low the "value added" tax is correspondingly low. In other words the *maquiladora* plants have functioned very much like a free trade program (much to the dismay of American labor unions) long before NAFTA was signed.

Now, with the 1994 signing of NAFTA, Brownsville's geographic location is even more of an asset. NAFTA calls for a fifteen-year phased elimination of all customs duties between America, Canada, and Mexico. Tariffs on some products have already gone; all tariffs on all products will be gone by 2009. By virtue of its location at the extreme tip of southern Texas, Brownsville is the closest American city to Mexico City and the cluster of urban areas that surround it and which house the vast majority of Mexico's ninety million population and form the main Mexican market. If NAFTA does, as many observers expect, help vitalize the Mexican market, Brownsville and the other cities of the Lower Rio Grande Valley might reap disproportionate benefit. Brownsville might become, as former Governor Ann Richards predicted, "America's front door," instead of its back door.

Of course, such a rosy future is by no means assured. The recent political and economic turmoil in Mexico is going to delay if not derail Mexican hopes of escaping the Third World and emerging as a First World consumer society. At the moment, Mexico is not escaping the Third World; what is escaping is Mexican and foreign investment capital — and new throngs of desperate illegals. This does not bode well for Brownsville, at least in the short term. Moreover, there are some disturbing signs that twin plant owners in the Brownsville-Matamoros area have been turned off by the rising wage demands of *maquiladora* workers adjacent to the border. Some companies are preferring to move their assembly plants deeper into the impoverished interior of Mexico where even cheaper, more willing workers may be obtained. Nevertheless, when all of Brownsville's natural advantages are considered and, indeed, with confidence that sooner or later the Mexican market will take off, Brownsville's long-term economic prognosis must be regarded as favorable. At the very least, it should be able to improve on its ranking as America's poorest city.

W.L.A.

CHAPTER 4

Down and Out in Brownsville

It's 8:00 Sunday morning, the day before Christmas, 1995. The sky is gray and overcast. A "norther" has come through, and the temperature hovers at 40°. I'm ready to go. My wife holds me tight for a moment, and then I slip out through the alley gate so the neighbors won't see me. I start walking. I am wearing reaggedy clothing carefully selected at ropas usadas *and then imaginatively sullied with car engine oil, charcoal ash, and dirt. I have on old, cracked sneakers, two pairs of socks, two pairs of jeans, three shirts, a padded vest, and a coat with a left sleeve that has been chewed up in some kind of a machine. I am also wearing a shoulder-length, Rod Stewart-style wig that I have dyed slate gray. I haven't shaved in five days and brown and gray stubble sprouts from my face. I wear a filthy ballcap. The front of the cap has scenes of blue skies, snow-capped mountains, and a big buffalo. It says "Yellowstone Park." I wear sunglasses. Evil looking things. They are the black wraparound style that conceal your eyes from front and sides and the bulbous, lozenge-shaped lenses are mirrored turquoise. I can see you, but you can't see me. I look like the dickens.*

When I get to the intersection of Expressway and Boca Chica Boulevard, I stake out the traffic island commanding the southbound left turn lane, and set down the battered carry-all

I've been toting. I take out my cup and pencils, and put a cardboard sign with a rope loop around my neck. The sign says: "Can you help a Vet? Pencils 25¢." I start working the cars. At every change of the light three cars are trapped for ninety seconds beside my stretch of the traffic island while they wait for the green left turn arrow. These people have to deal with me. I come to their windows. I rattle my cup of pencils at them. I point to the "25¢" on the sign. It takes several light changes and maybe twenty cars before I make my first hit: a handful of change and they don't bother to take a pencil. I work this intersection about an hour and a half and pull in about $7.

It doesn't take long begging before you learn people fall into one of four basic categories. By far, the most numerous group are the drivers whose faces start to harden up as soon as they spot you. They pretend they don't notice you and glue their eyes on that traffic signal. You shake your cup two feet from their window but they can't see you. You move on to the next car, but they're hunched over their steering wheels staring up at the light too. Faces of iron. Then you've got your folks who do notice you, but go through a little pantomime of making motions towards their pockets or fidgeting with their purses and then shrugging their shoulders and showing you empty, upturned palms. This means that these people would sure like to help you, but they've got no change. From the beggar's standpoint, you don't really mind either of these two groups. In fact, faced with the bums, squeegee kids, and cripples that abound at Brownsville intersections, I go with the iron mask myself. However, from a beggar's perspective, I must say you do feel a little better towards the people who employ the pantomime routine. At least these people acknowledge your existence. But either way, iron mask or pantomime, that's fine, that's okay. But what's not fine, not okay, are the people in the third category: those that laugh. You can see people in their cars talking about you, chuckling, sharing a laugh. There you are, standing in rags in the cold with a cup of pencils, and your situation gives them genuine pleasure. There is evidently something in the juxtaposition of their comfort and your discomfort that amuses them. What kind of human beings can they be? One young man pulls up in his expensive new car that daddy bought for him, and while he waits for the light, he keeps taking little sidelong glances over at me. And he gets a fit of giggling. He puts his hand to his mouth to hide his laughing, but he just can't help himself. He's really tickled. The fourth category, of course, are the people you live for: the givers.

A little before ten o'clock, I leave this intersection and walk a mile to Our Lady of Guadalupe Church on Lincoln Street. I want to work the crowd going in to ten o'clock mass. Unfortunately, I'm a little too late. Just as I'm arriving, I see the priest come around the side of the building and sail inside, a blur of advent purple. The mass has begun. I'll have to wait and work them coming out. I set up on the sidewalk directly opposite the main door where they'll exit. I prop my sign up against my carry-all bag. I set my pencil cup beside the sign. Then I pace up and down for an hour flapping my arms and stomping my feet to stay warm. At last, mass is over, and they start to come out. I move into position, and stand next to my pitiful little display. The first person out is a heavy-set lady in her forties wearing a tan coat. She spots me immediately, and her face begins to work with some strong emotion, but I can't tell what emotion. She comes straight at me and I try to back off — I'm afraid she's going to humiliate me with a tongue lashing in front of all these people. But no, she spreads her arms wide and embraces me in a bear hug. She holds tight for ten seconds and while she does so, she tells me that God will not forget me. God loves me and will provide for me. She gives me $2 and wishes me Merry Christmas. Afterwards, four or five more people come forward and give me money. Some give change, some dollar bills, one older gentleman gives me $5.

I wait there until the parishioners have dispersed, the last person gone. Then I pick up my stuff and walk two miles to the Expressway and Price Road intersection. Here, I again set up on the island commanding the southbound left turn lanes — two left turns lanes — with ninety-second light intervals. There's real potential here. Eight cars will be trapped in the two lanes opposite my island. Also I've learned by this time that I do better if I stay away from the immediate area of the drivers' windows. It's just too intimidating, especially for the women. Their faces just freeze up in iron behind their rolled-up windows. I'm scary looking. I'm six feet tall and although at 160 pounds I'm somewhat on the skinny side, with all my layers of clothes I look much heavier. But more than that, with my long, straggly hair and mirrored lenses, I'm not a figure that inspires much confidence. I look like I might have an attitude. And, of course, there is always that edge of danger that comes any time you confront a hobo: while you are a person with something to lose, he is a person with almost nothing to lose. As a result, lots of cars, far too many cars, avoid the first left turn lane immediately opposite my island. Instead, as the drivers approach and spot me, they edge themselves over into the farther lane so they'll have as much space between me and them as possible. Also many drivers, especially women drivers, when caught in the closer lane choose to hang well back — stay a car length back from where I stand. One timid lady hangs so far back — five car lengths back — that she blocks the U-turn lane that marks the far end of my island. She has cars behind her blocked off and honking, but she refuses to budge. When the light changes she moves out smartly. She wants to be going thirty miles an hour when she passes me.

So, to counter this fear which is eating into my profits, I stop approaching people's windows and shaking my pencil cup at them. Instead, I move back about eight feet from the curbside and stand propped against a signpost. I adopt a more passive, discouraged attitude. I hide my gloves and let people see how cold and red my hands are. I blow on them frequently for emphasis. I hold up my cup of pencils, point to the "25¢" on the sign around my neck, and, when no one responds, I sort of hang my head and let my cup hand droop to my side. The drivers have ninety seconds to contemplate this pathetic sight. I just slump there, apparently staring down at my worn out sneakers, but in fact, my eyes are slanted way over and I'm watching their every reaction from behind my mirrored lenses. I soon learn I've hit on a winner. People start rolling down windows and forking over their cash. Some people take a pencil, most do not. People honk their horns and I come running. This is important. When a horn is honked, you, the beggar, can't just saunter over — that would indicate you don't need the money that badly. You've got to show in your movement just how desperate you are for that money. Consequently, whenever a car honks, I jump like a goosed rabbit. Man, I'm at that window in a flash with my cup. And I'm heavy with the "thank you's" and "God bless you's" too. I always end the transaction with a well-rendered salute — after all I am a vet. If they give a dollar or more, I salute them two or three times like I can't believe my good fortune. This has a very good effect on the other drivers. When they see I'm no threat, but, on the contrary, grateful and probably dull-witted to boot, their iron faces melt and many start honking and rolling down their windows too. Now I'm cooking. Often, I'll score on two or three different drivers during a single light change. The money is really rolling in. I hear a honk way behind me. A black pickup coming through on Price Road has stopped and is holding up a whole line of traffic. The Hispanic driver in a cowboy hat waves me to him. I come running. He tells me, "Merry Christmas, pal," and hands me a fiver. I look at it as though I've been struck dumb and salute him out of sight. Back at my island, the driver's window rolls down on a battered old car without a front bumper. Two youngish Hispanic mothers are inside. The driver gives me 25¢ and tells me she wishes it could be more. I give them a "God bless you," and the window rolls back up. I appear to look away, but, in fact, I'm watching them from behind those wonderful mirror lenses. They're frantically digging through their purses. Just as the light changes, the window comes down a crack and they hand out another dollar or so in change. I'm there to take it.

By 1:00, I've taken in over $40 and decide to break it off. I've got no doubts I could pull in $100 or more if I stayed another couple of hours, but I've got enough. What do I think of these givers? Do I think they're schmucks? Not at all. I admire them. There is no question in my mind that they are our community's best people. People with their hearts intact. People who, when they see a fellow human in misery, respond.

Who are the givers? They're not readily classifiable. It's easier to say who does not give. Young people don't give and rich people don't give. Only one person under 25 gave me anything. No one in a "rich" car gave me anything. The people in the late model Cadillacs, Towncars, Lexuses, and Mercedes Benzes were a complete write-off. They just cast sour glances at you and put on their iron masks. The givers will be the working class, lower-middle class and middle class up to, say, $70,000 annual income. There seems to be no difference in giving rates of Hispanics and Anglos. They gave at about the same rates relative to their pro-

portions in the Brownsville population. Men were more likely to give than women, and they tended to give larger amounts — particularly men in the 45 to 75 age group. These men were possibly veterans themselves of either Vietnam or World War II and may have been responding to the "Vet" in the sign. The single trait that the givers all seemed to have in common was that they appeared to be happy people: people comfortable with themselves; people with a surplus of goodwill who could afford to squander a small amount of that goodwill on a worthless-looking beggar.

Anyhow, shortly after 1:00 in the afternoon, I pack up my sign and pencils and walk a mile to the McDonald's near Boca Chica and Expressway. It's not so much that I'm hungry, but I've been on my feet for five hours in the open, and I need to sit down for a minute and rest and get warmed up. I also have the problem of all hobos: the difficulty of finding a place to go to the bathroom. I enter McDonald's and order their smallest, cheapest burger. Customers and work crew stare. I sit in a corner of the room by myself. Word of my presence has circulated into the cooking area, and some of the fry cooks stand on tiptoe or peer out from behind equipment to check me out. I eat slowly to give myself time to rest and warm up. On my way out, I use the restroom.

I set out going east down Boca Chica Boulevard toward the airport. I have a four-mile walk to the Ozanam homeless shelter on Minnesota Avenue, just outside the city limits. I walk briskly down the side of the boulevard facing the heavy traffic. Everyone that passes gives me a good look, but after awhile I take no notice of them and just watch where my feet are going. Every few blocks, I shift my bag to the other shoulder. After three miles or so, I've moved beyond most of the traffic. I stop to rest at a small streetside park. From this point on, I'm unlikely to encounter any neighbors, colleagues, or students that I know, so my deep disguise is no longer necessary. I get rid of the wig and mirrored glasses and put my Phase II disguise into effect. With my wig gone, my Yellowstone Park ballcap is way too big and sits right down on my ears and eyebrow line. It makes me look stupid. I will now proceed to the homeless shelter, where my wig would have never held up under close scrutiny anyway, and present myself as a slow-witted tramp. I will pitch my speech and actions at about the 70 to 80 IQ level.

Shortly after 3:00 P.M. I draw near the shelter. A soft drizzle begins to fall from the deeply overcast sky, and cars are turning on lights and windshield wipers. It's turning cold. I can see the compound now, a compound surrounded by a tall, chain-link fence. On the side of one of the main buildings is a cross and the words: "When a stranger knocked, the door was opened."

At the locked gate a man comes out of the gatehouse wearing a long, green lady's coat against the cold. I ask to come in. He leaves, comes back a few minutes later, and lets me in. He takes me to an office where Sister Fatima greets me. She is Indian, looks to be thirty to thirty-five, wears glasses, and has a large cross on a necklace. She has one of the kindest faces you'll ever see. The face of an angel. She takes me into an office and sits me down opposite her at a desk. She says she has some questions to ask me and some forms to fill out, but that can all wait if I'm hungry. Food can be gotten for me right away if I'm suffering from hunger. Once it is established that I have eaten, we start on the questions. This could be tricky. What is my name? Bill. What is my full name? William Adams. She asks if I'm sick or if I need medication. She can see that I'm mentally very limited, and she treats me with great tenderness and dignity. She asks where I have come from. I say Oklahoma. She asks where exactly in Oklahoma, but I'm unsure. I spread my arms with palms upward and shrug to indicate anywhere, everywhere, nowhere. She asks if I have a social security number, and I strain my memory to come up with numbers. But no, I don't have the actual card or any identification of any kind. Because of this, she says she has to take a photograph of me "if I don't mind." She pulls a Polaroid out of her desk and focuses it on me. I whip off the Yellowstone Park cap and stare into the camera. The photo develops in a few seconds and she passes it over to me saying, "Would you like to see your picture, Bill? It's a good picture." I hardly recognize the dirty stubbled face with greasy, grizzled hair sticking out in all directions. (I had intentionally worked Vaseline into my hair in the morning to achieve just this effect.) The questions go on, but I have few answers. She asks how I support myself, and I tell her I sell pencils. She asks where I'm going and what I'll do, but I'm pretty vague. I just want to stay one night and then I'll move on. She lets me know I can stay longer if I need to. The questions are about over, but she has one more unpleasant duty. She needs to see everything in my bag. She's very sorry to have to do this, hopes it will not embarrass me, but she needs for me to unload it. Immediately, I drop down on the floor on my knees and start pulling out the contents. Fortunately, I had anticipated such a search and have nothing that could compromise my identity. I pull out a bunch of typical bum stuff: meager toiletries, two soiled towels, a spare pair of dirty socks, dirty pillow case, cardboard sign, spare cardboard and rope, and over a hundred pencils. She says, "Oh, and these are the pencils you sell, aren't they, Bill?" I say yes. And she says, "And you don't have any knives, or drugs or alcohol do you, Bill?" I say no. She has me pack my bag back up and apologizes again for having made me do this.

She then gives me a clean sheet, a pillow case, and tiny plastic containers of soap, shampoo, and a body lotion to put on my skin. Just before I'm led off to the dorms by a helper, she opens the palm of my hand and puts a little present in it "to show you that you're welcome here, Bill." It's a plastic bag with an apple and five candies in it.

A tall, slender, soft-spoken black man shows me to the men's dorm. On the way he points out the men's shower rooms and toilets labeled "Caballeros." Now this is right next to the women's shower rooms and toilets marked "Damas." Looking at me with my too-big ballcap that comes down to my ears and eyebrows, you can tell he doesn't have much confidence in my ability to keep these straight. He goes over this toilet information three times with lots of hand gestures thrown in. "Right toilet. Wrong toilet. Men's toilet. Women's toilet. This one's good. That one's no good." As we move on, it's evident he thinks I'm just the kind of dope who'll still get it wrong.

In the men's dorm eleven bunkbeds face eleven other bunkbeds across a center aisle. The bunk beds are almost all triple deckers, and the space between both decks and beds is very narrow. I'm assigned bed #53, an undesirable middle bunk with just 18 inches of headroom. I put my sheet on the thin foam mattress, put on my pillowcase and hoist myself in fully dressed except for my shoes and coat. I'm exhausted from the cold, the walking, the lying, the constant need to be alert. I nap for an hour.

When I awake, I stay in bed and observe my dorm mates —

the homeless. The room has sixty-three beds, and all but three have people living in them. Their beds are made; their few belongings are stored on shelves behind them. Most of these men are Honduran refugees with a smattering of Mexicans, El Salvadorans, Nicaraguans, and Guatemalans thrown in. There are ten Americans, at the most. Three of these are blacks, the rest Anglos. Aside from myself, there are only a couple of true hobo types — middle-aged men with the characteristic beards and wounded eyes. And one of these is obviously trying to stage a comeback. He's keeping clean, caring for his clothes, talking to people. But there is another one that just lies in bed. Gray beard; seared eyes.

The Central Americans are an interesting lot. A few of this group are in their thirties and forties and the twenty or so women and children who live in the women's dorm next door belong to them. These men seldom smile and show signs of being under considerable stress. They gather in small groups, sit on the edges of beds and conduct serious conversations. No doubt they are trying to figure out where to go, what to do next. Two middle-aged men near my bed carry on a discussion in which several times I hear the word "coyotes" (alien smugglers). But the bulk of the Central Americans are young men in their late teens and early twenties and they are very lively. They have the irrepressible optimism of youth. They laugh, joke, wrestle about. One of them has a boom box and this plays high volume Tejano music constantly. A group forms in a circle between the beds and the members dance in place — one at a time they take turns moving into the center of the circle and giving a display of their most outlandish dance steps. In another circle in the center aisle six youths tap a soccer ball back and forth to one another. Meanwhile, two of the youngest boys — fourteen or fifteen — have gotten ahold of squirt guns and are conducting a running battle all over the room. The music blares.

At 6:00 a worker walks through the room swinging a bell and clapper which is the signal for food. We go into the cafeteria and line up. An orange is handed to each of us from the kitchen window. Supper is usually at 6:00, but since this is Christmas Eve, we're on a special holiday routine. The usual rigid schedule of chores, English lessons, religious opportunities, roll calls, and meals has been superseded. Mass will be at 9:00 this evening with dinner to follow. The orange is just to tide us over.

By 9:00 we have all gathered in the cafeteria for mass. Because of the shortage of men's coats, many men wear ladies' coats or have blankets wrapped around them. We sit at wooden picnic tables with benches. The "padre" arrives and sets up a makeshift altar for a dry mass. He begins by picking up a guitar and leading us in singing a couple of Christmas carols in Spanish. He then gets down to the mass in earnest — his homily is rendered in Spanish, but with a brief summary in English for the benefit of the Americans. The priest is an excellent speaker and the homily is built around homelessness. How there is no shame in homelessness. That Christ was Himself born homeless in a stable and therefore has a special love for the homeless — will not forget them. The priest then signals for everyone to rise. He says that since everyone present is homeless and in extra need on this Christmas Eve, it would not be wrong, it would not be selfish, for each person to pray for His help at this time of great difficulty. As we stand in long, silent, intense prayer — and you can tell that many of the mothers and fathers are praying for all they're worth — Sister Fatima and three other nuns who have come in specially for this mass move through the crowd and place their hands on different people's shoulders. I feel the pressure of an elderly nun's hand on my shoulder. She whispers, "God will help you. You're not alone. Don't give up." She passes on. Am I moved? Oh, yes.

After mass, we have some skits while supper is prepared. Six of the men have agreed to be made up by the women as women, and the results are predictable: the inevitable overdoing of brassiere padding, the shaky performance on high heels. When the skit is over, everyone's anxious to finally have supper, but there's been some foul up. The organization or church that was to supply the tamales for our Christmas Eve feast have not come through yet. We wait and wait. Calls are made. We wait a little longer. Some people lay their heads down on the dining tables. Finally, it's learned the tamales won't be coming after all, and so at midnight, Sister Fatima decides to go ahead with what we have: beans, tortilla chips, sliced pickles and fruit. A cafeteria cart is rolled out, and while the men and children sit, the wives serve us.

It's nearly 1:00 A.M. when we finally get to bed. Sixty men bed down in very close quarters. Foot odor permeates the room.

Most everyone, including myself, wears several layers of clothing against the cold. I fall asleep almost immediately.

At 6:00 I awake. It's Christmas morning. The room is warmer now from the body heat of sixty tightly packed men. The room seems to heave with breathing and snoring. I quietly put on my sneakers, coat, and Yellowstone Park ballcap. I pick up my carry-all and creep out. A gatekeeper in a woman's coat unlocks the gate and lets me out of the compound. It's dark and cold and I have a six-mile walk ahead of me. I tie one of my towels around my head to protect my ears. I put my cap back on. I walk west down Boca Chica, turn south on 14th, then west again on Madison. Deserted streets. It grows light. I love these tiny homes downtown that have just one or two rooms that are strung with Christmas lights and have red bows decorating the doors. Poverty, but no despair.

Finally, I reach Our Mother of Perpetual Help Home. I pour all my begging money, bills and change, into my old pillow case and tie it up with a knot. Beyond one of the Home's iron gates is an alcove with a statue of Our Lady. I pitch the pillow case over the fence and it lands at Her feet. The offerings of dozens of well-meaning, generous Brownsvillites.

Less than a mile to go now. I arrive home. Blue Christmas lights glow. The newspaper lies on the lawn. My family is still asleep. I go inside.

W.L.A.

Welfare

The 1990 census revealed that the U.S. had 284 Metropolitan Statistical Areas (urban areas of over 100,000 population with at least one core city of over 50,000 people), and that of these 284 metropolises Brownsville ranked 284th, dead last, in average per capita income. In other words, Brownsville had narrowly beaten out the McAllen-Edingburg and Laredo MSAs to earn the dubious distinction of being America's poorest city. Naturally, then, efforts and programs to assist the impoverished are of tremendous importance to Brownsville.

At the very bottom of the economic barrel in Brownsville are the individuals who seem to have fallen through society's cracks altogether and may be seen drifting around Brownsville eking out the most meager of existences: the people pushing shopping carts about loaded with aluminum cans or cardboard, the families who pick through dumpsters in downtown alleyways, the human scavengers who root through the mounds of garbage at the city dump, the hobos, urchins, and beggars who congregate at city intersections and underpasses. The stories of these people will vary: some of them are poor Mexicans who slip across the border from Matamoros each day (a society which has no welfare programs at all for the able-bodied), some are resident illegals ineligible for most U.S. welfare programs, some are illegal Mexicans and Central Americans piled up here at the border waiting for the means and opportunity to move further north into America, and others are American hobos who have sifted down to Brownsville from more northerly climes to enjoy the warm climate that allows them to sleep outdoors in parks or in dumpsters and to avoid the strictures and teetotaling atmosphere that is *de rigueur* in most public shelters. And some are simply the poor — the poor the Bible foretold would always be with us, the people who through misfortune, personal limitations, and weaknesses, or some combination thereof, are just not able to provide themselves with life's basic necessities.

To assist these most needy members of the community, Brownsville has a number of "helping" agencies. One of these is the Good Neighbor Settlement House at 1254 East Tyler Street. This charitable organization occupies the old Alvarez family grocery store catty-corner to the old Methodist Church (now the *Iglesia del Pueblo Pentecostal*). Begun by Methodist women in 1953, the Good Neighbor Settlement House now receives funding from the United Way, the First Methodist Church, the Board of Global Ministries in New York and interdenominational support from other churches in Brownsville, including the Catholic Church. Under the guidance of Executive Director Natalia Zapata and long-time Program Director Richard Parker, this forty-three-year-old Brownsville institution serves a free lunch from 12:00–1:00 and a free supper from 5:00– 6:00 Monday through Friday to anyone who presents themselves. Richard says, "We ask no questions," and admits that the majority of the two hundred people fed each day are "mostly hungry people from Matamoros." In addition to feeding the poor, Settlement House has a free clothing program and a program to train adult Down's Syndrome sufferers in reading, basic arithmetic, arts and crafts, and survival skills "so they don't become dormant." The House also offers after-hours tutoring every weekday to BISD-referred homeless children, including children of migrant farm workers, children whose families live in cars, children of working prostitutes. Settlement House also has a home rehabilitation program funded by a private donor who wishes to remain anonymous that annually allows for refurbishing twenty dilapidated homes of the very poor, using the building trade skills of Winter Texan volunteers, some of whom park their RVs within Settlement House's fenced compound.

Another local helping agency is Live Now Ministries, Incorporated. Founder and director Cicely Ratcliff (a modish grandmother who was honored as one of President George Bush's "Thousand Points of Light") operates out of a Brownsville Housing Authority building rented to her for one dollar a year at 556 West Elizabeth Street. Although Live Now Ministries' main mission is to train the underprivileged and, frequently, illiterate poor towards economic self-sufficiency (courses are offered that could lead to careers in janitoring, cooking and the restaurant trade, sewing and garment manufacturing, professional cake decorating, and floral arranging), the organization does also have a food pantry and offers free clothing and counseling to the poor. Moreover, Cicely maintains a registry of generous landlords who have agreed to temporarily domicile homeless persons referred to them by Live Now Ministries.

There are three shelters for the homeless in Brownsville. One of these is the Victory Outreach Ministry at 805 East Madison, whose primary mission is drug and alcohol rehabilitation, but which does offer some limited sheltering capacity as well. Another shelter is the Brownsville Family Center at 815 Arthur Street, which caters exclusively to families, often families fleeing an abusive father. The Family Center can shelter up to ten families at a time, for maximum stays of thirty days. Its funding comes from the federal government's Emergency Shelter Grant Program. But, by far, the most important shelter is the Bishop Enrique San Pedro Ozanam Center at 656 North

Minnesota Avenue. Jointly funded by the Catholic Diocese of Brownsville and the City of Brownsville, the Ozanam Center occupies a six-acre compound just outside the city's eastern limits. It has 124 beds divided equally between a men's dorm and a women's and children's dorm. Residents receive three cafeteria meals a day, and all residents are required to participate in chores and maintenance. Structure is given to each day with set times for waking, showering, bed-making, eating, chores, instruction, religious observances, roll calls, lights out, and so forth. Persons are checked in and out of the locked compound when they have employment or other business to conduct in the city; Ozanam Center is not a come-and-go-as-you-please shelter. Ordinarily, residents are permitted to stay no more than thirty days. Emilio Crixell is chairman of the Center's governing board, and Alex Fuentes is the director.

Back in the late 1980s, the Ozanam Center (then known as Casa Oscar Romero in honor of an activist El Salvadoran bishop slain by a death squad while presiding at mass) was the subject of considerable local controversy. It was accused of being a magnet that attracted thousands of Central American refugees to Brownsville from strife-wracked Guatemala, Honduras, El Salvador, and Nicaragua. These desperate refugees not only filled the shelter's compound, but adjacent fields and properties as well. Hundreds of squalid tents and shanties surrounded the compound and were initially without benefit of latrines or sanitation facilities of any kind. There has been no subsequent inundation to equal that of 1986–1987, but there is no question that Central Americans still make up the bulk of the sixty to one hundred residents normally sheltered at the Center at any given time. However, because the Ozanam Center keeps its gates closed and its residents do not drift about the city, the refugee problem remains relatively "low profile" and the controversy has largely blown over. Also, because it shelters American citizens as well, most Brownsvillites perceive it as performing a much-needed service for the city. After all, in winter time, whenever temperatures plummet towards the freezing mark, it is to the Ozanam Center that the police are instructed to take the city's unsheltered, homeless people.

Of course, local churches and charitable organizations are only able to assist the most needy of persons, those who, so to speak, have "fallen through the cracks" of the welfare net. It is upon the joint state-federal welfare system that the bulk of Brownsville's poor, and that's half the city's population, depend. In Texas, as in the other states, a single person or family becomes eligible for a variety of assistance programs whenever they fall below the federal "poverty line" — the annually-adjusted, estimated amount it takes to feed, clothe and shelter a single person or a family. The most current figures are:

1996 Federal Poverty Line
1 person = $ 7,680
2 persons = $10,320
3 persons = $12,960
4 persons = $15,600
5 persons = $18,240
6 persons = $20,880
7 persons = $23,520
8 persons = $26,160
9 persons = $28,800
10 persons = $31,440
Over 10 persons continue to add
$2,640 for each additional person.

Keeping in mind that the current minimum wage is $4.25 per hour and that a minimum wage earner working 40 hours a week grosses $8,840 per year, it is easy to see why so many Brownsvillites are on assistance. Any household consisting of more than one person which is supported by a minimum wage earner falls below the poverty line. Even families in which both parents work at minimum wage jobs will be below the poverty line if they have more than two children. In Brownsville, where both minimum wage jobs and large families are the rule rather than the exception, welfare abounds. Indeed, in January 1996, Michael Uhrbrock, Public Relations Officer for the Texas Department of Human Services' McAllen District (under which the Brownsville office falls), said 53,539 Brownsvillites were receiving food stamps valued at $3,781,139 monthly.

Typically, he said, a single mother in Brownsville with two children receives $295 in food stamps per month. A Brownsville family of four headed by a male on minimum wage receives $300 in food stamps. In that same family of four, if no one worked, they would receive $400 worth. In a household of seven people, if no one works, they receive $608 worth.

Indisputably, the food stamp program has positive benefits for Brownsville: it helps feed nearly half the city's residents and yearly pumps over $45 million of federal and state money into the Brownsville economy. Nonetheless, there are some negative repercussions as well. There is the worry that persistent dependence on the food stamp program and other forms of public assistance is becoming generational among border Hispanics and will create a welfare culture similar to that of the black underclass in urban America. A point is reached where there is no shame attached to living off public assistance — it's an "entitlement." Brownsville may be especially susceptible to such an attitude since so many are doing it — half the people in the supermarket checkout lines are using the benefits. So why be embarrassed? Another problem is that the food stamp system is prone to abuse. The problem of persons selling their stamps for 50% of their cash value was only partially solved with the phase in of the "Lone Star" card in 1995. Used like a credit card at checkouts, purchases are electronically deducted from food aid recipients' accounts. The system will eliminate some forms of fraud — food stamps can no longer be stolen from recipients' mailboxes, and multiple addresses cannot be used to collect multiple benefits — but people may still sell the use of their cards and PINs (Personal Identification Numbers) for cash payments, and, no doubt, some ineligible individuals will still obtain cards by fraudulent means. Certainly, many Brownsvillites feel the program is abused and one hears frequent tales of welfare queens decked out in expensive clothes and jewelry paying with Lone Star cards and them navigating their late model, top-of-the-line automobiles out of supermarket parking lots.

At this point (Wednesday afternoon, January 17, 1996) I decide to conduct a little investigation to check out these rumors. I will go to ten different Brownsville supermarkets and at each of them tail the very first person I see who pays with a Lone Star *card. I'll learn for myself what I can about their cars, homes, and general circumstances. First, I go to the H.E.B. Supermarket at 2250 Boca Chica Boulevard. I park my car in a central location toward the back of the parking lot so I can keep sight of my quarry at all times, and quickly reach whichever parking lot exit they choose to take. I buy a Pilot pen and get in one of the 14 checkout lines. The person immediately in front of me pays with the Lone Star card. She is a woman in her early twenties dressed in black shorts and black T-shirt. I follow her out. Walking across the parking lot, she pulls a cellular phone from her purse, flips it open, and commences a call. She slides into a late-model Ford Crown LTD. I get in my car and wait five minutes while she completes her call. It's obviously a social call, and she is laughing much of the time. Finally, the call over, she pulls out. I shadow her, fifty yards back, to a newer housing addition in the southmost area. She pulls up at a brick home, single garage, which I appraise at $50,000. Two other late model cars are already parked one behind the other in the driveway.*

Next, I go to the small Pronto Supermarket at 3831 Boca Chica. Only four or five checkouts here. I buy a can of Campbell's chicken noodle soup and get in line. The group in front of me consist of three small children, not much more than babies really, and three young women ranging from about nineteen to twenty-four. I can't tell whether these young women are sisters, relatives, or just friends, but one of them pays for all the groceries with a Lone Star card. My transaction only takes a moment, and I'm right behind them as they go out to the parking lot. They get into a 1987 Mercury Cougar and drive to an apartment complex near the airport where I'd estimate rent runs $400–$500 a month.

El Centro Supermarket at Four Corners is next, and at this six or seven checkout store I buy another can of chicken noodle soup. The person in front of me pays with cash, but at the next booth an attractive 20-year-old girl in dungaree jeans and vest, accompanied by what I take to be her mother and baby daughter, uses the Lone Star card. I follow them to the lot where they get into a 1990 Pontiac Grand Prix. This girl drives way over the speed limit and I, trailing too far behind, lose her at a stoplight.

I go to the Lopez Foodstore on McDavitt Boulevard. This is a small, four-checkout establishment with little activity. I pay for a can of tomato soup, but there's no one else checking out at the moment. I hang around the gumball machines pretending to read a Bargain Booklet until a drab, unhappy-looking woman wearing bedroom slippers checks out with the card. She is a walking customer and shuffles across the street to a public housing project.

Next, I go to King Mart on Palm Boulevard and buy another can of tomato soup. Most of the people at the checkouts are paying with checks or cash, and I have to stand near the door like I'm waiting for someone until I see a customer use the card. I follow this fiftyish mother and twentyish daughter out to the lot. They get into an old, banged-up Toyota Corolla and leave. I'm right behind them. They pull up in front of a swanky home in Rio Viejo, which puzzles me. I swing around the block for another look and by this time, they're getting back into their car. Perhaps they're maids and had a message to drop off. Anyhow, we now proceed to a much poorer neighborhood off Paredes Line Road where they park in front of a tiny, wooden frame home without a garage or driveway which I appraise at $20,000 — land included. I shoot around the block for another pass. Their trunk is open, and they're unloading their groceries.

At 4:30 P.M. I'm at El Globo Supermarket off the Expressway. People are now getting off work and there are more men in the stores. I buy a quart of Havoline engine oil, use the express lane, and then walk the length of the thirteen checkouts until I spot a man with his card out. I follow him into the parking lot. This man looks tired. He wears jeans and a plaid shirt. He gets into a ten-year-old Mercury Topaz and drives down FM 802 and goes into a Coastal Minimart. This is awkward. I pull into the minimart's parking lot, but whereas the man goes inside the store, I stay outside and pretend there's something wrong with my car. I'm looking under my hood with my back to him when he comes out. It's all to no avail, however, because I lose him a few moments later in the heavy rush-hour traffic at the intersection of Expressway and FM 802.

I next turn off 802 and run down to the H.E.B. on Central Boulevard. Here I pick up some candy circus peanuts to nibble while I drive, and I pay for them in the express lane, but I can't spot anyone at any of the fourteen busy checkouts using the Lone Star. Everyone seems to be paying with cash or checks. I stand near the door like I'm waiting for a wife and keep watching. After a few minutes, I spot someone with the card. I follow them out: a forty-year-old man with a twelve-year-old daughter. They have a full cartload of groceries with a sack of Pampers on top. They get into a big, white panel van, by no means new, in which several other people are waiting. They set off with me behind them, and they travel very slowly as though the driver is unsure of streets and directions. I follow the van all the way to the B&M Bridge where they get into line to go across to Mexico. Interesting. The van has Texas plates.

This incident prompts me to drive next to the H.E.B on Elizabeth Street. This supermarket is primarily used by Mexican nationals, and I want to see if they're also using Lone Star cards. This store has ten checkouts and, now, at dusk, all of them are very busy and have long lines. I get into the express lane with a purchase and see people paying with dollars, pesos, and the card. A cheerful, chunky couple in front of me in their late teens, both wearing wedding bands, pay with the Lone Star, and I'm on their heels as they leave. He wears laborers' clothes and his hands are soiled with grease. They get into a five-year-old white Mercury Marquis that has been well taken care of. It has been customized with lots of chrome. Both of us soon get snarled up in the heavy traffic waiting to get across Gateway International Bridge, and I eventually lose them, but not before ascertaining they did not cross the bridge into Mexico.

At the Lopez Supermarket on Ringgold Street, there are six checkouts. I buy a can of corn on sale and get in line. Most of the customers in line are men just off work and most are paying with cash. Actually, many of these male workers are buying beer for which the Lone Star cannot be used. The first person I see who does use the card is an elderly lady two booths over. She must be eighty at least, and her feet obviously pain her. She has one of those side-to-side, teeter-totter sort of gaits that very old people often develop. I figure she ought to be a cinch to tail, and she is. The dear old thing comes out the door with her small sack of food and totters ever so slowly across the street to a public housing project.

The tenth and final supermarket I visit is the new fourteen-checkout H.E.B on Southmost Road. It's dark now, and difficult to tail cars. I buy a six-pack of Coke and get in the express lane.

There must be three hundred people milling around in the store, but I'm the only Anglo. The person in front of me pays in cash, but in the non-express lane to my left, a family with a full cart of food is paying with the card. I shadow them out. The mother and father are about forty. The mother wears her hair in a youthful ponytail, but it's mostly gray hair in the ponytail. The father wears a work outfit: shirt and trousers are both of the same heavy, dark-green material. They have a ten-year-old son with them. They load their groceries in the bed of an old blue pickup, and then all three get in the cab. I follow them all the way across town. At every stoplight their three heads are illuminated in the cab window by my headlights. They finally pull up before a simple, wooden frame home near the courthouse. No garage. No driveway. They park at the curb. I roll around the block for another pass. My headlight beams sweep over them: the boy is standing in the truck bed handing down the sacks of groceries to his mother and father.

What have I learned from this? I'm not sure. I think the girl with the cellular phone, brick home and three late-model cars was a case of fraud — so too, probably, was the panel van that drove over to Mexico at dusk. I would say then, based on what I saw in this brief, unscientific investigation, perhaps 20% of local food assistance is fraudulently obtained. I suppose most of the other people I followed met federal/state eligibility criteria, and I don't begrudge them the free food, but I must say I was everywhere dismayed by the casualness with which the cards are used. There was not any indication of anyone's being even the slightest bit embarrassed to be receiving "free" food. This does not bode well for the community's future.

The other main assistance program managed by the Texas Department of Human Services is Aid to Families with Dependent Children (AFDC), a program funded 60% from federal monies, 40% from state monies. According to the Texas Department of Human Services' Michael Uhrbrock, as of January 1996, there were 13,614 Brownsvillites on AFDC rolls who were sharing $853,144 in monthly payouts. Sample payouts are $188 per month to a single mother with two children, and $226 per month to a single mother with three children. In 81% of the cases AFDC recipient families are headed by females: 39% by mothers who have never married; 42% by divorced, separated or abandoned mothers. And even though Texas AFDC payment are among the most niggardly in the nation (48th among the 50 states in average family payout), the program still generates statewide controversy. As of January 1996, Uhrbrock reported there was still no ban on single women joining the rolls if they give birth to an illegitimate child, and assistance is stepped up whenever unwed, divorced, or abandoned mothers produce additional illegitimate children. There is legislation pending at both the state and national levels to end this taxpayer subsidization of illegitimate births, but actual enactment is by no means certain.

The U.S. Department of Health and Human Services' Social Security Administration is another source of public assistance for city residents. After very significant downsizing over the past ten years due to computerization, the Social Security Administration's Brownsville office now has just twenty-nine employees, headed by District Manager Alberto C. Galvan. Galvan's most recent statistics show that his office is dispersing $7,238,000 monthly to 16,729 Brownsville retirees, retirees' spouses, disabled workers, and widows and their children. These so-called Title II benefits are, of course, not considered welfare since they were paid for, at least in part, by the workers' payroll deductions. However, Galvan's office also handles the Social Security Administration's Title XI Supplemental Security Income (SSI) program which is very definitely a federal welfare program. It provides monthly payments to the aged (65 and over), to blind children and adults, and to disabled children and adults who have limited incomes and resources and who are U.S. citizens, legally admitted permanent residents, or legally admitted resident aliens. Galvan's most recent records show that 7,904 Brownsvillites are sharing $2,2245,942 in monthly SSI benefits. Of these people, 3,636 are meeting the federal guidelines for being the aged poor, 130 are blind, and 4,138 are classified as disabled. In general, beneficiaries of SSI in Texas must have accountable incomes below $470 per month ($705 per couple), and while they may own a home and car, they cannot have over $2,000 ($3,000 per couple) in other real estate, bank accounts, stocks and bonds or cash. To establish whether a person meets eligibility criteria for blindness or mental or physical disability, the Social Security Administration refers applicants to the Texas Rehabilitation

Commission for a determination. If deemed eligible by the commission, the Social Security Administration starts the payouts: a typical SSI payout to, say, a blind adult would be $470 per month, or $705 if the person has a spouse.

There has been considerable controversy sparked by SSI's broadening its disability criteria in recent years to include fat people. SSI considers a person disabled if they are more than twice as heavy as their recommended weight. Moreover, SSI now considers alcoholism and drug addiction as disabling diseases, not personal weaknesses, and therefore these diseases' victims are also worthy of taxpayer assistance — although District Manager Galvan was quick to point out that only nine Brownsville addicts and alcoholics ("not the hundreds that some might think") are currently receiving payments. Also, since 1991 and the notorious *Zebley* court case, SSI benefits must also be paid out to adults and children who exhibit certain forms of "maladaptive behavior." Galvan says this area is especially vulnerable to fraud, and the current Congress is working to exclude it from eligibility. He says there have been instances of parents coaching their children to wildly misbehave during interviews with Social Security personnel in hopes of qualifying for these *"disability"* benefits.

There are no Social Security fraud inspectors per se working out of the Brownsville office, but they can be requested and sent down form the Dallas office. Furthermore, according to Galvan, all of the local Social Security workers are alert to fraud, have been trained in the detection of false and counterfeit documents, and all applications for Social Security and SSI benefits must be reviewed by two staff workers to prevent one staff worker from accepting bribes or otherwise working in collusion with the benefits applicant. As a further guard against fraud, the Social Security Administration system randomly generates one Brownsville case per day for District Manager Galvan or Assistant District Manager Jose Villarreal to personally scrutinize for evidence of fraud. As a result, Galvan says, "I really believe there is very little fraud because of the built-in checks. But that is not to say it doesn't exist."

One current SSI issue Galvan foresees as having a major impact on Brownsville is the proposed change to SSI contained in the welfare reform bill currently stalled in the 104th Congress. As the unenacted bill read in January 1996, it called for cutting off SSI benefits to all but U.S. citizens. Since 40-50% of SSI beneficiaries in Brownsville are either permanent resident aliens or resident aliens, this will have a profound impact not only on these affected persons, but also on the city's economy as a whole — a loss of about one million federal dollars per month.

Yet another form of assistance Brownsville's needy may receive is federally-subsidized public housing. The Brownsville Housing Authority, with fifty-two permanent employees under the direction of Ernesto Pena, assists in housing 2,400 Brownsville families — 8,144 people, nearly seven percent of the city's population. Executive Director Pena works under the guidance of the five-member Brownsville Housing Authority Board directly appointed by the city mayor. Ninety-eight percent of the Authority's funding (approximately $10 million a year) comes from the U.S. Department of Housing and Urban Development (HUD).

The Brownsville Housing Authority had its beginning in 1937, in the heady days of Roosevelt's New Deal, and Brownsville's first "project" was completed and opened for occupancy in 1941 — this was the 150-unit, optimistically-named Buena Vida housing project off East Tyler Street. This project was followed by nine others over the course of nearly five decades: 1943 Bougainvillea (50 units); 1943 Victoria Gardens (50 units); 1952 Poinsettia North and Poinsettia South (together comprising 250 units); 1961 Citrus Gardens (150 units); 1971 Villa Del Sol (200 units); 1981 Los Brisas (50 units); 1982 Linda Vista (50 units); and 1987 Citrus Annex (37 units). All of the housing projects are single-story duplexes or free-standing, single-unit homes with from one to three bedrooms — the one exception being the fourteen-story Villa Del Sol tower downtown which exclusively houses elderly and handicapped persons. All of the projects are designated by HUD as "low income," except for Linda Vista on Old Port Isabel Road and the Citrus Annex on Grapefruit Street which are designated "very low income" projects.

After 1987 the federal government decided it was unwise to lump together large numbers of low income/welfare families in public housing estates, and so for a short time, the Brownsville Housing Authority built individual homes in ordinary neighborhoods around town. They had built just five such units, however, when Washington had another change of heart and decided to stop building homes and projects altogether. Instead, they favored issuing rent vouchers to persons eligible for public housing. This is what Director Pena's office now does. They have the 1,040 project units which they own outright, and they then distribute rent vouchers to an additional 1,360 families who are responsible for finding a house or apartment to rent wherever they choose in Brownsville. The rationale is that it is preferable for these "assisted" families to be rubbing shoulders with normal, self-reliant, hard-working neighboring families rather than to be trapped in a less wholesome project environment which may breed a welfare mentality.

The eligibility criteria for receiving rent vouchers or residing in the projects is wonderfully complex and based on literally *volumes* of HUD regulations. Depending on family size and income, residents at the projects may pay from zero percent to virtually all of their rent. On the average, the families living in the projects pay about $100 to $150 in rent for a unit that would command about $350 on the open market. With such a bargain, it is not surprising that over 3,000 families are on the Brownsville Housing Authority's waiting list. Most of these families will inevitably be disappointed since Pena says only fifteen to twenty vacancies occur in any given month. Once families move in, they usually stay for years. Pena says some current project residents have been there over fifty years. Pena is not at all happy with this situation and feels public housing should be strictly temporary: families should be able to get on their feet, get financially stabilized, and then move on and give the opportunity of public housing to other *temporarily* needy families. The welfare bill pending in Congress may correct this situation, Pena believes, since it calls for setting a three- to five-year cap on the length of time families can receive housing assistance. Pena thinks this is a fine idea.

One major change Pena is bringing about at the projects is the method of handling utility payments. All of the projects are group metered for electricity, water and gas, and so there is no incentive for families in the projects to be frugal in their use. Pena says irresponsible families leave their lights on all the time, while others leave water sprinklers going all night. The Housing Authority's utility bills are, therefore, huge.

To solve this problem, Pena is converting every project (except for the Villa Del Sol tower) to individual unit metering of gas, water, and electricity. This conversion is underway and will take until the year 2000 to complete. Residents will then receive a utility allowance sufficient to cover "reasonable use," but profligate families will be made to pay for their extravagance.

As with virtually all other welfare programs, public housing assistance may be in for a rocky future. Pena says his maintenance funds have already been cut back 30%, and he expects even deeper cuts in the future.

Of even more consequence to the Brownsville projects was the mid-1995 passage of a federal law that prohibits housing assistance to illegal aliens. Prior to passage of that law, it was illegal for Pena's staff to even ask housing applicants about their citizenship or residency status, and, consequently, Pena estimates 30-35% of his units have at least some illegals living in them. This is a situation that has angered many U.S. citizens mired in the Housing Authority's 3,000-family waiting list. But as things stand now, new housing applicants are queried on their citizenship/residency status, and Pena's staff are bound by law to report any and all suspected illegal applicants to the Immigration and Naturalization Service. As for illegals already housed in the projects, they are allowed to remain if at least one household member is a U.S. citizen or legal resident, but the rent is jacked up to higher levels depending upon how many illegals are also residing in the unit. These rent hikes, Pena says, frequently force these mixed legal-illegal households to move out.

The hardening of Washington's (and Austin's) attitude towards both welfare recipients and aliens also threatens to seriously erode Medicaid assistance available to Brownsvillites. This "Great Society" program of the 1960s was enacted to parallel the Medicare program. But, whereas Medicare for the elderly is not welfare (since it is partially paid for by the recipients' payroll deductions), Medicaid is welfare. Funded jointly by state 35%, and federal government 65%, it pays the medical bills of the elderly poor not qualified for Medicare, and also for the blind, the disabled, and poor families with children. According to TDHS spokesman Michael Uhrbrock, 16,202 Brownsvillites are enrolled in Medicaid and annually generate medical bills of $34 million — an average of $2,080 per person! Uhrbrock says the majority of Medicaid beneficiaries are poor families with children and fatherless families on AFDC. About one-fourth of Medicaid recipients in Brownsville are the elderly poor, and these people, understandably, have more ailments and submit disproportionately high medical bills. But there is no question either that the high, $2,080 per person, average medical bill is also due to the chronic overuse of the benefits on the part of many Medicaid enrollees. Whereas most Brownsvillites, even those with medical insurance, must pay all or substantial portions of their hospital, doctor, laboratory, and pharmacy bills, and are, therefore, inclined to use medical facilities sparingly, there are no disincentives at work on Medicaid enrollees. A cold, a touch of the flu or other minor complaint may prompt a visit to the doctor; nor is there any reluctance to show up at budget-busting emergency rooms which paying patients seek to avoid if at all possible.

If, as pending Washington legislation calls for, Medicaid's rate of growth is reduced, Brownsville hospitals and many local physicians who treat mainly Medicaid patients will be affected. The *Brownsville Herald* reported in a Lisa Marie Gomez headline story on July 1, 1995, that the city's two largest medical facilities, Brownsville Medical Center and Valley Regional Medical Center, received respectively 45% and 39% of their financing from Medicaid reimbursements. Any reduction in Medicaid growth "is going to have a dramatic impact on the Valley," said State Senator Eddie Lucio. "The person who has Medicaid won't be affected, but rather the hospitals are going to have to absorb the cost."

Lucio's statements were presaged four days earlier by Cameron County's Health Director, Dr. Gus Stern, who told the *Brownsville Herald*:

> If you cut down the number of Medicaid recipients, cut down the number of payments for Medicare, plus you don't provide any access to care for undocumented aliens — then you have a big segment of the population who live here who have no way to access health care. Since these people will not seek preventive care from family physicians, they will wind up in Valley hospitals when their diseases progress. The hospitals will have to foot the bill. You will see hospitals closing and physicians leaving . . . and [the Valley] not able to attract any health care providers to this area.

And although Stern's forebodings were probably intentionally hyperbolic in order to attract public attention to the issue, there will be serious consequences in store for Brownsville's medical establishment if Medicaid slow-growth funding is enacted by Congress, and alternative state funding cannot be procured. Physicians *might* leave the Valley. They are already being jostled along by Medicaid patients' penchant for suing their doctors. As the *Herald* reported in a May 15, 1994, story, the Texas Medical Association described the Rio Grande Valley as a "liability war zone" with doctors more likely to face malpractice suits there than anywhere else in the state. Of Texas' 254 counties, Cameron County ranked third, with, annually, 19% of its doctors having lawsuits filed against them. Next door Hidalgo County was first in the state, with 30% of its doctors being sued each year.

Perhaps the form of public assistance most indicative of Brownsville's unique status as America's poorest city is the local school district's application of the federal government's Child Nutrition Program. In most schools across the nation, the majority of students take a sack lunch to school or buy a cafeteria meal, while a handful of needy students qualify for "free lunches" or "reduced payment lunches" depending upon their degree of poverty. But Brownsville is different. Demographic statistics that reveal the depth and extent of poverty in Brownsville set off all sorts of alarm bells in Washington and automatically trigger certain assistance mechanisms. For instance, instead of individual students having to prove their eligibility for a free or reduced-payment lunch as they do elsewhere in America, federal guidelines *require all* of Brownsville Independent School District's 40,000+ students be offered a completely free lunch and breakfast every school day. Consequently, according to BISD Food Service Director Dora Rivas and Field Supervisor Beatriz Rodriguez, 500 cafeteria workers are employed at Brownsville's forty-two public schools to serve out about 20,000 breakfasts and 40,000 lunches each day at an average value of $0.99 for a breakfast and $1.79 for a lunch — with virtually all of the cost borne by the U.S. Department of Agriculture.

W.L.A.

CHAPTER 5

At the Great Bilingual Debate

You wonder what it is that compels you to put yourself in these situations. I am seated at the front of one of the oversize classrooms on the University of Texas at Brownsville campus. The room is filling up nicely with a wide selection of students, faculty, newspaper reporters, and local citizens. The audience is anticipating a debate (though billed as a "symposium") between myself and Dr. Graciela Rosenberg on the issue of bilingual education. Dr. Rosenberg's area of academic expertise is bilingual education. Mine is not.

Fortunately, the symposium is structured to minimize opportunities for Dr. Rosenberg to highlight my ignorance. We've been allotted twenty minutes each for presentations, and she goes first. To my relief, she focuses on defining and describing bilingual education, using overhead transparencies in a professorial presentation.

My turn. I had agreed to participate in the symposium because I had been invited by Dr. Eliana Bennett, organizer of the series, who assumed that I would be hostile to bilingual ed., and because I did have some strong opinions on the subject. During the week prior to the event, I'd done a quick research job on the "anti" side so I could give the audience some of what they'd come to hear. My main point was that bilingual ed., as it exists in

Brownsville and many other cities, was not really effective in improving learning.

A bad moment. In the middle of my presentation I spot "the boss" in the audience. UTB/TSC President Juliet Garcia does not look happy. Twitching nervously, I press forward to make my demand for "real" bilingual education: some classes taught completely in Spanish and others taught completely in English for all students in Brownsville, beginning in first grade and continuing through high school. My goal is to see that all graduates have the skills to succeed in the bilingual border environment.

Some in the audience are dissatisfied or confused by my presentation. You're supposed to be for it or against it, and I seemed to be muddying the waters. But there's support for my view, particularly from the Modern Language Department. The issue of "Spanish for Anglos" has been raised in letters to the Brownsville Herald, *and* Herald *columnists have argued aspects of the subject. Ultimately, citizen pressure will elicit a tepid response from the Brownsville Independent School District Board of Trustees: some intermediate schools will begin offering Spanish as a second language. Not nearly satisfactory from my perspective, but at least my reputation as an academic provocateur, or "crank," is secure.*

A.K.K.

Education

For a city with a population of limited educational attainment, Brownsville has an enormous education establishment. The Brownsville Independent School District alone has 40,000 students, 6,000 employees, and a budget of $235 million. For many citizens, however, awareness of the impact of education on the community begins and ends with their own children or the fortunes of high school athletic teams.

As in most any community, efforts to provide education began early in Brownsville's history. While a public school was established in 1855 by Cameron County, the effort soon lapsed, leaving a gap to be filled by private religious schools. Since the population was predominantly Catholic, the schools established by Catholic religious orders achieved the greatest success.

In 1853 French nuns belonging to the Sisters of the Incarnate Word and Blessed Sacrament opened Incarnate Word Academy for girls. Despite the difficulties of frontier life, which included a postulant (apprentice nun) being eaten by Indians while in transit between Brownsville and Laredo, the sisters persevered and established a permanent presence. By 1885 the sisters were providing a twelve-year curriculum, and in 1890 they opened a school for boys.

Meanwhile, priests and brothers of the Order of the Oblates of Mary Immaculate, another French religious group, established St. Joseph's school for boys in 1862. A permanent building was constructed after the Civil War, but not occupied by the Oblates until 1869, due to its temporary use by the Incarnate Word sisters, left homeless by the hurricane of 1867.

By the 1870s the State of Texas had mandated a system of free public schools. The Brownsville Public System began in 1875 with seven teachers and a principal, but had no permanent housing for the first fifteen years. In 1888 steamboat Captain William Kelly, chairman of the School Board, organized support for construction of the Grammar School on land donated by the Stillman family at Washington Park. The first principal was J. F. Cummings, a West Point graduate, who taught close order drill to the male students. State-ordered segregation resulted in a separate school for the few black children. At the turn of the century only about one-fourth of Brownsville children were attending school.

The Brownsville Independent School District was created in 1915 with five city schools and five rural schools. Over the years BISD absorbed small adjacent districts as Brownsville expanded. In 1916 a high school building was constructed on Palm Boulevard; it now comprises part of Central Intermediate School.

The slow development of public education in Brownsville was partially due to the inclination of the wealthy and influential families to support the Catholic schools. New St. Joseph School buildings were added in 1920 and 1926, and Villa Maria High School for girls was built on Jefferson Street in 1926.

It was during the twenties that local leaders recognized the need for a source of higher education in the Valley. Encouraged by the president of the University of Texas, who desired the creation of junior colleges as "feeder" institutions for "UT," BISD Superintendent Thomas Yoe and others established the Junior College of the Lower Rio Grande Valley under the auspices of BISD. The college was housed with the high school until 1948, when the major part of the de-activated Fort Brown was allocated for the college. Fort buildings dating to the late 1860s were adapted for classroom and administrative uses. The institution was re-named as Texas Southmost College.

Population growth and geographical expansion in the fifties and sixties prompted the replacement of the city-wide high school by three new high schools: Hanna, Pace, and Porter. Elementary and intermediate schools expanded apace. Mandatory enrollment was taking hold, and federally-funded programs added to the growth of the late sixties. These programs included establishment of a school for children of migrant farm workers and Head Start for pre-schoolers.

The succeeding period of continued rapid enrollment growth was overseen by Superintendent Raul A. Besteiro, a veteran BISD teacher and administrator, who took office in late 1976. Affectionately known as "Mr. B.," Besteiro was popular in the community and non-threatening to the education establishment of which he had long been a part. During Besteiro's tenure, enrollment grew from around 20,000 to more than 36,000. New programs designed to involve parents in the education process and to provide alternative opportunities for potential or actual drop-outs were inaugurated. The close of the Besteiro era saw the opening of Rivera High School in 1988, but financial exigencies had compelled the construction of "temporary" wooden classrooms capable of being moved to high-growth campuses. A complacent education establishment and the community at large were shocked by the results of a Texas Education Agency accreditation review in the spring of 1989. Accusing the Board of Trustees of micro-managing district operations, the TEA lowered the district's status from "Accredited" to "Accredited Warned with the Assignment of a Monitor." Under the supervision of a monitor, the district gradually regained its "Accredited" status over the following two years, but the community had become aware of additional problems concerning the quality of education provided in Brownsville.

Data compiled by the Texas Education Agency revealed that in comparison with similar school districts, BISD had a significantly higher dropout rate, nine percent for 1992-93. A comparison of

Texas Assessment of Academic Skills (TAAS) test results demonstrated that while BISD third-graders fell marginally below their peers statewide, the gap widened considerably for those taking the exit TAAS (high school). Strangely, BISD happily awarded over half of high school graduates an advanced seal on their diplomas, denoting completion of "a more rigorous set of courses than required for graduation," a substantially higher percentage than awarded statewide. BISD administrators appeared to be living in a fool's paradise in terms of the scholastic achievement of their students.

Apparently recognizing that strong measures were called for, the Board of Trustees chose Dr. Esperanza Zendejas to be the new superintendent in the spring of 1992. Zendejas, a Ph.D. in administration and policy analysis from Stanford University, came to Brownsville with experience as the superintendent of a much smaller district in California. Not only did she not fit the stereotype of middle-aged, Anglo male superintendents, she was an outsider in a very insider-oriented city. Nevertheless, she aggressively tackled the task of bringing change to a troubled school system.

Controversial from the start, Zendejas quickly moved to restructure Central Office (the "Glass Palace") organization and personnel and began transferring school principals. While Zendejas claimed the personnel shifts were designed to promote the development of new ideas and problem-solving approaches, she appeared to be breaking up the "old boy" network and undermining the "compadre" system of personal loyalties. In truth, some principals had established personal fiefdoms with employees beholden to those principals for their employment.

Zendejas' shake-up of the system did not go unchallenged, and it was widely acknowledged that she had "stepped on toes." Opponents claimed that the abrupt transfer of principals threatened the smooth functioning of the instructional program. Some wondered why ineffective administrators were transferred instead of being dismissed. The discontent was reflected even on the Board of Trustees, especially in the person of Board President Joey Lopez.

Despite the turmoil among the educators, Zendejas proved to be effective in promoting public relations. As an amateur ventriloquist (no kidding), the new superintendent used Kiko (her dummy) to help her relate directly to school children. As in California, she had her own call-in radio show and appeared with great regularity on the BISD television channel.

But there was more to Zendejas' plans than publicity. She initiated the Homework Hotline for students to call in for help, created the Saturday Academies, and brought the Help One Student To Succeed (HOSTS) Program to Brownsville. Since the state had provided a yardstick to measure minimum achievement levels in math, reading, and writing through the TAAS tests, Zendejas focused on overcoming the poor performance record of BISD.

"You have to hold people accountable," Zendejas announced. "Our school system is the way it is because there hasn't been that accountability." In 1993 the Texas Education Agency rated eleven BISD schools as "low-performing" based on a combination of TAAS scores, attendance, and drop-out rates. The superintendent added eight other schools to the list by raising the state standards. The probationary schools were targeted for extra help, including additional funding.

Zendejas' commitment to improving the low-performing schools appeared to have paid off by the next year when no BISD schools were listed as low-performing. The superintendent had the rug pulled out from under her, however, when it was revealed that Texas Education Commissioner "Skip" Memo had "adjusted" the criteria in a manner which reduced the number of low-performing schools statewide by 83%. Results from the 1994 TAAS tests showed improvement but still left BISD near the bottom in a ranking of Valley school districts.

By 1995 it was clear that under Zendejas BISD had achieved a significant degree of success in raising TAAS scores and improving low-performing schools. The superintendent had already been rewarded by the Board of Trustees with a five-year contract. On July 4, 1994, Zendejas was honored by Senator Eddie Lucio as the "1994 Outstanding Brownsville Citizen." She acknowledged, however, that "we have a tough road ahead," and asserted that it would "take a good five years of no compromise, push ahead, first-quality education."

Zendejas would not be around to fulfill her five-year contract or to oversee the achievement of success in her own terms. In the fall of 1994 rumors circulated to the effect that she had been approached about a position with another school district. Additionally, rumblings from disgruntled employees and others were reflected in the attitudes of several candidates for the Board of Trustees election in the spring of 1995. Concerned in part that she might lose support of the Board majority and tempted by a $30,000 increase in salary, Zendejas accepted the superintendency of Indianapolis Public Schools in April of 1995. Probably her time in Brownsville had run out, because the ensuing election confirmed the likely loss of Board support for the superintendent.

The departure of Zendejas and the appointment of an interim superintendent put BISD in a holding pattern while a new search began. Toward the end of 1995 the Board ended its search and announced the selection of the acting superintendent, Wally Jackson, a veteran of twenty-four years as a Valley educator and administrator. Jackson had been an area administrator under Zendejas and was noted for his easy-going style. According to one trustee, Jackson "likes to take his orders and get things done."

In typical Brownsville fashion, Superintendent Jackson came in for immediate criticism. A former trustee claimed Jackson "just doesn't like to make decisions." Others noted his lack of a doctorate and the nine years dedicated to owning and managing a Harlingen fence company. Some believe that BISD could have "done better" with a wider search. On the other hand, even some Zendejas enthusiasts acknowledged the need for a period of calm and adjustment after the turmoil of the four or five previous years. Jackson himself acknowledges that Zendejas was "right for the times," but that he intends to pursue a "team" approach to problem-solving. Asserting that he is neither autocratic nor *laissez faire*, Jackson will listen to all sides in seeking a consensus. This will take more time, but might produce more quality in decison-making. Rather than seeking confrontations, Jackson says he "will pick the battles to fight." Nondefensive, open and congenial in person, the new superintendent defends his qualifications, notes his years of service in a variety of positions, and points out that he was asked by trustees to apply for the job. The big question is whether the momentum for reform would continue and grow, or whether BISD will sink back into complacency now that the "heat" is off.

There are ample reasons to be concerned. The "Behind the Lines" column in the December 1995 issue of *Texas Monthly* served as an indictment of public education in Texas and, by implication, Brownsville. The author noted a "relentless pressure to keep students in school at all costs and to pass them almost no matter what," in part because districts receive state aid based on attendance. Districts often "saw strict discipline and difficult courses with too many F's at report card time as certain to cause more and more dropouts." Teachers found it necessary to develop strategies to ensure that "an acceptable number of students passed," regardless of whether they had actually learned. Many teachers claim that these conditions exist in Brownsville.

By almost any measure of performance, Brownsville students rank well below state averages despite recent gains on TAAS tests. Some of the explanations offered for this circumstance seem justified: poverty, the influx of non-English-speaking aliens, and local sub-cultures which undervalue extended education. But these do not explain the accelerating decline in students' performance as they move through the upper grades and middle school. One BISD administrator attributed the decline to puberty. "This is the time youngsters are changing — it's very difficult for them of focus on instruction," he claimed. "It's the nature of the beast." Statewide, however, TAAS scores show no such decline. While the percentage of Brownsville students passing the TAAS declined from 62% in the fourth grade to 31% in the eighth, at the state level 75% passed in the fourth grade and 71% in the eighth.

The issue of students' performance has been the subject of discussion in several venues, notably the *Brownsville Herald.* Respected editorialist Marcelino Gonzales claimed that the "public schools graduate many students who can hardly read or write, much less cope with the higher standards of colleges and universities." Gonzales asserted that "Matamoros students graduate from elementary schools and high schools with higher degree of skills than their Brownsville counterparts."

What's the problem? Superintendent Jackson maintains that expectations for children are too low, a conclusion concurred in by Dr. Eileen Johnson, Professor of Education at the University of Texas at Brownsville. Rivera High School teacher Penny Hartwell also agrees with this assessment. "Expectation levels are, in my opinion, too low. And when a teacher tries to maintain a high expectation level, students complain and try to drop your class—and sometimes administration backs them up." This situation leaves students who go on to out-of-state universities wishing they had been better prepared. Jackson intends to set expectations in the lower grades so that Brownsville children will be reading at the fourth grade level, when they complete the fourth grade, and then require higher level courses in the middle schools. It may prove very difficult, however, to change long-established patterns based on what were sometimes racist assumptions concerning the academic limitations of Mexican-American children — the *pobrecitos* syndrome. Supposedly, benign racist attitudes of some teachers and administrators (and the community) led to lower standards designed to accommodate the presumed limitations of Mexican-American children, and that pattern became ingrained in the system.

Compounding the problem of quality are the issues of quantity: continued rapid growth of the school age population, the influx of illegal alien children, and the consequent need to expand facilities. Enrollment increases leveled off for the 1995-96 school year, but Superintendent Jackson and others consider this to be only a temporary respite, perhaps related to the peso devaluation. Jackson sees this as an opportunity to "catch up" in the effort to end persistent overcrowding of schools. Attempts to cope with the overcrowding led the district to resort to "multi-tracking" at Perkins Middle School, despite the apparent lack of success in an earlier program of year-round schools.

Contributing to the numbers crunch are the thousands of illegal aliens attending Brownsville schools, some transported across the border for this very purpose. Since the district cannot, by law, inquire into the citizenship status of students, there is no way to ascertain actual numbers. Various estimates range from four to seven thousand. In late 1993 *Brownsville Herald* editor Rey Guevara Vazquez claimed that these students were "saturating our schools, slowing down classes, contributing to the TAAS failures and creating the overcrowding that now plagues the Brownsville school district."

BISD already has forty-two schools, including five of the largest high schools in the state, to service over 40,000 students, and a new elementary school was scheduled to open in 1996. Many schools still utilize temporary wooden buildings (portables) to cope with the overflow of students. Despite state aid for construction in "poor" school districts, local school officials see the need for a bond issue to fund new projects. The BISD facilities committee has estimated the need for construction of ten new schools in the next ten years. Together, with the upgrading of current facilities and the elimination of 465 portables, the cost of the facilities committee plan would run over $134 million. Much of this cost would have to be met by tax-supported bonds.

Taxpayers are already supporting a $235 million BISD annual budget. The district employs nearly six thousand personnel. This makes BISD the biggest "business" and the biggest employer in Brownsville. Remarkably for a "poor" district, BISD is able to spend significantly more dollars per student than any other district in the Valley and more than the average for the state. This money makes it possible to pay teachers' salaries comparable to those in such urban areas as San Antonio and Austin.

Of course, much of the budget goes to support the programs and services designed to meet the needs of "special populations," ranging from the 60% of students who qualify as underprivileged to the 40% enrolled in bilingual and English-as-a-second-language classes to the students with various disabilities. BISD has not been deficient in devising and developing programs to meet students' needs. A district list of "Initiatives" includes forty-nine centers, partnerships, academies, and sundry other programs. High school centers for fine arts, medical and health professions, engineering, and law and criminal justice have been established. There are programs for gifted and talented students as well as "at-risk" students.

Despite the efforts of many sincere and dedicated administrators and teachers, BISD faces numerous intractable problems and controversial issues beyond those generally encountered in American education. The drop-out problem is particularly stubborn and particularly endemic in Mexican-American society. A former Texas education commissioner claimed that inability to speak English played a prominent role in the Mexican-American drop-out rate. BISD seems to be having some success in coping with the problem, thanks to a variety of programs, but statistical re-jiggering leaves the degree of success in doubt. Contributing to the dilemma is the problem of chronic truancy. District attendance monitors have reported as many as fifty truancy cases per week per school. In addition to missing out on education, truants cause trouble and commit crimes and, thus, involve the juvenile authorities. Neither the district nor the authorities have the manpower (or will) to effectively control truants.

Controversy swirls around other issues affecting BISD. Regarding bilingual education, district officials have an easy answer: they do what the state requires. Students deficient in English begin school learning almost entirely in Spanish and gradually move toward functioning completely in English. Placement in bilingual classes is recommended but not mandatory, and in 1994-95 over two thousand parents opted to place their children in English-only programs. The controversy is over the efficacy of bilingual programs. Proponents claim it facilitates learning, while opponents claim it interferes with the efficient learning of English. Adding to the controversy are those who would like to see all students learning in both English and Spanish. Wally Jackson wants all graduates to be able to function in Spanish as well as English. Such an accomplishment seems a long way off at present.

Yet another controversy involves homework. While homework assignment has been erratic for years, it surfaced as a public issue when schools began restricting access to textbooks. To try to save money on lost textbooks, schools began limiting their use to the classroom, frustrating parents who believed that students needed the books for home study. Superintendent Jackson supports homework, but is concerned about making learning too dependent on textbooks. Nevertheless, he urged principals to provide the books to low-performing students. Some observers remained concerned that BISD was not really committed to homework and high standards of performance.

High school athletics provides a source of ongoing controversy, a condition not unique to Brownsville. Local citizens often expend far more emotion over the selection of a football coach than they do over major educational issues, despite the fact that Brownsville football teams are rarely successful in inter-Valley competition. Debates rage over how much money should be allocated for athletic teams and how much for which sports. Athletic Director Joe Rodriguez is a former trustee who is considered to wield a great deal of influence—some say an inordinate amount of influence—in the district.

Brownsville sports fans disappointed by the performance of their favorite football team could take consolation from the performance of the high school bands at half-time. The BISD music program has achieved success in high rankings for band performances and has contributed members to all-state bands. District students have also been successful in competition in other areas — ranging from Porter High's military drill teams to Russell Elementary's state champion chess team.

The problems and achievements of BISD are reflective of national trends accentuated by local conditions. Superintendent Jackson acknowledges that the impression of public school failure has stimulated the privatization of education. This is true in Brownsville as well, with many middle-class parents choosing to enroll their children in private schools. Many would grant that it is quite possible to have a good education in the public schools, but only if one is able to select schools and teachers. Since the degree of choice is not available, a variety of private schools thrive despite the general poverty in the community.

The Episcopal Day School is clearly the elementary school of choice in Brownsville. On occasion, parents of prospective students have waited in line for the school office to open in order to assure themselves of being able to register their children. Catering to the middle and upper classes and Protestant in religion, the school has a disproportionately high percentage of Anglo students. Uniforms and homework are required, discipline is enforced, and standards are high for Brownsville.

Catholic schools comprise the major component of private education in Brownsville. St. Mary's and St. Luke's are diocesan schools operated through their local parishes. Incarnate Word Academy, first established in 1853, continues to be conducted by the Sisters of the Incarnate Word and Blessed Sacrament. The school provides instruction through the middle school level and is noted for the high number of upper-income families from Matamoros who enroll their children generation after generation. The Catholic schools all require uniforms, discipline, and performance.

In 1992 the IWBS sisters closed their historical high school, Villa Maria Academy. Most of the students enrolled in the sole remaining Catholic high school, St. Joseph's Academy, operated by the Marist Brothers. Beneficiary of a long tradition, "St. Joe's" is the secondary school of choice for Brownsville's well-to-do. Many non-Catholics attend. St. Joe's appears to serve the dual function of providing both a college preparatory education and the opportunity for adolescents and families of the community's elite to interact and socialize. A large majority of the graduates attend upstate and out-of-state universities.

Tiny Valley Christian High School, the only other private secondary school, offers a stoutly Christian-oriented education. So do the First Baptist School and Faith Christian Academy at the elementary level. Three Montessori schools round out Brownsville's private education offerings.

Higher education in Brownsville is provided exclusively by the University of Texas at Brownsville and Texas Southmost College. This nearly unique entity is the result of a merger between the junior college and what had formerly been a branch operation of Pan American University in Edinburg. The merged entity has been the source of some confusion in that both institutions continue in existence. TSC has no faculty and only half a dozen employees. It owns the land, most of the buildings, collects local taxes, and contracts with UTB to provide the junior college courses. UTB provides faculty, staff, and administration, receives funds through the University of Texas system, and offers the upper division and graduate courses. The combined entity has the same chief executive and answers to both the TSC and UTB Boards of Trustees. And that's the "nutshell" version.

When the new entity (UTB/TSC) appeared in 1992, the junior college contributed the vast majority of personnel, facilities, and students. TSC had emerged from a post-World War II period of slow growth during the presidencies of Arnulfo Oliveira and Albert Besteiro beginning in the early 1970s. Enrollment surged from less than a thousand to over five thousand during the seventies and eighties. UTB/TSC President Juliet Garcia began her career as a TSC speech instructor early in that era. Garcia, a Brownsville native, obtained a doctorate from the University of Texas and was appointed Dean of Arts and Sciences. Respected for her abilities and accomplishments, Garcia was selected for the TSC presidency less than a year after Besteiro's resignation.

An important factor in Juliet Garcia's promotion to the presidency was a major shift in the membership of the TSC Board of Trustees, a locally elected body. Trustees elected in the eighties began to develop a new vision for the growth of the institution.

Trustee leaders Michael Putegnat and Mary Cardenas found an ally and conceptualizer in then Dean Garcia. Their apparent goal was to overcome the image of "Tamale Tech" and "Texas Almost College" by establishing a plan for development, especially by building high-quality facilities.

To carry out their strategy, Garcia, Cardenas, and Putegnat successfully organized a campaign to raise funds through a $13.5 million bond issue in 1986. The funds enabled construction of the institution's most prominent buildings and the refurbishing of others. In contrast to previous construction, the new buildings maintained an architectural integrity with the old Fort Brown buildings. The basic appearance of the campus was transformed into one of the most visually pleasing aspects of the city, despite the desires of some students, who would have paved over the interior campus ground to provide "convenient" parking. The quality of the campus would prove to be a factor in the University of Texas' agreement to the partnership.

A second initiative of the Garcia, Putegnat, and Cardenas team gained national recognition. Accepting the offer of a challenge grant, the triumvirate set out to raise $1 million in eighteen months (1988-89) toward the establishment of an endowment. The money would ultimately be used for tuition payments at TSC for local students who performed well in public school. Again, the TSC leadership succeeded in rallying the support of the community and met their goal.

When Pan American University became part of the University of Texas system, so did its branch operation in Brownsville. This set the stage for the merger with TSC which would bring the resources and prestige (and bureaucratic entanglements) of UT to the border city. Indeed, the merger, combined with the impetus of a lawsuit over allocation of state higher education funding, soon resulted in the awarding of $28 million for construction — $23 million of it dedicated to a science and engineering technology building. Construction began early in 1996.

The transition to UTB/TSC brought with it a host of problems as well as benefits. The integration of faculty, staff, and administration necessitated the establishment of twenty-four project teams. The application of UT standards for promotion and tenure of faculty provoked consternation among former TSC faculty who believed they had been promised job security when the merger was proposed. The new entity was required to adapt to the complicated and confusing policies and bureaucratic procedures of the UT system. An expanded institution mission required the rapid development of new programs which would satisfy the scrutiny of state authorities. Uncertainty, overwork and stress resulted in a less than happy atmosphere during the transition period.

Despite the difficulties, UTB secured state approval for a doubling of degree programs during the next few years, especially in the areas of education, business, and science and technology. As a consequence, enrollment in upper division and graduate courses expanded rapidly. Much of the credit for program expansion went to "point man" Vice President Phillip Kendall, who also received much of the blame from faculty members who experienced problems with the merger.

By early 1996 UTB/TSC had grown to over 7,000 students in credit-carrying courses, plus hundreds more in non-credit English language and community education courses. Few would dispute the perception that the dynamic force behind the growth and expansion of the institution was President Garcia. Her leadership skills have received national recognition, including election to the board of trustees of the Southern Association of Colleges and Schools and selection as head of the American Council on Education.

Affable, self-confident, and enthusiastic in her vision for her institution, Garcia readily recalls the challenges of her presidency. In the beginning it was a problem of efficiency in business operation and the need to create a sense of unity. She sees her most significant accomplishment as "survival" in the sense of maintaining credibility with the community by accomplishing what she had promised. The danger, she acknowledges, is in getting so caught up in the "cause" as to lose sight of the broader perspective of the community by "taking ourselves too seriously."

Despite her accomplishments, President Garcia is not without critics, both in the community and in the university. The late Henry Sanchez, former state representative, accused Garcia and TSC Executive Director (former trustee) Michael Putegnat of engaging in "sweetheart" deals for their personal enrichment and gutting TSC in the process of creating the new entity. Journalistic gadfly Jerry

McHale weighed in with accounts of faculty discontent based on arbitrary decision-making and inadequate communication.

Concerns over the fiscal operations of the partnership, including the sale of the UT-owned president's home to Garcia, prompted Senator Eddie Lucio to call for a state audit in early 1995. An audit report in April cleared Garcia and the partnership of any irregularities, and the controversy died down. At the same time, many faculty concerns regarding job security were allayed by a new interpretation of tenure eligibility by Vice President Kendall. Other issues remain: extensive expansion of the bureaucracy in the face of restricted faculty hiring during enrollment growth, tendencies toward micro-management by top administration, and questions about the quality of education provided by the institution.

An informal poll of fifty students conducted for this project reflected concerns about quality. Over 80% of the sample rated the university as overall "average" as opposed to "very good " or "poor." While "average" was the response of at least 50% of all questions, students registered somewhat more positive responses to those concerning facilities and instructors and somewhat more negative to those on student services and number of courses and sections available. Those who have attempted to visit the campus during the work week will not be surprised to learn that the students expressed more frustration over the crowded parking situation than any other single issue.

President Garcia is well aware of issues of quality. The endowment scholarship program for local public school graduates will undergo refinement to assure that recipients are prepared to do college-level work. Only 10% of TSC students enrolled in remedial courses succeed in standard courses. University Completion Testing (EXCET) reveals low levels of performance in comparison with other universities, although performance has been gradually improving. Garcia urges clear establishment of a single college preparatory "track" for secondary students and hopes that funding changes will enable the hiring of more well-qualified university professors.

In the meantime, the TSC Board of Trustees has decided to begin a new wave of physical expansion. Having acquired several tracts of land to the southeast along the Rio Grande over several years, the trustees opted early in 1996 for a $30 million bond issue for the construction of buildings with purposes ranging from occupational technology to athletics and featuring a $14 million fine arts complex. The bonds would be paid off with funds from lease payments to be made by UT for use of TSC facilities.

Since no immediate threat to taxpayers' pocketbooks impended, and no citizen vote would be required, response to the bond proposal was generally muted. Critic Jerry McHale, however, announced that "Dr. Juliet Garcia, Michael Putegnat and Rose Mary *(sic)* Cardenas have concocted a scam that will put $23 million in the wallets of bankers, lawyers, brokers, architects, contractors and other professional carpetbaggers at the expense of the institutions they purportedly serve." McHale feared the preemption of local resources more needed by the city or the school district. He concluded that truly necessary TSC expansion could be funded by TSC reserves.

Despite the criticism and such obvious shortcomings as a woefully inadequate library, UTB/TSC is becoming a source of pride to the community. Disputes over sense of direction were bound to arise in such a rapidly expanding institution, and UTB/TSC can hardly be blamed for the atmosphere of malaise which afflicts American education generally. Indeed, UTB/TSC may well be poised to play an inspirational leadership role in the community and help lift Brownsville above the negative image that obscures it.

A.K.K.

CHAPTER 6

On Patrol with BPD

It's November 10, 1995. A warm Friday afternoon is drawing to a close; evening is approaching. I am dressing for night patrol with the Brownsville Police Department. I put on black trousers, a long-sleeved white shirt (for high nighttime visibility as Chief Ben Reyna instructed), and a tie. As I leave my house, I double-check my wallet to make sure I have plenty of donut money.

I drive to the police station and at 5:00 P.M. report to Lieutenant Angel Gomez, supervising officer for the 2:45-10:45 shift in progress. He assigns me as a "ride along" to Officer Robert Nieto. Robert is twenty-four years old, married with one child, and structured to the proportions of a brick: his width and depth are about one-third his height. Not fat; but powerful and with a low center of gravity. Sanguine personality.

I sit in the Report Writing Room with Robert while he finishes the paperwork on his last call which concerned a sixteen-year-old boy living on his own. The parents had left town some weeks ago to look for work in Lubbock. The boy stayed behind in Brownsville with some relatives until they pulled out too. The boy wanted to stay behind and finish high school and was living in an abandoned home. Robert turned the boy over to Child Protective Services.

At 5:10 we climb into patrol car D-49 and go "10-8," meaning we are on call and on patrol. Brownsville is divided into twelve sectors, and we are patrolling the downtown sector along with two other units: Officer Jessie Garza in patrol car D-26, and Officer Rolando Trujillo in D-17. We will be backing each other up throughout the evening.

At 5:14 we get our first call on the radio. We are dispatched to Lucio's Café on Washington Street for a "Subject Down." We double park on the busy street behind an ambulance that has just arrived. A crowd has collected around a semi-coherent old man who has slid himself out of his wheelchair and laid himself down on the sidewalk in front of the café. Bystanders have tried to get him back in his wheelchair, but he has slinked himself back down. Robert and the EMS people look over the old man and talk to him. EMS informs us the man is tubercular and drunk. The man has a house to live in, so it's decided we will just take him home. Robert puts on rubber disposable gloves from a big box of them we have in the front seat, and with the help of EMS people the old man is laid out in the back of our unit. The wheelchair goes in our trunk. We drive him to West Brownsville with our windows rolled down — because of the odor and because TB can spread by air. At a very humble home in West Brownsville, humble even by Brownsville standards, his daughter, a wiry, fortyish woman wearing a hernia-prevention belt, comes matter-of-factly out and helps Robert wrestle him into the house. She says, "Gracias." Robert takes off his rubber gloves and washes his hands thoroughly with the garden hose.

At 5:43 we head back towards downtown and go "10-8" again. Six minutes later we get our next call and are dispatched as a backup to a downtown alley for an "Intoxicated and Violent Subject." When we arrive, officers Trujillo and Garza already have the man in handcuffs and wave us on, so at 5:59 we call in that we're "10-8" again. On call and on patrol. We cruise the congested shopping blocks downtown. Traffic is backed up for blocks at the International Bridge. Pedestrians are everywhere, and one notices how people, drivers and pedestrians alike, immediately are aware when a patrol car is present — you can see their eyes registering on the vehicle from a block away. We are, as Robert says, "Making sure we're seen." Night is falling and lights are coming on all over the city. We cruise along and go up and down streets and alleys at random. Robert has the car's radio tuned at low volume to K-TEX, and soft country ballads tell us about broken hearts and love gone sour. Meanwhile, the police radio chatters incessantly calling numbers and codes meaningless to me, but not to Robert. At 6:06 we suddenly pick up speed. We are en route to J. C. Penny and Amigoland Mall where the security guard is holding two juvenile shoplifters — one with a knife.

We arrive at 6:08. Officer Jessie Garza's patrol car has arrived just before us. We walk through the J.C. Penney store and then wind our way through the shelves in the large stockroom to the security room. Two brothers, a fifteen-year-old and an eleven-year-old, are quickly frisked and cuffed with their hands behind their backs. The fifteen-year-old is as sly and insolent a package as society produces, and the eleven-year-old is well on his way. They are both dressed "grunge" style with extra-large sweatshirts to tuck merchandise beneath. The knife is a wicked looking four-inch wooden-handled dirk. The boys look at each other and smirk. At 6:17 we bring them out cuffed through the store — shoppers stop and stare. We load them in the back of our car and head for the station. The two boys have their heads together in the back seat getting their stories straight and mapping strategy. We drive up to the back of the station and Robert radios inside for another officer to come out and help with the boys. He's afraid the strategy they've decided upon might be to bolt and run as soon as the door's opened. These two boys do look nimble, and Robert is not built for speed. So, when the other officer arrives, we triangulate ourselves just outside the door as it's opened, and the boys' arms are grabbed. Officer Garza is left to deal with the boys and the paperwork.

Back at the car, Robert pulls out the back seat to make sure the boys haven't stuffed any drugs or weapons behind it. Then at 6:38 we go "10-8" again. We cruise the city blocks — background of soft country music, foreground of our chattering police radio. The prostitutes are now out in full force downtown in groups of two or three at nearly every corner. Some are very young, many in their mid and late teens, mostly Matamoros girls, Robert says. We roll slowly by them — some ignore us, some stare insolently. Then, up ahead, Robert sees one in the act of actually negotiating with a "John." As we approach, they spot us. The girl runs down a narrow path between two buildings, while the "John" walks rapidly on.

In the alleys poor people with shopping carts pick through the dumpsters looking for stuff — clothes, aluminum cans. We pull up beside a guy peeing in the alley. Robert gets out and talks to him. The man moves along. At 6:50 we spot a guy sitting cross-legged Indian style in the alley. He's got a quart bottle of Budweiser in a brown sack in front of him — and a squeegee. Robert shines our unit's spotlight in his face. No response. We get out. Robert talks to him in Spanish. He's cooperative. Robert stands him up against the wall of a building to check his eye responses. He has the man stand on one foot and count to twenty. "Uno . . . dos . . . tres … " He does it. Not perfectly, but he does it. Robert tells him to pour the beer on the ground and leave. He says, "Gracias, gracias. Thank you, chief," and leaves with his squeegee.

Back on "10-8," we wind through town, passing lots of groups of adolescents playing in groups, sitting on cars, loitering outside convenience stores on International Boulevard. Robert pulls up to many of these groups, rolls down his window and talks to these kids. "How's it going? What are you doing tonight? Don't stay out too late. Be careful." Most of the groups are okay. Reasonably polite. No trouble. We're "being seen."

At 7:05 we are dispatched to a house next to Casa Linda Restaurant on Palm Boulevard. A citizen has something to report. When we get there a man is waiting in front of his house and flags us down. He's a handsome thirty-year-old — bare-chested in the heat — with two birds tattooed on his back. We get out. He talks to Robert while his womenfolk and children watch from the open second-floor windows. The children giggle and wave. The man said he spotted a man and woman on top of the restaurant roof looking into his open second floor windows. As soon as he saw them, they quickly climbed down and fled in separate Suburbans — one brown, one white. Robert called the descriptions in on his radio.

We go back on "10-8" at 7:18. We cruise the "Muralla" neighborhood off Fronton Street near the railyard. A neighborhood known for car thieves. Knots of people are out in front of houses or run-down apartment blocks drinking beer, sitting in lawn chairs, talking on this sultry evening. Reba McIntyre's sin-

uous voice comes from our car radio. Suddenly, Robert tenses to some numbers and codes on the police radio. He listens, makes a U-turn, and begins adding speed rapidly. He tells me "something's going down." Up to this point, all our dispatches have been suffixed with the words "Code I" — meaning we are authorized to go no more than 15-20 miles over the speed limit, and no flashing lights. This call is a "Code II" — instructing us to travel at speed with flashing lights, sirens at intersections are optional. We are responding to a violent domestic dispute in progress with people screaming for help. We are one of six units and an ambulance converging on a home in West Brownsville near the water plant. We travel rapidly across town at high speeds on the straightaways. We brake at traffic lights and stop signs and then peel out. The siren helps get us through crowded intersections.

As we arrive at the house, Robert tells me to stay near the car. I do, and smell the scorched rubber of our smoking tires. Officers are piling out of cars and surrounding the house. The situation is this: a male is in the front room with a knife. Two women, one bleeding badly, have barricaded themselves in a side bedroom. The officers pull the two women out through the side bedroom window. One woman's hand is badly cut. She's the mother. Her adult son had attacked her adult daughter with a knife. The mother intervened and grabbed the blade to save her daughter. EMS takes her away, three fingers cut to the bone. Meanwhile, the officers are still surrounding the house. They coax the man out. He comes out and is swarmed and cuffed. Robert retrieves the knife. We examine it in the beam of our headlights — a sturdy ten-inch blade set in a wooden handle.

On the way back to the station to book in the evidence, I ask Robert if he likes his job. He says, "I love it. I love getting my adrenaline pumping. I love helping people — like those people back there. There's nothing like being a cop."

Back at the station, Robert fills out an evidence report and locks the knife in a locker. He then informs me that each eight-hour shift is permitted one 15-minute break and one 30-minute break. He asks if I'd like to take the 15-minute break now. Sure! I assume this means my donut shop trip. But no, we sit in the police lounge where I smoke a cigarette and Robert chats happily away on the telephone with his wife for fifteen solid minutes.

At 8:20 we go back on "10-8." On call and on patrol. Not one minute elapses before we are ordered to respond to a burglar alarm that has gone off at the Lin Buk Company on Adams Street. This is a rambling Chinese establishment incorporating several store fronts in a row — and advertising "Ropa Semi-Nueva" (half-new clothes). We check every door, every window, front and back. It's secure. Robert reckons a rat inside has set off the motion detector.

At 8:30, back on "10-8." We patrol the area between the south side of the Fort Brown Resaca and the levee bank of the Rio Grande. This is one of several "lover's lanes" in the city and eight or ten cars are parked beside the resaca *or under trees near the levee. We cruise slowly past them, Robert fixing our spotlight on each car in turn. In most cars no heads are visible, but now some heads pop up from front or back seats. Some engines start up. We run up onto the dirt road atop the levee and drive along it. Robert is giving the lovers five minutes to get themselves dressed and sorted out, and then we return for a second pass with the spotlight. This time the remaining cars get their engines started and creep off.*

At 8:53 we're back downtown in the Market Square prostitute area when we're dispatched to a "Subject Down" at 14th and Expressway. We arrive a couple of seconds before our back-up, Officer Trujillo. A man is face down and motionless in the grass beside this busy intersection. We get out and triangulate around him. Robert tries to rouse him. The man doesn't respond. Robert rolls him over on his back. Nothing. I'm not sure he's alive, but then his eyes roll open like a doll's. Rapidly he becomes conscious — and wild! He's totally incoherent, not knowing where he is or even who *he is. He's cussing and trying to break loose. He's cuffed and wrestled into the back seat. As we head for the station, he gets wilder by the second, thumping and thrashing about. We pull up to the jail entrance at the station with Officer Trujillo right behind us to help get the man the ten steps from the car door to the double-locked steel chamber that leads into the municipal jail's reception area. Buzzing and clanging steel doors, and we're inside. Strong, clear-eyed jailers meet us and help to handle him. His shoes are removed. He's thoroughly searched. Everything in his pockets is removed, and his shoes and belongings are turned over to the matron inside a barred safety cell with thick plexiglass windows. She tags and stores his few possessions. She takes his driving license and punches the name and license number into a computer which instantaneously brings up his mug shot and criminal history on the computer screen. Meanwhile, the man himself is becoming completely unglued. His pupils, even in the bright, unforgiving lights of the jail, are fully dilated, and his eyes are watering copiously. He is not crying, but is as distraught as a human can be. It is taking four officers to hold him. He's shrieking, kicking, wrestling. They manhandle him towards a padded cell. In he goes. We then go into the matron's security booth where she has six closed circuit TVs monitoring different cells. We study this wild man from a camera fixed in the ceiling of the padded cell. The man is berserk. Screaming, whistling, hopping up and down, battering the padded walls with his fists and head. In a span of two minutes he puts his body through a kaleidoscope of positions. Standing. Standing with arms stretched straight up above his head. He then lays himself out in a star shape on the padded floor. Now he balls himself up in a fetal position. And then up and hopping and shadow sparring. He's yelling at the top of his lungs and pounding the walls so hard they vibrate. The matron calls the duty sergeant. He arrives and joins us in watching the man on the TV monitor. After five minutes of watching he orders EMS called in. Everyone knows the man has some drug or, more likely, combination of drugs in him — but the question is whether the dose is life-threatening. EMS personnel arrive and, with the help of police and jailers, check him. He is not in danger. He's locked back in the padded cell until he comes down.*

We're back on "10-8" at 9:35. At 9:36 we are pulling over a car on Van Buren traveling without lights. We get out, and Robert shines his flashlight on the two occupants who we suspect might be drunks. But no, two very pretty girls, perfectly made-up, stare back like startled, bright-eyed does. Robert tells them to turn on their lights and waves them along.

By 10:20 we're back at the station for Robert to finish up some report writing, and, after thanking Robert, I'm passed along to the next shift, which begins with 10:45 "Roll Call." Fifteen fresh new officers, one female officer, and a plainclothes detective sit at tables two by two with their briefcases in front of them. At 10:45 Lieutenant Ruben Rios and the sergeant of this shift come in and sit side by side at what would be the teacher's desk in a classroom — which this in some ways is. There is a telephone on the desk in front of them. The sergeant checks that everyone for the shift is present and then says to especially watch for two vehicles stolen in the last couple of hours — and for five children who have run away from their homes today. As he begins to give descriptions of cars and kids, the phone rings and the lieutenant answers it. He orders two of the officers to go to a certain address for a domestic dispute in progress. These two officers immediately leave the room. The other officers shout after them: "Be careful." The sergeant continues with the descriptions of the runaways, boys and girls between thirteen and sixteen, but then the phone rings again. The lieutenant dispatches another two officers to another problem. He tells the sergeant to "hurry." The sergeant quickly wraps things up, and the officers bolt for their cars. The lieutenant tells them to "Be careful out there."

For the next hour, I ride with Lieutenant Rios in his car. Lieutenant Rios has been with BPD since 1971 and, like myself, is deep in middle age. A big, shambling man balding somewhat on top. He drives much slower than the younger men and, as the supervisor of this shift, he does not answer calls. He does, however, listen carefully to the radio. As patrol cars are dispatched here and there on various calls, he is registering units, locations, problems. Occasionally, he activates the radio and asks a question. The response is always immediate and punctuated with "Sir!" When you think about it, whenever Lieutenant Rios is on duty, night after night or day after day as the case may be, he, along with his sergeant, is responsible for the safety of 130,000 city residents and, of course, the patrolmen under him.

It does not take long to realize that each police officer has his own "style," and I soon get a sample of Lieutenant Rios'. We are traveling in a southmost residential area when we turn a corner and see about a dozen young people standing around, sitting on car hoods, talking and drinking beer. The lieutenant pulls up beside them and chats with them. Within a minute or so, one young man in his early twenties clearly takes the lead in responding. Everything is very civil. And then the lieutenant addresses this evident leader directly — and exposes the steel hand beneath the velvet glove. He says words to this effect: Everything's quiet here and that's good. But that boy there is well under age and drinking. That's against the law. So let's finish up pretty quick now. I'll be back in a while and if you're still here I'll do something about it. He then looks straight at the leader and says: "You're the oldest. I'm holding you responsible." The kids respond with okays, good nights, yes sirs. We drive on.

I ask Lieutenant Rios if he likes his job. He chuckles, says "Yes I do," and chuckles again. After a long pause he goes on to say — in words much like these — the following: "I'll tell you why I laugh. Do you know what p———means? No? Well, I'll tell you. It's a word that means something like 'dumb ass.' But very rude. Very rude. Fighting words. My father used to call me that a lot, and that's what I sometimes call my patrolmen and rookies. We call it the 'P' word around the station. I'll put it like this. The newest patrolmen make just a little over $10 an hour. Now you were there when that lunatic — a young, strong man — was brought in and put in the padded cell. How long did that take? About a half hour, right? Well, if I went up to you and said: Look, here's $5. I want you to go face up to a lunatic — or go face up to a 6' 2, 250-pound man, drunk and disorderly. And I want you to arrest that man, put handcuffs on that man, and bring that man into the jail Now would you do that for $5? Of course you wouldn't. No one would No one but a p——— would. And yet every night that's what I ask my officers to do again and again and again. And that's why I call them p———. And yes, I'm a p———— too. I think I could have made more money doing something else, but I like it. The only things that bother me are the external things———like the court system. But I like being a policeman.It's   not   boring   You're   handling   people."

In the parking lot of the Jack in the Box on 14th Street, we rendezvous with Officer Arturo Mena with whom I'll ride along for the graveyard shift, the shift on which, according to Lientenant Rios, the "real animals" come out. Officer Arturo Mena is a twenty-four-year-old single man and a Hanna High School graduate. He has been on the force for a year. Immediately prior to joining the force he served six years in the Marines. Like Robert Nieto and so many other BPD officers, Arturo has the brick build. His friends on the force have nicknamed him "Tattoo" in reference to the dwarf that starred in the television series "Fantasy Island." And, indeed, there is some facial and physical resemblance. Arturo has short arms and legs that sprout from a barrel of a torso. His hair is oddly cut: the sides are cut short, but the hair on top of his head is long and combed straight back. And the hair projects out beyond his head at the back. The overall shape of his hair is reminiscent of one of those racing bike helmets and it gives him the appearance of speed even when he's standing still. Arturo is very cheerful, very open, very talkative. He's an immediately likable person.

As soon as we crawl into his patrol car, at 12:08, we get our first call. A naked suspected burglar has been reported behind the Strawberry Square Mall. The animals are coming out. We race to the scene and join two other units behind the mall. There is a large, shadowy area of dumpsters, air conditioning machines, and loading bays behind the mall. The two other officers' cars are there, but they are not. They are somewhere in the shadowy area. Arturo tells me to stay near the car, and he runs crouching towards the dark area. His gun is still in its holster, but his hand is on his gun. His hair gives him a speedy look. I pace for three, four, five minutes. I can hear and see nothing. And then at 12:15 the three officers emerge out from behind some air conditioning machinery with a handcuffed man. He's not completely naked, but nearly so. The only thing he's wearing is a pair of raggedy jeans that are several sizes too big for him and they keep falling down, and he's not wearing any underwear. The crotch area of his jeans is wet. He's about thirty years old, and he looks like Hollywood's conception of a Mexican "bandito." Deeply unreliable looking. He has gold spray paint on his fingers — the paint sniffers' favorite. The man is put in the back of one of the patrol cars while we wait for the Border Patrol to arrive. The man writhes around in the back seat trying to get out of the cuffs. At 12:25 the BP van arrives, and they take custody.

At 12:26 we're back on "10-8" and are immediately dispatched to Los Ebanos for a loud music complaint. We cruise slowly through the block indicated with our windows rolled down but can hear nothing and drive on.

We begin patrolling on Paredes Line Road and we're near the Vermillion Bar and Restaurant when we see two men walking north in the block ahead. They are not walking together, but *are about one hundred yards apart. We cruise by them slowly, looking them over — neither of them are too steady. Arturo doesn't like the looks of them, so we "shoot a U" and come back again. Arturo talks to the first man, frisks him and then lets him go on his unsteady way. We then drive up to the second man who has now decided to change directions. Arturo pulls up to him and gets out. He talks to the man and then tells him to put his hands on the hood of the patrol car. Arturo pats him down for any weapons and then begins pulling out all the contents of his pockets. Bingo. He starts pulling out jewelry from various pockets: six, eight, ten, twelve necklaces and three sets of earrings with the price tags still on them. About $200 worth altogether. The man says he found them on the street and then a minute later remembers it was a man called "Mople" that gave him the jewelry. Arturo speaks into the radio microphone clipped to his collar and in less than one minute we are joined by a patrol car and two unmarked detectives' cars from which two plainclothes detectives emerge. They spread the merchandise out on the patrol car hood and examine it and the price tags carefully. They are trying to determine if what we have here is a theft or if the merchandise matches descriptions of any goods taken in a store burglary. Burglary, of course, is a much more serious charge. The detectives advise Arturo to book this fifty-year-old man for "public intoxication" with a "hold" for possible burglary. They will check their records in the morning.*

We book this man into the jail, and I notice most of the cells are filling up rapidly. About thirty to forty people are now locked up. There is a zoo-like atmosphere. Some people are pacing in their cells, some are yelling, most are curled up in blankets on the floor sleeping it off. A couple of people are sitting on the benches lining the cells, face in hands, crying. The lunatic in the padded cell is still as active as ever banging the walls, whistling, yelling. He calls for "Madre" over and over again, and then switches and starts calling for "Pedro" over and over again. Pedro is his own name.

At 1:20, after Arturo has written up an incident and evidence report, we go "10-8." At 1:22 we are dispatched to the public housing project off McDavitt Blvd. Someone had dialed the 911 emergency number, and then the phone call was cut off before anything was said. This could mean a number of things, but the worst possibility must be assumed. The dispatcher's "caller ID" has given us the address. We drive down Ash Street in the projects illuminating the house numbers with our spotlight. Just as we find the number, our backup arrives. No lights show in the house, and Arturo and the other officer knock on the door. A woman answers the door. They had some problems but now everything is okay. The officers say good night.

At 1:43, while patrolling Boca Chica, we are dispatched to the same projects off McDavitt for a "Juvenile Disturbance." Some youths, males and females, are sitting on the curb and on car hoods drinking beer and talking. Arturo pulls up, gets out and talks to the kids. Our backup arrives, but Arturo waves him along. The kids all look 21, or pretty close, and they're no problem. We drive off; they wave as we go.

Arturo remarks, "I have good memories of this project." It is where he grew up. He says it was nice there. His family eventually got better jobs and moved away to a house of their own. Arturo's father is the Bell Captain at the Radisson Hotel at South Padre Island, and his mother is a BISD cafeteria worker. The family's five children are now all doing well at school or at jobs. They are naturally very proud of Arturo's being a policeman.

I ask Arturo if he likes his job. He replies, "I like this job. It's different from everything. I work with great guys. Everybody takes care of everybody else. Everybody. Even if we might have some differences off the job, on the job we all take care of each other." He goes on to say that when he was just a kid, he promised himself that he would accomplish four things during his life: one — graduate from high school; two — be a Marine; three — be a police officer; four — get a college degree. He is happy that three of these goals have already been accomplished, and he plans to start attending college part-time next year.

At 1:54 we are dispatched to a domestic dispute in the Lincoln Park area. No lights show in the front, and a high chain-link fence surrounds the house. The front gate is chained. We cruise into the alley way in back, and meet the backup patrol car there. We park hood to hood, headlights to headlights. Arturo and the officer get out and call over the fence to the back of the house.

A woman comes out to talk. There had been "some yelling, but no hitting." Everything's okay now. We say good night.

At 2:00 we head to the gritty bars that line 14th Street: Charlie's Bar, Charlie's Lounge, Papucho's Bar, JP Lounge, Monkey Bar, El Tejano Bar, Cabanita Bar. We monitor the 2:00 closing time to make sure there are no fights and to arrest anyone obviously drunk who tries to get in the driver's side of a car. We look into one or two bars to make sure the customers move out. Everything's pretty peaceful and most of the patrons toddle off on foot in different directions.

By 2:15 we are back patrolling on Boca Chica when it starts to rain. Within five minutes, at 2:20, we are dispatched along with other units and an ambulance to an "Accident with Injury" near Perkins Intermediate School. As the closest unit to the accident scene, we are instructed to go "Code III." With flashing lights and continuous siren, we tear down Boca Chica. We take the interior lane and traffic melts off into the right-hand lanes as we approach. We are traveling rapidly, very rapidly, but we're still braking and slowing at major intersections. At "Four Corners," where seven lanes intersect with six lanes, we activate a foghorn device to clear our way through.

As we approach the accident scene, we see a number of people standing in the street and in nearby yards. A car has jumped the curb, crossed a yard, and plowed into the side of a wooden frame house. Seeing this, Arturo immediately radios for a fire engine in case the gas line going into the home has been cracked. We get out. Two teenage girls who were in the car are now standing in the rain beside it, badly shaken. One of the girls, wearing a t-shirt with Selena's photograph stenciled on it, has a bloodied face. The blood is coming from a gash over her eye and a tear down the length of her nose, which I am certain is also broken. It is already swelling wide. She also complains that her leg is hurting. The girl says she does not want to use the ambulance, can't afford it. But Arturo convinces her she's hurt, could have a concussion, and needs to go in the ambulance. There are other problems. Neither of the girls has a driver's license; the car is not theirs, but a "friend's," and, no, they don't know whether it is insured or not. This information, especially the question of the insurance, has gotten the homeowner's family very excitable.

Who's going to pay for the damage to their home? Good question. They begin to badger Arturo, me, and the other police officers for an answer.

After a few minutes, another BPD patrol car rolls up to join the three patrol cars, ambulance, fire engine, and tow truck already on the scene. This patrol car is driven by an officer from the traffic division, and he now takes over the situation. He measures some skid marks. He talks to the girl who was driving while EMS personnel are loading her into the ambulance. She says a van hit her car and ran her off the road. However, the traffic division officer can find no dent or paint residue on the side of the car she claims was hit. One by one, the emergency vehicles begin to pull away, leaving an increasingly panicky homeowner and his family. They plead with the traffic officer not to have the car towed away. It should be left with them as collateral in case no one pays to repair their home. The officer thinks about this a moment and then speaks into his collar mike to the sergeant back at the station to see what he thinks of this proposal. The sergeant says it sounds okay. As we pull away, the homeowners are cheerfully rolling up the car's windows and securing it for the night.

We go "10-8" again. "On call and on patrol." A few minutes later, we're sent to yet another domestic dispute at the projects off McDavitt. When we get there another officer is already present and talking to a woman in the front yard. He needs no backup and waves us on.

At 3:19 we're dispatched to the southmost area where a "Domestic Dispute with Violence" is occurring. Always dangerous. However, Arturo never refers to these as "domestic disputes;" he just says there's "a family that needs our help." We begin to head for the address, but not as rapidly as I expect. I ask Arturo why we are not speeding with flashing lights. He informs me his backup is two miles further away than us, and he's coming as fast as he can. We're going somewhat slower so that we converge on the house at about the same time. As it is, we get there first and get out. Although it's well after three in the morning, six or seven sad looking kids from about seven to fifteen years old are standing fully-dressed in the front yard. One boy is bouncing a basketball on the walkway. A sullen looking man in his forties sits in a chair on the porch. He's wearing shorts, white knee socks, and sandals.

He's not wearing a shirt. The front door is wide open, and a woman can be seen moving about inside. I stay out front, and Arturo speaks to the man and goes inside. Thirty seconds later the back-up unit comes barreling up, and that officer, too, goes inside. For a while it's quiet, and then violent commotion: shouting, cursing, struggling. The two officers then bring a tiny, drunken spitfire of a woman out handcuffed from behind. As she's brought out, she tries to charge her husband and screams curses at him. He starts to come at her, but the older boys push him back while the officers pull the woman away. The woman is now cursing us all and screaming: "Take me in! Take me in!" Once she's in the back seat, Arturo and the other officer confer on charges. Apparently it was she who assaulted the husband, and she also struck the two officers, but the officers decide to let that go. They settle on "disorderly conduct."

At 3:31 we're inbound to the station. The woman in the back eventually stops yelling at us and starts crying. Sobbing her heart out. She pleads with us through the plexiglass shielding to see that her kids are looked after. We arrive at the jail at 3:37. When the car door is opened, she comes out crying and terribly bitter. As we head for the jail door, Arturo asks her if she's been to jail before. She hisses: "I won't lie. I've been in trouble in Florida before." She marches straight to the jail door.

Inside, she stands before the matron's booth waiting to be booked. Still in cuffs, she's sobbing like there's no tomorrow. Her face is so ravaged, so terribly unhappy, that it hurts to look at her. She wears a super-sized t-shirt that comes down to her knees. The t-shirt says: "Everybody gets 15 minutes of fame. I'm on overtime."

I look around the cells. They're all filled up. There must be fifty or sixty people locked down, and sad looking people in cuffs are still arriving. The lunatic in the padded cell is still going strong with his yelling and banging.

At 4:05 we step outside the jail. I feel very tired. I had intended to see this second shift through to the end, but I decide I've had enough. I tell Arturo I'm just going to go home.

We shake hands, and I thank him. Then, I don't know why, I shake his hand again. As I turn to leave, Arturo Mena, with the speedy looking hair, is standing with one foot already inside his

patrol car. He's smiling. He speaks into his collar mike, gives his code number, and says, "I'm 10-8."
Brownsville's Finest.

W.L.A.

Law Enforcement

Any newcomer to Brownsville will quickly deduce that Brownsville is a high-crime area. The evidence is everywhere: the clubs on car steering columns, the heavy shutters on store fronts, the barred windows on houses, and the prevalence in many city neighborhoods — unusual elsewhere in America — of homes having both their front and back yards enclosed by high chain-link fences, and, as often as not, with watchdogs patrolling within. This evidence is corroborated by flipping through the local 1996 telephone directory yellow pages and taking notice of the attorney listings running from page 28 to page 64 — touting specialities in everything from criminal defense to "slip and falls." A few pages deeper into the directory one comes upon the depressingly extensive Brownsville bail bond listings : A-Fast Bail Bonds ("You ring; We spring"), AM-PM Bail Bonds, Aguila Bail Bonds, Cameron Bail Bonding ("In Trouble . . . Call Us on the Double"), and on and on through the alphabetical listings.

To combat the criminals, Brownsville relies on an array of law enforcement agencies. These include local agencies (Brownsville Police Department and Cameron County Sheriff's Department); state agencies (Department of Public Safety); and federal agencies (Customs Bureau, Border Patrol, Drug Enforcement Agency, Federal Bureau of Investigation, and U.S. Marshals Service).

Brownsville's first and foremost line of defense against criminal activity is the Brownsville Police Department, the largest Valley crime-fighting outfit and, according to Leslie Parks (Director of the Criminal Justice Institute attached to the University of Texas at Brownsville and an official who oversaw twelve regional police academies in 1995), the "most highly-regarded, most professional police department south of San Antonio."

In November 1995 thirty-eight-year-old Ben Reyna took over as chief of this exceptional force, following able predecessors Victor Rodriguez and Andy Vega. Chief Reyna is remarkably young looking. When he took the podium at a 1995 Dallas convention of metropolitan police chiefs, one startled chief's wife exclaimed, "My goodness, child, how old are you?" But youth aside, there is little doubt Chief Reyna will succeed in maintaining the BPD's squeaky clean image. As the *Brownsville Herald* has revealed, the chief has never smoked a cigarette or drunk a beer. (Although the chief, when pressed, does allow he once tasted a beer. He just didn't like it.) At any rate, having headed BPD's Internal Affairs Division for nine years immediately prior to assuming the force's top spot, there is no question Reyna is sensitive to, and intolerant of, police malfeasance. When, within the first few weeks of his stewardship, a policeman was brought before him accused of kicking an obstreperous handcuffed suspect, the chief fired him on the spot when the officer gave as his excuse: "My foot slipped."

The force that Reyna heads is composed of 197 licensed police officers (forty of whom are detectives) and an additional ninety-seven civilian employees (dispatchers, jailers, etc.). Although there is some variation with time of day and day of the week, at any given moment there are usually about twenty-five officers patrolling the city and, in an emergency, these can be immediately reinforced by another twenty officers from headquarters. These numbers are well in line with nationwide staffing levels where the rule of thumb is that modern American cities need 1.5 licensed police officers for every thousand of population. Since Brownsville has a population of 130,000 that would translate into a recommended force of 195 (130,000 x .0015 = 195). In actual fact, owing to its high poverty level and border location — wherein Matamoros' crop of criminals supplements the activities of Brownsville's homegrown variety — Chief Reyna feels a force of 225 licensed officers would be desirable and justifiable.

One aspect of the department's personnel statistics that Reyna is not happy with is the dearth of female officers: only six are on the force. But increasing that number will not be easy due to what Reyna sees as a deep cultural aversion: Hispanic fathers and husbands do not want their daughters and wives involved in such "dirty" and dangerous work.

On the whole, the BPD is young, Hispanic, bilingual (although Spanish is not an absolute requirement), and fairly well-educated. All officers must have a high school diploma or equivalency, and most new hires also have some college education or compensating life experiences such as military service.

The force has a vehicular fleet of fifty marked patrol cars, fifty unmarked cars and ten motorcycles. Not all of the unmarked cars are the big, monotone black-tired, lot-bought Caprices half the city residents immediately recognize as police vehicles. The force has dozens of perfectly-disguised forfeited and seized vehicles (pick-ups, vans, rusted-out hulks, *chuko* cars, and others) that blend in with city traffic. These undercover cars are renewed constantly to prevent detection.

Chief Reyna is reluctant to label any Brownsville neighborhood as a high-crime area, except for the downtown sector. He admits the downtown commercial district's proximity to the river and international bridges makes it vulnerable to the criminal element from "across" (purse-snatchers, shop-lifters, burglars, car thieves, and prostitutes), but this vulnerability he hopes to alleviate by increasing foot and bike patrols pairing police officers with their Border Patrol counterparts. Theoretically, this could double effectiveness, since Border Patrol agents have the authority to ask anyone — particularly suspicious looking persons, for citizenship or residency documentation, whereas police officers do not.

But as for singling out any residential neighborhood such as the Southmost area or any of the several public housing projects as being particularly crime prone, this he will not do. He will allow for the fact that the department receives more calls to certain city areas than to others and that these are generally the poorer areas, but many of these calls are for domestic disputes. Reyna thinks there may very well be just as many domestic disturbances occurring in wealthy neighborhoods like Rio Viejo, but due to the large, semi-secluded nature of the homes, these disturbances are unlikely to be heard or reported by neighbors. Moreover, troubled families in such wealthy areas have the resources to seek professional counselling or psychiatric help, luxuries poorer families cannot afford. When families in the poorer sections of the city need help, their first, and often only, recourse is to call the police. Quite understandably, Chief Reyna does not wish to discourage those calls. On the contrary, responding to those cries is in keeping with the oath all BPD officers make "To protect and serve," and to do so, Reyna leans forward to give the words emphasis, "with courtesy, kindness, and concern."

On the whole, while not being complacent, Chief Reyna is pleased with declining crime statistics in Brownsville. Compared to 1994, 1995 criminal statistics were promising: rapes were down 14%; robberies were down 18%; vehicle thefts were down 24%; and burglaries were down a hefty 39%. Most encouraging of all, only seven murders were recorded in Brownsville during the course of 1995 as compared to 14 in 1994. Unfortunately, murder was up more than 100% in Matamoros where there were 41 homicides recorded between January and October of 1995 — a worrisome sign since any epidemic in Matamoros, criminal or otherwise, has a way of eventually infecting Brownsville.

Three problem areas the chief has strong feelings about as he begins his tenure of office are gang activity, prostitution, and spring breakers. So far, the chief believes BPD has done an excellent job of discouraging the gang activity and vandalism that plague McAllen, Edinburg, and other Valley cities. The relative absence of graffiti in Brownsville is but one sign of BPD's success in this area. Chief Reyna intends to continue his predecessors' strategy of snuffing out gang activity before it gains a hold. For instance, when from time to time patrolmen notice groups of youths congregating at Strawberry Mall or at fast food parking lots, or spot three or four low riders cruising in convoy down Boca Chica Boulevard, they get right on it: break up the groups of kids, pull over the low riders, bring in drug-sniffing dogs to search both cars and kids. To put it bluntly, they hound and harass these groups out of existence before they become a fixture of the community. Likewise with gang graffiti. When it appears in a neighborhood, the police put some manpower on the case and go knocking door to door asking questions, looking for suspects. And while the chief allows that such efforts rarely net an arrest, the very fact that the police are out in force looking for the culprits puts a chill on incipient gang activity. Reyna believes this approach is more effective than any curfew (which he does not favor), and that this approach is one reason he can claim with certitude that there is not a single "crack house" in Brownsville.

The long-standing prostitution problem, particularly downtown in the Market Square area, in the vicinity of Immaculate Conception Cathedral, and, more recently, along International Boulevard, is another blight on the community Reyna and the BPD hope to eradicate or, at least, radically reduce. It will not be easy. In speaking of the problem to *Brownsville Herald* reporters in March 1995, former chief Victor Rodriguez said: "We're just flat tired. The problem prevails and it will continue to prevail. I wish I could find the one thing to clean it up once and for all. We shouldn't have to see that in the downtown area around a cathedral." Rodriguez was commenting upon a March 1995 sweep made by four BPD detectives that netted twenty-one prostitutes — eight of whom eventually proved to be male transvestites when they were sorted out at the county jail. According to Jerry Martinez, a Cameron County Detention Officer, the guideline used in assigning these folks to male or female cells was whether or not they had a penis. No other criteria would work because most transvestites have breasts and "use hormones to enhance mammary glands . . . hormones designed for farm animals, like cows and stuff." For their own protection, these male transvestites are never jailed or exercised with the "general population," but instead are placed with the mentally and physically handicapped and the "crazies."

The new chief plans to tackle the problem somewhat differently. He had first wanted to arrest the "Johns" and have their names, addresses, and photographs displayed in the *Brownsville Herald,* but the newspaper either did not wish to devote so much photographic space to the topic, or, perhaps, realized what a devastating impact such action would have on marriages, families, and reputations. So instead, Reyna intends to carry out raids on the seedy hotels, motels, and apartment blocks used for the illicit trysts. He feels that by barging onto the scene with police, officials of the state attorney's office, health inspectors, and rolling video cameras, he will force the owners and landlords to either clean up their act and end prostitution on their premises or risk having their buildings condemned for health violations and demolished — literally bulldozed.

The Spring Break scourge may be an even more difficult conundrum to solve. The chief sees the nightly swarming from South Padre Island to Matamoros as "an extreme hazard for the kids" and "a dead loss to the city," as far as his department is concerned. "It ties up a lot of police hours." As in past years, BPD's goals will be to "channelize" the kids — get them in and out of the city as quickly and efficiently as possible to minimize the harm to the community. BPD will try to get the breakers to park or, preferably, de-bus as close as possible to Gateway International Bridge, and then to re-embark with as much dispatch as possible when they return. He wants to do everything he can to prevent them from drifting drunkenly about town making trouble. Reyna doesn't buy the argument that parents (either out-of-state parents or local parents) are ignorant of what really goes on at Spring Break: "Parents know exactly what their kids are going to do, and they tolerate it. I've seen ten-year-olds come back [from Matamoros] plastered." Reyna believes the problem "needs to be addressed by everyone from here to Padre Island."

Aside from the Brownsville Police Department, the only other exclusively local law enforcement agency is the Cameron County Sheriff's Department headquartered at the Cameron County Hall of Justice complex on East Harrison Street in Brownsville. The sheriff"s department, under the command of elected Sheriff Alex Perez, employs seventy-eight full-time deputy sheriffs to investigate crimes and patrol the county's 4,400 square miles. For the most part, although the sheriff is the chief law enforcement official in the county, law enforcement within the corporate limits of Brownsville, Harlingen and the other main cities of the county is left to their respective municipal police departments, while the sheriff's department concentrates on enforcing the law in rural areas and assists police officials in smaller towns. For instance, the sheriff's dispatchers serve such small county towns as Primera, Combes, Laguna Vista, and Rio Hondo where the town may have only one or two policemen and must rely on sheriff's deputies for assistance and back up in many situations, particularly when violence may be anticipated. As for the single "hottest" crime area in the county, according to the department's Lt. Arnold Flores, deputies are dispatched more often to Cameron Park than to any other locale. (This *colonia* situated on the northern edge of Brownsville is a maze of unimproved dirt roads and 1,600 mainly poorer homes and makeshift shacks housing 4,000 people — many of whom are recent Mexican immigrants or illegals — which Brownsville's city government refuses to annex into the corporate limits for fear of the drain it would be on city resources.) Naturally, this poor *colonia* warrants considerable policing, and, since it is unincorporated, the sheriff's department must provide it.

In addition to the seventy-eight licensed deputies, the sheriff has 159 licensed jailers. Seventy-nine of the jailers work at the maximum-security Cameron County Jail in the Hall of Justice complex which has a prisoner capacity of 258; fifty-four work at the minimum security Detention Center I which has a capacity of 288; and twenty-six are employed at Detention Center II which has a capacity of 192 and also is minimum security. The two detention centers, two blocks east of the Hall of Justice, hold both county and federal suspects awaiting trial, while the county jail holds convicted prisoners being held for sentences not exceeding one year, plus serious convicted offenders awaiting transfer to either the Texas or federal prison systems. Those destined for incarceration in the Texas prison system are periodically collected, usually within two to three weeks of sentencing, by a Texas Department of Corrections secure bus and transported to Huntsville. Convicts destined for the Federal Bureau of Prisons are collected by the U.S. Marshals and flown to their designated prison on secure airplanes owned and operated by the U.S. Marshals Service which periodically call at the Brownsville Airport.

One issue that should be of concern to all law enforcement officials and county residents alike is the absurd ruling by a federal jury in November 1995 that awarded damages of $80,000 against Cameron County and $50,000 against Sheriff Alex Perez personally for the 1988 strip searching of a Harlingen pawnbroker being booked into the county jail for having a suspected stolen gun in his possession. The gun was later proved not to be stolen, and the pawnbroker's emotional trauma for having had to strip naked, bend over and spread his cheeks was valued at $130,000 by the jury. So, despite the well-known fact that suspects frequently try to smuggle drugs and weapons into jails — and in his defense, Sheriff Perez cited an incident where a prisoner was found with a pistol stuffed in his anus — the county jail has rescinded the routine strip-searching of its prisoners until an appeal can be heard. In the meantime, of course, if there is any homicide or suicide at the jail involving a gun or a knife, you can be sure the county and sheriff will face another suit — this time for negligence. It's another no-win, damned if you do, damned if you don't, situation for law enforcement.

The main state law enforcement agency in Brownsville is the Department of Public Safety located on the west end of Boca Chica Boulevard. Here, there are two state troopers who conduct road tests for driver's license applicants and eight troopers who patrol the nearby highways — mainly highways 44, 77, 100, and 281. The ten troopers are led by Sgt. Raul Vargas and aside from their road testing and patrolling duties, they assist in manhunts, respond to accidents, and help local police officials during major emergencies such as hurricanes or building collapses. Corporal Minerva Peña also reports that DPS catches numerous wanted criminals during the routine photographing, fingerprinting, and document checking of driver's license applications and renewals.

Recently, the Brownsville DPS office has been augmented by the arrival of its first ever, permanently-assigned Texas Ranger. There are fewer than a hundred rangers statewide in this legendary branch of the DPS, and Texas Ranger Rolando Castaneda will be available, upon request, to conduct investigations of political and police corruption at the municipal, county, or state levels.

The largest federal law enforcement group operating in the city is the Brownsville office of the U.S. Customs Bureau of the Treasury Department. The local office, headed by trim, plain-spoken, fifty-six-year-old Chief Inspector Paula Greene, has 153 inspectors and fifteen dogs. They are responsible for enforcing customs, especially those pertaining to federal drug laws, at seven locations: Gateway International Bridge, the Brownsville & Matamoros Bridge, the Los Indios Bridge, the Port of Brownsville, the Brownsville Airport, the Southern Pacific Railyard, and the Union Pacific Railyard. The difficulty of the task may be gleaned just by looking at average monthly bridge crossing statistics during 1995: 30,000 vehicles (no pedestrians) crossed the Los Indios Bridge each month; 200,000 vehicles and 12,000 pedestrians crossed the B&M Bridge; and a whopping 250,000 vehicles and 250,000 pedestrians came over Gateway International.

Each of these entrants will be questioned at the toll gates or pedestrian entry booths by either U.S. Customs officials or U.S. Immigration and Naturalization Service inspectors. Any person or vehicle suspected of smuggling contraband, plus a random number of all persons and vehicles, are then "secondaried" for more thorough questioning and inspection. Efforts are made to avoid any semblance of a routine creeping into the work: for instance "secondarying" every eighth car or every tenth person. Also, on any given day, several "blitzes" are conducted in which for a time every vehicle or every person is subjected to a secondary search. The customs inspectors are, of course, trained at their academy in the nuances of suspect behavior — and develop further expertise on the job. What they are looking for, according to Chief Inspector Paula Greene, is the inconsistent statement, the averted eyes of a liar, the whole gamut of a person's body language. In general, the driver or pedestrian who appears either too nervous or, on the contrary, too nonchalant, too studiously "cool," is a good candidate for more thorough questioning and searching. The innocent driver or pedestrian falls somewhere in the middle: not too nervous, but not completely at ease either. Paula says there is no stereotypical drug smuggler. Innocuous-looking Winter Texan types have been caught; women feigning pregnancy have been caught; meek looking persons wearing priests' collars have been caught.

The fifteen dogs that assist the customs inspectors are of no particular breed, and the one thing they have in common is that none of them are pedigreed. All of them have been trained to detect drugs — all drugs: heroin, cocaine, marijuana, amphetamines. Their olfactory sense is so acute that they frequently detect the drugs just by walking around a person, car, or truck. The background odors of most cargoes will seldom confuse them, nor, usually, will the smugglers' trick of concealing the drugs within gasoline or diesel fuel tanks. Most wonderfully, the dogs are proficient at detecting paper currency that has been handled by drug traffickers. So efficacious are the dogs that in the past, drug organizations have put out "contracts" on the lives of particularly successful individual dogs.

One ongoing problem Paula Greene and the bridge inspectors face is the existence of "spotters" at the bridges. These are individuals employed by the drug organizations to hang around the bridges from either the Brownsville or Matamoros sides to keep watch on the inspection booths and lanes and signal information to smugglers who are crossing. This is something of a cat and mouse game, because not only are the spotters watching, but customs is also watching for the "watchers" by both human and electronic means, including hidden television cameras. If Customs can detect the spotter, they can surmise that a shipment is about to come across and respond accordingly. The spotter, of course, is doing all he can to maximize the chances of getting the shipment through: seeing if there is a "blitz" in progress, seeing if any pattern has emerged as to which vehicles are being "secondaried" at the booths, and seeing, according to Greene, which booths are manned by INS inspectors and which by Customs inspectors, each of which have easily identifiable uniforms. It is Greene's belief that INS inspectors are best at detecting illegal aliens and Customs inspectors are best at detecting illegal drugs. Consequently, drug smuggler spotters are directing their vehicles to INS-manned lanes, alien smuggler spotters are directing their vehicles into Customs lanes. When asked if what really might be at work here is that the spotters are directing the smugglers towards a booth where they have a bribed official in place, Paula responded: "Oh God, I hope not."

Another large, high profile federal entity enforcing law in the Brownsville area is the U.S. Border Patrol, an agency of the Immigration and Naturalization Service which, in turn, is a branch of the Justice Department. The Brownsville Border Patrol office is responsible for patrolling a sixty-three-mile stretch of the U.S.-Mexican Border (the Rio Grande), commencing at a point ten miles west of Port Isabel and continuing sixty-three miles upriver. To deter or detect and catch some of the tens of thousands of illegal aliens, *coyotes*, border bandits, and drug smugglers who cross that section of the river each year, the Brownsville BP deploys 138 agents (eight are women), eighty-five vehicles, six horses, and one dog — all at the command of thirty-nine-year-old Patrol Agent-in-Charge David Agular. Their task is daunting. Many of the illegal aliens (or, as the politically-correct crowd would have it, "undocumented residents") come across on their own accord — most frequently in the 2½ mile river frontage marked from one mile upriver from the Brownsville and Matamoros Bridge to one mile downriver of Gateway International Bridge. They may wade across when the river is low, cross on submerged stepping stones, swim, or paddle across sitting in tire innertubes. They may also cross atop the bridges with false documents or hidden in or under cars, trucks, and trains. Of course, these freelance crossers are the most likely to be apprehended right at the point of their arrival in Brownsville, or soon after on the streets of the city, or at the airport or bus terminals, or at one of the Border Patrol checkpoints on all major highways leading north out of Brownsville and the Rio Grande Valley. The more serious illegals, those wanting to move north out of the Valley and to lose themselves in the interior of the United States, are more likely to employ a *coyote,* a professional alien smuggler. These *coyotes* actively recruit their *pollos* ("chickens") in Central American countries, in major Mexican interior cities, and in Matamoros. Spotters ply the large, busy Matamoros bus terminal looking for poor Mexican families and single men arriving on buses from the Mexican interior, and the spotters also have ties with the cheapest Matamoros hotels where such poor people stay while they're checking out the lay of the land and choosing the time of their crossing.

The *coyotes,* for a fee of about $200, will arrange a river crossing, but the charge to deliver a chicken to an interior city, say Dallas, Houston or Chicago, ranges from several hundred to even several thousand dollars. For this money, the *coyotes* can offer much better odds of making it. They have staging houses in Matamoros and, says David Agular, staging houses in Brownsville "too numerous to name." And, with only 138 agents to guard sixty-three miles of river, obviously not all portions of the river can be guarded all of the time. The *coyotes* will choose the place and the time of the crossing — with periods of heavy rain and low visibility being especially preferred. Once in Brownsville the *pollos* will be held in another staging house until spotters and *coyotes* judge it propitious to move them north — in cars, trucks, U-Hauls, and train boxcars. Agular says, "It's ungodly what the *coyotes* put a fellow human being through." [At this point he takes this writer out to the large lot of impounded cars behind the BP's headquarters on North Expressway to inspect a small U-Haul seized the previous day that had twenty-six Mexicans and Peruvians crammed inside it. The U-Haul, when stopped and unlocked north of Brownsville, had been on the road an hour, and already many of the women and children had passed out — and they had another five hours to go to Houston.]

To combat the illegals and the alien and drug smugglers, BP pursues a defense-in-depth strategy. The Border Patrol maintains dirt roads and trails atop the levees of the Rio Grande throughout most of the Brownsville office's sector, and these roads and trails are patrolled by the green and white Broncos and Suburbans that make up the bulk of the BP fleet, and also by agents on horseback. The BP also has embedded infrared and geoseismic sensors along the banks and levees capable of detecting humans by body heat or the tread of a human foot. Soon, the BP will add low-light television cameras to their technological arsenal, whereby a single agent can monitor twelve screens at a time capable of viewing long stretches of the river day or night.

Within Brownsville's city limits, the BP concentrates on deterring illegal crossings by maintaining high visibility. That is why the BP has very few unmarked vehicles, and the agents usually wear their prominent forest green uniforms. (However, some BP agents do operate undercover, particularly in the ongoing work of ferreting out dealers in counterfeit documents such as birth certificates, Texas driver's licenses, and social security cards. "A booming business" in Brownsville according to David Agular.) The agents also operate foot patrols and bike patrols in which they are paired with Brownsville police officers and nab suspected illegals from the streets of Brownsville, although they assiduously avoid schools and churches. They take special care to watch departures at all three Brownsville bus terminals, the airport and the railyards. Virtually all trains that cross the B&M road/train bridge are searched, as are the trains that depart from the Union Pacific Railyard. This is the main work of "Harris," the Brownsville office's only dog. Like all BP dogs throughout the nation, Harris is a Belgian Malonois, a breed that looks much like a German shepherd but darker in color and with a smaller frame which allows for greater agility in searching among cargo in truck trailers and in freight cars. Moreover, whereas most dogs can only be trained to respond to one odor — say drugs, humans, or explosives — Harris is something of a wonder dog that can detect drugs or humans equally well. With a sense of smell 4,000 times more acute than a human's, at the railyard Harris lopes along the sides of trains preparing for departure, and stops outside any boxcar concealing people.

If illegals make it beyond Brownsville and the immediate Valley area, the BP's next best chance of catching them is at one of the BP checkpoints on the major highways. The Sarita checkpoint on U.S. 77 and the Falfurias checkpoint on U.S. 281 are situated in very sparsely settled ranch areas in dry chapparal country. These are not easy bottlenecks for illegals to pass. Virtually every vehicle is stopped, and the occupants, particularly non-English speakers, are questioned concerning their citizenship and residency status. Belgian Malonois are also present. The agents are, of course, alert to nervous respondents and look carefully at the set of a car's chassis and rear tires which might indicate a person hidden in the trunk. Because of such scrutiny, *coyotes* transporting their illegals in cars, trucks or U-Hauls will typically unload the *pollos* well south of the checkpoints and make them run through the open range land and then collect them at a roadside rendezvous well north of the checkpoints. However, the BP again has infrared and geoseismic sensors buried in these range lands to detect the aliens' presence. Other *coyotes* try to avoid the checkpoints altogether by moving their cargoes north through a patchwork of little frequented farm and ranch roads, but the BP have tried to counter this with "Operation Backroads," which employs helicopters and light aircraft.

On a typical day, Brownsville BP agents catch between 100 to 450 illegals. Most of the illegals caught are Mexicans, but by no means all. For example, when Agent-in-Charge Agular was interviewed on November 16, 1995, he checked his computer which showed that so far during that month his agents had also caught 101 Hondurans, 83 El Salvadorans, 50 Guatemalans, 35 Asians (mainly from China and India), 30 Nicaraguans, 8 Iraqis and 6 Ecuadoreans. When BP catches persons from Iraq or other nations adjudged especially hostile to the U.S. (e.g. Iran, Libya, North Korea, Cuba), the FBI must be called in to interview and debrief these people to ascertain if they pose a terroristic threat, to determine how they managed to reach the U.S., and to discover any information they might possess concerning conditions in their usually closed societies.

But what makes BP work most discouraging is the fact that the U.S. Justice Department policy is that if there is no evidence of a crime having been committed — *other than illegally entering the U.S.*, which is itself a misdemeanor crime for a first offense (a felony for a subsequent offense) — the apprehended person has a choice of either being "voluntarily returned" or going before an immigration judge and making a plea for political asylum. The vast majority of Mexicans choose to be returned voluntarily, in which case they are escorted to the middle of Gateway International Bridge and set free *within one to four hours* of their apprehension!

Naturally, many of these Mexicans will try crossing again — often the same day.

Those persons who are apprehended who seek political asylum and other long-term detainees are usually held at the Immigration and Naturalization Service's Bayview Detention Center northeast of Brownsville. This facility usually holds about 800 detainees, but by erecting tents can quickly be expanded to accommodate up to 3,000 persons during such immigration inundations as occurred in the winter of 1987-1988 when thousands of Nicaraguans fleeing the Contra-Sandanista civil war arrived in Brownsville.

One bright new prospect for alien control is the BP's new high-tech "IDENT" system. The first "IDENT" machine arrived in Brownsville in November 1995, and David Agular arranged a demonstration of its use. He plucked one man at random from the Brownsville office's holding tank (a large, locked room with steel mesh and plexiglassed viewing windows in which poor, unhappy looking men, women and children sat on benches) and led him into the IDENT room. The person selected was a polite, humble, cooperative young man who gave his name as Vicente Robles. He said he had come up from Guerrero state in southern Mexico and had been caught near the Sarita checkpoint. He was sat before a computer screen and a flexible probe with a tiny camera lens at its tip was aimed at his face — which then appeared, to this unsophisticated man's utter amazement, in full color on the computer screen. Next, his right and left index fingers were placed on two pads wired into the computer, and these two fingers' prints then appeared in two boxes below the man's face on the computer. A button was pushed and face and fingerprints were transmitted to INS headquarters in Washington where the man's face and fingerprints were instantaneously filed and analyzed by computer to see if they matched any already on file. In less than 90 seconds the answer came back: negative. Vicente Robles had never been caught trying to enter the country before, and had no criminal record on file. Hence, Vicente Robles was to be released, but if ever caught again trying to enter the U.S., the IDENT system would know it, regardless of what alias he might use, and he could be prosecuted and incarcerated for a federal felony. This system has the potential of ending the revolving door policy of illegal entry if, and that's a mighty big if, the Justice Department and federal courts have the will to prosecute the cases.

As for Patrol Agent-in-Charge David Agular, he believes the best and surest solution to illegal entries would be an impenetrable fence on the border from one mile upstream of the B&M Bridge to one mile downstream of the Gateway International Bridge. Despite selective media clips showing illegal aliens climbing over or tunneling under such fences in California, David says he's personally seen what the fences can do. He was very emphatic: "The fences work! They help tremendously! Tremendously!"

Whereas the Border Patrol, like the Brownsville Police Department, intentionally pursues a high-profile stance for its deterrent value, at least one law enforcement agency in Brownsville chooses to maintain as discrete a presence as possible. This is the U.S. DEA (Drug Enforcement Agency), today one of the world's premier law enforcement/intelligence organizations. As far as involving work that is intellectually demanding, physically dangerous, and emotionally depressing, it rivals and perhaps eclipses Israel's MOSSAD, Britain's SIS, France's Sureté, and the U.S.'s CIA, each of which are agencies that maintain worldwide networks and are deeply dependent on undercover work. The danger inherent in such work was brought home to the local area's population when Kiki Camarena, a DEA agent with local ties, was revealed to have suffered an agonizing death in Guadalajara, Mexico — a death in which torture was carefully supervised and expertly prolonged by a Mexican physician in the employ of drug lords.

The Brownsville office of the DEA is situated well back from the side of one of the city's main northern thoroughfares. Like all DEA offices, the Brownsville office's location was carefully selected: a nondescript building designed not to attract attention; a freestanding building that allows for 360° surveillance of approaches while minimizing risks to adjacent businesses; and, most of all, an office that eschews a vulnerable ground floor location. The doors that lead into the local office are sturdy steel affairs with viewing peepholes. The visitors' waiting room — which must be very, very seldom used — has an upholstered couch, an upholstered chair, and a round electric wall clock that can be heard humming in the silence. Another heavy steel door with coded locks gives admittance to the inner sanctum. The overall atmosphere of the chamber inspires a vague sense of dread, like sitting in the waiting room of an unpopular dentist. Behind a glass partition, an ancient secretary can be seen moving slowly about. She is a grandmotherly figure who looks like she would be more comfortable somewhere else, perhaps in a rocker by a fireplace shucking peas. She addresses one through a slot in the bottom of the glass partition. In time, one is admitted.

The DEA Resident Agent-in-Charge is Ron Lard, a middle-aged man with salt and pepper hair and alert, unwavering blue eyes. He is relaxed, informal, entirely at ease in his position. He is somewhat reluctant to be specific about how many agents work out of his office, but when asked if "a couple of dozen" would be roughly correct, he says, "Yea, a couple of dozen or so." Since worldwide the DEA has 2,800 agents, this would mean about 1% of the agency's entire strength is concentrated in Brownsville. And Ron believes his numbers should be and will be increased, because the sector which he covers (Cameron and Willacy counties) is a major drug corridor for the Juan Garcia Abrego Gulf Drug Cartel and for several other drug organizations which have cells in both Matamoros and Brownsville. Also, as far as drug interdiction is concerned, the local sector faces a "double threat": there is the land threat posed by the border with Mexico, and the sea threat posed by the Port of Brownsville. Ron says the drug organizations move South American cocaine and Mexican heroin and marijuana through this area. Marijuana which may be bought for $300 a pound here at the border will fetch $1,200 in Florida and in major cities elsewhere in the U.S. Cocaine will sell for $12,000 to $15,000 per kilo, and heroin may sell as high as $180,000 per kilo. According to Ron, "staging groups" in Mexico move the drugs to "staging groups" in Brownsville, Harlingen, and other Valley cities. The traffickers "use any method you can think of" to get their products across the border: human "mules," cars, trucks, trains, light aircraft, pleasure boats, shrimp boats, shark boats, ships. From Brownsville and the other Valley cities, the drug shipments are transported to Houston — "almost all the local drugs are heading for Houston" — from whence the drugs are dispersed nationwide.

To combat the traffickers, Ron Lard's agents "try to work the whole picture." Most of his agents, three of whom, incidentally, are women, are usually conducting four or five investigations simultaneously. They target major suppliers, transporters, and distributors, and they conduct wiretaps, make wide-scale investigations, and periodically organize major "round-ups." Ron says, "We [the DEA] excel in undercover work and informant recruiting and handling."

Many of his office's operations, especially the larger ones, require assembling task forces that involve officers from virtually any and all of the other law enforcement agencies in the area: BPD, FBI, IRS, BP, DPS, ATF, and the Cameron County Sheriff's Department. Some of the operations also require cooperation with Mexican law enforcement authorities, but when asked if he has much "confidence" in the Mexican authorities he must sometimes work with, Ron's reply is a firm: "No comment."

Brownsville's FBI (Federal Bureau of Investigation) offices are located in the downtown area at 700 East Levee Street. Once again, these are offices that occupy a non-descript, free-standing building, and the offices are not on the ground floor. The office is headed by Agent-in-Charge Raul E. Carballido, a slim man with brown hair and moustache who appears to be in his late thirties. He dresses like a lawyer and his every motion and his every word is precise and deliberate. He gives the impression of being on some kind of time delay, and you can tell he thinks twice or even three times before committing himself. For instance, when asked a preliminary question of how many FBI agents work at his office, there is a long pause. Finally, when it is suggested to him that informed sources estimate that there are "about a dozen," there is another considerable pause before he says, "My staffing level is thirteen, but I do not say that is how many I have." When asked in a follow-up question if all these agents are male, he studies on this a good while before eventually replying, "At present."

The sector his office covers is Cameron and Willacy counties, just like the DEA, and in fact, the FBI and DEA are territorially identically structured throughout the U.S. However, whereas the DEA is authorized to operate worldwide, the FBI's investigations and intelligence gathering activities are restricted by law to the nation's territorial limits. The FBI's main task, of course, is to investigate violations of federal laws.

In the Brownsville sector, a "very unique area because of the border situation," Raul reports that "drugs are the number one priority." His agents target major drug groups, and "Juan Garcia Abrego's organization is the dominant drug trafficking organization that controls the drug trade on both sides of the border." Raul says that in investigating the Abrego organization and other large drug organizations, his agents do not work undercover because "these crooks work with only long-term associates or family members, so they are very difficult to penetrate . . . and it is very dangerous." And, although Juan Garcia Abrego grew up in the Rio Grande Valley town of La Paloma just a few minutes west of Brownsville on the Old Military Highway, Raul believes Abrego stays in Mexico and no longer comes to Brownsville or the Valley. "It would be too big a risk for him." After all, the FBI offers a $2 million reward for his capture, and he is on the Bureau's "Ten Most Wanted" list. [Less than a month after this interview, on January 16, 1996, Juan Garcia Abrego, also known as *"La Muneca"* or "The Doll" in reference to his baby face, was captured by Mexican agents at a *villa* in suburban Monterrey. He was turned over to the American Embassy in Mexico City, and then flown to Houston to stand trial. Meanwhile, Abrego's underlings are scrambling to see who will take over control of his organization.]

Other federal crimes that the FBI investigates locally are assaults on federal officials (most often involving Border Patrol agents), crimes on the high seas (which frequently occur on shrimp boats "that have been out there a long time" and where the crew takes to fighting among themselves), armored car robberies, and, perhaps most ominously, corruption of public officials, some of which Raul says is drug related and some of which is non-drug related.

Another federal crime the local office gets involved in is "interstate flight." Whenever a criminal flees the state in which he committed a crime, regardless of what the crime was, the crime becomes *ipso facto* a federal crime. This, of course, applies also to criminals who flee the U.S. into Mexico and vice versa. Raul says much of the work in his office involves cooperating with Mexican municipal police, state judicial police, and federal judicial police to apprehend and exchange these trans-border criminals. Raul reports that, "Generally speaking, Mexican authorities are cooperative. They're trying their best."

The U.S. Marshals are a final federal law enforcement group in Brownsville. They have their offices on the third floor of the Federal Building on Elizabeth Street. They are headed by acting U.S. Marshal Alfonso Solis and Supervising Deputy U.S. Marshal Robert

Cervantes. There are seven deputy marshals and three civilian employees attached to the group, and their job is to protect the federal courts, the federal judges, and the federal court "family." They serve and process federal warrants, summonses, writs, and subpoenas and seize property in drug cases. They also transport prisoners to and from the county jail for their trials at the Federal Building's upstairs courtrooms. (The U.S. Marshals have two cages on the third floor where they can hold these prisoners on a temporary basis.) The U.S. Marshals in Brownsville also participate in the Federal Witness Security Program in this area, but, understandably, Supervising Deputy Robert Cervantes refused to reveal any details about this ultra-sensitive program.

Since Brownsville is both the county seat of Cameron County and also the home of the U.S. District Court for the Southern District of Texas, there are a goodly number of courts in the city. There is, first of all, the Brownsville Municipal Court located on the first floor of the police department's headquarters on East Jackson Street. This so-called "traffic court" is presided over by Municipal Judge Kip Van Johnson Hodge and Assistant Municipal Judge Ben Neece both of whom are appointed by the Brownsville City Commission. This court is open every day, weekends included, and plows through 6,000 traffic cases a year which net the city over a million dollars in revenue. The court also assesses fines for violations of a plethora of city ordinances, some well-known (albeit poorly enforced), such as the requirement to keep vacant lots mowed, but some arcane ones as well — lawns may not be mowed between the hours of 11:00 P.M. and 7:00 A.M., cars may not be washed at curbside in a public street, no one may own over three adult dogs. Another function of the Municipal Court is to arraign and refer to the appropriate court of jurisdiction anyone arrested by the BPD in the previous twenty-four hours. This procedure applies to everyone from public drunks to murderers. The municipal courts of Texas cannot themselves sentence anyone to confinement or assign fines greater than $2,000 for ordinance violations or $500 for class C criminal misdemeanors (representative crimes being disorderly conduct and public drunkenness).

County and state courts are housed on East Harrison Street within the "new" Cameron County Courthouse — a most regrettable building appearance-wise. This brawny concrete edifice, devoid of any grace, calls to mind the "heroic period" of Soviet architecture. Inside its solid ugliness are to be found two justice of the peace courts, two (soon to be three) county courts-at-law, and five state district courts.

There are eleven elected justices of the peace scattered about Cameron County, but only two of these hear cases at the Cameron County Courthouse. These are J P Tony Torres and J P Ed Sarabia. Like the municipal court judges, they can arraign suspected criminals, set bond, and assign fines of up to $500 for Class C criminal misdemeanors. Additionally, they can handle small claims and civil suits where financial stakes do not exceed $5,000. The JP courts also handle landlord-tenant disputes and evictions. And, as everyone knows, JPs can perform civil marriages.

In Cameron County, as in all the more populous counties of Texas, the county judge and county commissioners' court serve a purely administrative function. Their judicial powers have been broken away and assigned instead to one or more county courts-at-law. At the beginning of 1996, Cameron County had two county courts-at-law, and a third was approved during the course of the 1995 Texas legislative session. Cameron County Court-at-Law No. 1 and Cameron County Court-at-Law No. 2 are presided over respectively by elected judges, Everardo Garcia and Migdalia Lopez. The county courts-at-law try suits in which monetary sums involved do not exceed $100,000. However, whereas JP and municipal courts can only handle the most minor (Class C) criminal misdemeanors, county courts-at-law try Class B misdemeanors (e.g. prostitution, indecent exposure, theft of items valued $20-$200, assault, keeping a vicious dog, telephone harassment) and Class A misdemeanors (e.g. bomb threats, resisting arrest, theft of items valued $200-$750, bigamy, cruelty to an animal), and can sentence convicts to up to one year's confinement in the county jail and fines up to $4,000. Moreover, county courts-at-law hear cases in family law, assign guardianships of minors and the mentally ill, and serve as probate courts for settling wills and estates.

One serious concern regarding the Cameron County courts-at-law has been their inability to keep up with the body of cases confronting them. Thousands of cases have become backlogged. The gravity of the situation was highlighted in a series of Elizabeth Allen articles that appeared in the *Brownsville Herald* in December

1994 and January 1995. Allen documented retiring County Court-at-Law No. 2's Judge Adolpho Betancourt's efforts to throw out 2,700 cases he still had pending from 1986 to 1992, and to pass along 4,000 unheard cases from 1993 and 1994 to his successor, Judge Migdalia Lopez.

Not only does such throwing out of cases deprive the county of much needed revenue from criminal fines, but it also makes a mockery of the efforts and risks taken by local law enforcement officers in executing thousands of arrests. What is even more unfortunate, it convinces both law breakers and law abiders of the increasing impotence of the legal establishment to protect the innocent in this county and in this country.

Certainly, Judge Betancourt is not solely — probably not even primarily — to blame for this legal travesty. Indeed, the backlog incident prompted mutual finger pointing between the judge, County Clerk Joe Rivera's office, and County Prosecutor Louis Saenz's office. Nor is Cameron County unusual in the severity of its backlog — nearby Hidalgo and Starr counties also have thousands of waiting cases. Nevertheless, something is wrong and needs to be fixed, and it is going to take more than a third county court-at-law to do it. The public may put up with case backlogs, even though "justice delayed is justice denied," but when thousands of criminal cases are tossed out wholesale, that is hard for the community to swallow.

The third floor of the county courthouse is home to five state district courts: Judge Menton Murray's 103rd; Benjamin Euresti's 107th; Roberto Garza's 138th; Darrell Hester's 197th; and Rogelio Garza's 357th. These state district courts settle divorces, hear civil cases involving more than $5,000 (and often millions), and try the most serious crimes — state jail felonies (e.g. criminally negligent homicide, assisting a suicide, interference with child custody, unauthorized use of a vehicle); 3rd degree felonies (e.g. perjury, theft of items valued $750-$20,000, credit card abuse, incest, possession of child pornography); 2nd degree felonies (e.g. voluntary manslaughter, rape, theft of items valued over $20,000, robbery, arson, aggravated assault); 1st degree felonies (e.g. murder, burglary of a habitation, aggravated robbery, aggravated kidnapping); and capital crimes (e.g. multiple murders, murder for pay, murder of a law enforcement official, murder while committing robbery, murder while committing arson, murder of a kidnapped victim).

Sentences meted out by the five state district judges on the third floor occasionally call for execution by lethal injection but usually involve incarceration within the nearly 200,000-bed Texas state prison system, the world's largest, for periods ranging (at least theoretically) from two years to life. (The newly created state jails hold state jail felons for periods of 180 days to two years.) As soon as practical after sentencing, the Texas Department of Corrections transports the criminals to the diagnostic facility at Huntsville, Texas, where they are examined and observed by psychiatrists and correctional officials for thirty days before being assigned to one of the fifty-eight Texas state prisons most suitable to their needs and the State's needs based on their sex, age, education, skills, physical and mental health, and the degree of threat they pose to themselves, other convicts, and correctional personnel.

Since the five district judges handle all state felonies and capital crimes committed in both Cameron and Willacy counties, and since the cases are distributed on a rotational basis among them to ensure equitable trial loads, suspected felons in the two-county area can never be sure which of the five judges they will appear before. There is no question, however, who they most dread. As every criminal, every lawyer, every law enforcement official, and virtually every informed citizen knows, Judge Darrell "Hang 'em High" Hester is fierce — and fourteen times has invoked the death penalty. Bane of criminals; hero to police and public.

The federal court in Brownsville is but one element of the U.S. District Court for the Southern District of Texas (a district that stretches from Houston to Laredo). This court is housed in the upper floors of the Federal Building on East Elizabeth Street — a building in the grand manner of the 1930s, with four ornate courtrooms. The presiding judge, Filemon Vela, was appointed in 1970 to the lifetime post by President Jimmy Carter. Previously, Judge Vela had served as state district judge of the 107th district (Ben Euresti's current post). In the closing months of 1995, President Bill Clinton elevated Hilda Tagle, a forty-eight-year-old Robstown native and state district judge in Corpus Christi, to the federal bench. She was to join Judge Vela and help handle the very heavy caseload of federal crimes and civil suits generated by the district's proximity to Mexico and an international border. Due to its location, the district handles not only the usual federal court traffic (suits involving parties of different states, counterfeiting, interstate flight, tax evasion, postal crimes, bankruptcy, and civil rights violations) but also federal crimes inherent to a border location (immigration violations, alien smuggling, drug smuggling, etc.).

One serious handicap Vela and Tagle confront is the dilemma of balancing suspects' Eighth Amendment rights ("excessive bail shall not be required") with the reality of an international border crossing that beckons just four blocks from their federal courthouse. Over two hundred arraigned suspects have absconded from Judge Vela's court and remain at large, most likely in Mexico.

The hazard of the courthouse's siting within a bullet shot's distance of the border was further emphasized in the summer of 1995 when the Cameron County Sheriff's Department and the FBI arrested six persons for conspiring to free two suspected drug smugglers, the Cisneros brothers, when the U.S. Marshals were scheduled to transfer the duo from the Cameron County Jail to the federal courthouse for trial. The plot called for a possible shootout with the marshals in downtown Brownsville. As the *Brownsville Herald* reported U.S. Magistrate Fidencio Garza as saying, "If this matter had gone down it could have been a bloodbath for everybody."

Hopefully, such dangers will be somewhat alleviated — although they will never be entirely removed — when the court is relocated to a new, larger, more secure building immediately north of Brownsville police headquarters. This $27 million facility should be completed sometime in 1998.

W.L.A.

CHAPTER 7

At Charro Days

It's Saturday, the 25th of February 1995. A warm and sunny day, and once again the annual Charro Days festival is in full swing. With my beautiful twenty-three-year-old daughter as my companion, I stroll to the corner of 7th and Elizabeth streets, at the western edge of the downtown area. We're just in time. Already the spectators line the street four or five deep. Early arrivals sit in their lawn chairs at curb's edge. These veteran parade-goers even have coolers beside them from which they pluck snacks and cold drinks. Further east, in the heart of downtown, the crowds are even thicker. Second and third floor windows of stores have been pulled up and people sit on the ledges. Other people are right up on top of the flat store rooftops staring down from the parapets. The Grand Parade is approaching. The blare of horns and thump of drums can be heard. The parade is working its way in our direction from the west. Heads crane.

First come the charros. Five horses bearing riders. And what horses! Lively, spirited beasts with bobbed and ribboned manes. Their twenty steel-shod hooves sound on the pavement: a rapid-fire staccato of clipping and clopping. Astride them, the vaqueros in embroidered short jackets and riding breeches. All five wear sombreros, and three of them bear flags: the flags of the United States, Mexico, and The Virgin. Roars of applause. They are fol-

lowed by vaqueros afoot twirling lariats. New, stiff-roped, manila lariats. Some of the vaqueros twirl the lariats over their heads, others twirl them at their sides, and still others twirl them at their feet and jump in and out of them. Roars of applause. And now the body of the parade — a parade that takes a full hour to pass a given point: police cars, politicians in open cars, marching band after marching band, floats, beauty queens, Mr. Amigo, veterans groups, Shriners, Army Reserve and National Guard, baton twirlers, clowns, more floats and school bands. A blur of perceptions: an open-cabbed firetruck with a well-behaved unintelligent-looking Dalmatian perched beside the driver. Politicians in chauffeured convertibles with easy, artificial smiles wave at the crowds while their less comfortable wives and children on display beside them endure the purgatory. Baton twirlers, vanguard of a high school band, become stalled before us due to some snag up ahead. The girls march in place. They wear short purple skirts and tasseled white boots. Lovely, high-stepping girls. Dark skinned, dark eyed, dark haired. Beaming smiles and twirling batons. Parked by the curb in a wheelchair, an adolescent girl — homely and overweight — watches them. What can she be thinking? The delay is resolved; the twirlers march on; the crowd applauds. The girl in the wheelchair applauds too. An orange-haired clown with two-foot long shoes goes flopping by, tossing candy to the crowd from a bucket. Kids squeal and run to the pavement to pick up candy. One five-year-old, fascinated by the clown's walk, takes a few experimental floppy-footed steps by the curb until his dad pulls him back. An old Winter Texan couple — white haired and easy to please — vigorously applaud every contingent. Survivors of a more innocent age, they clap with their fingers pointed up. Prayer fashion.

As the parade winds down, we wander over to Washington Park. More crowds. We buy tacos at one of the food stalls. It's hot. I have a beer. We watch the "Waiters' Race." A score of uniformed waiters in full rig — even to the point of having towels draped over their forearms — race around and around the park fountain. They carry trays of drinks which they must not spill. They are very serious competitors. Their wives and children cheer them on in Spanish. A crowd watches with lukewarm interest.

Many of us are just killing time until the main event: the Jalapeno Eating Contest.

Well before the scheduled 2:30 start, my daughter and I prudently secure good seats in the sure-to-be-packed grandstands. The open-air stage where the contest will be held is directly in front of us. While the crowd and the excitement builds, we watch the preparations. The peppers being carefully counted out ten to a styrofoam cup and placed on the long row of tables. Umpires and festival officials conferring on rules. The ambulance rolling into place nearby — ready for the dash to the emergency room and the stomach pump.

And now the eaters themselves begin taking their places on the stage. They are mostly stout men who have arrived at the peak of their eating powers. Stomachs in full flower. But there are a few skinny ones too, and even one woman. All are Hispanics, of course. But then, what's this? Two gringos have appeared on stage! Are they out of their minds? The audience greets them with laughter. Not cruel laughter, but the good-natured, tolerant laughter society accords to drunks and idiots. As for drunks, it is apparent that one or two of the contestants have fortified themselves with a few beers — either to buck up courage or to dull the senses. The cognoscetti say this is a real mistake. An empty stomach is best.

But amidst this mixed bag of contestants, many of whom will never stay the distance and have little more than comedic value, two competitors, serious and sober, have appeared. Murmuring in the crowd. The two Brownsville icons who the audience have come to see have arrived. One is Danny Garza — four-time champion — returning to defend his crown. So dedicated is this champion that it is rumored he religiously devours a plate of jalapenos every day of the year — Sundays included — to stay in shape. Guts of steel. A mere glance at his belly tells you that, when it comes to eating, this is not a man to be trifled with. The other man is Garza's dogged challenger, David del Castillo. He is tall and reasonably thin. Truly, he has the "lean and hungry look" of a Cassius. Year after year, del Castillo has relentlessly been closing in on Garza. At the 1994 contest he came within a hair's breadth — three jalapenos — of unseating the champ.

Clearly a worthy opponent. Looking at him now, he's a man who commands attention: grim-faced, pucker-browed. Wired.

Ready. Set. Go. The contestants have ten minutes to eat as many jalapenos as they can. Ten minutes to eat the hottest peppers ever cultivated by man. Peppers so hot that their juice blisters the lips. Peppers so hot that the smallest bite brings tears to the eyes and traumatizes the tissues of mouth and throat. Peppers from Hell.

Most of the participants adopt the strategy of wolfing down as many as possible, as rapidly as possible, before the nerves can register the pain. This is a losing strategy. Within a couple of minutes these folks begin to falter. The gringos pack it in first and are helped from the stage. They are walking funny. They pick up their feet and put them down very deliberately — Frankenstein-like. Their motor functions have been impaired. The big beer drinkers don't last much longer. One stops and howls. They eat a couple of jalapenos, guzzle a beer, eat a couple more, guzzle another beer. In under five minutes their eyes are awash with tears and their eating stops. They just sit there in their chairs, dazed.

After five or six minutes only half a dozen serious competitors are left, including, to most everyone's surprise, the lady. The two icons are still going, of course, and it is now that their greatness begins to demonstrate itself. Their styles are different. Garza is an absolute machine. Very steady. He sits with his elbows on the table staring unhappily at the jalapenos before him. The crowd doesn't exist. He chews and swallows the peppers at the rate of about one every six or seven seconds. Every 30 seconds or so he takes a small sip of beer, and then right back at it. You can tell he is hurting, but he works through the pain and keeps going. No emotion. No theatrics. On the other hand, del Castillo works more in bursts. He eats maybe ten in a row rapidly, very rapidly, and jerks his head back. He is an ecstasy of pain. His eyes are tightly closed, his nostrils flared. After several moments he quaffs half a beer and then plows back in for another binge on peppers. It's going to be close.

Less than a minute to go. The emcee is counting off the seconds. Both Garza and del Castillo are pulling out all the stops and sprinting for the finish line. Time! The umpires count the pepper stalks. Pause. A second count. Tension builds. It's announced that the lady, Vicki Hernandez, has eaten 45 jalapenos.

*Good effort. Respectable applause. And now the results all have
been waiting for: del Castillo an amazing 84! Pause. Garza, 85!*

W.L.A.

The Tourist Industry

According to Nick Reyna, director of the Brownsville Convention and Visitors Bureau, Brownsville received 1.1 million visitors in 1995, and visitors have been increasing about 5% annually. Some of the visitors are day-trippers over from Mexico, some are out-of-towners visiting relatives, some are corporate officers with business at the *maquiladoras,* some are conventioneers, retirees or vacationing college students, and some are leisure visitors that have driven down to the area — what Nick refers to as his "rubber tire market." Best months for visitors are January, February, and March when most of the nation is experiencing its worst weather — but when Brownville is enjoying some of its best. Average daytime highs are a relatively balmy 69° in January, 72° in February, and 78° in March. The worst month for tourism is August (due to the heat and increasingly early school openings in the nation) and May is not much better since by then all the Winter Texans and Spring Breakers have gone, and the summer vacationers have not yet arrived.

To accommodate its visitors Brownsville has twenty-five hotels and motels with 1,600 rooms (the Fort Brown Hotel with 278 units being the largest), while South Padre Island has an additional 19 hotels and motels with 3,000 rooms (the Sheraton Beach Resort with 256 units is the largest). SPI also has 3,000 rentable condominiums. Room rates in Brownsville are quite moderate by national standards despite the fact that Brownsville's 13% hotel/motel tax is the second highest in the nation, exceeded only by New York City's 14% levy. Room rates at South Padre Island are somewhat more expensive and vary greatly depending on the season.

The three tourist groups that have the largest economic and social impact on the area are the Spring Breakers, the Winter Texans and the Mexican tourists. Unquestionably, the Spring Breakers — or simply "Breakers" in the double-meaning local parlance — have the largest social impact on the area. These students (mostly college students but some high school students as well) deluge the area every year. They come in waves stretched over a six-week period in March and early April. The waves coincide with various college closings in the midwestern and plains states. Obviously, a week-long, seaside vacation in a warm climate has an undeniable attraction to students on snow-bound campuses in Michigan, Ohio, and Nebraska. In March alone, upwards of 200,000 students will cycle through South Padre Island, and that makes the Island one of the nation's three premier destinations for Breakers. Panama City, Florida, which services the East Coast crowd, is currently the most popular destination and entertains over half a million Breakers annually. Lake Havasu, Arizona, which caters mainly to West Coast students, is also very popular.

The behavior of the Spring Breakers is horrendous. Their actions, manners, and language would make a drunken sailor blush. Any parent who thinks Spring Break is the innocent fun portrayed in such sixties genre movies as "Beach Blanket Bingo" had better think again. Spring Break is no longer about Frankie Avalon, Annette Funicello, and budding puppy love; Spring Break nineties-style is pure raunch. It's about boozing babes in string bikinis — many of them minors — trolling the beach for a quick "lay." It's about bleary-eyed, foul-mouthed fraternity louts chugging beer and fornicating. It's about obscene T-shirt shops. (Sample: No more Mr. Nice Guy; on your knees, bitch.") It's about wet T-shirt contests, planes trailing sky signs advertising "Rubber Ducky" condoms, and bungee jumping where girls going topless jump for half-price and completely nude girls jump free.

Each year the local electronic and print media will run stories and news clips stressing the economic benefits of the Spring Breakers who, national studies show, spend an average of $340 during their break. Unconvincing stories will also be run excusing the Breakers' behavior as a necessary "rite of passage" and a well-deserved break from the books and an opportunity for these hard-working students to "blow off steam." Inevitably, there will be some Christian college youth group that will devote the break to painting one or two homes for the elderly poor in Brownsville. This will get inordinate media attention and show the "good side" of the Spring Breakers. As though one or two dozen decent kids can make up for the actions of the other 200,000.

However, at least one local reporter, Oscar Cisneros of the

Herald, seriously questioned the impact of the Breakers' behavior on cross-border relations in an excellent March 13, 1995, front-page article entitled "Good Tourists or Ugly Americans." Since many underage Breakers make a nightly run into Matamoros, where the legal drinking age is just eighteen, Matamoros streets, particularly in the area adjacent to the International Bridge, are nightly filled with drunken, rowdy teenagers who puke and urinate in the streets. As Cisneros pointed out, many Mexicans — who are generally much less tolerant of lewdness and drunkenness than are Americans — deeply resent the Breakers and their penchant for shouting insults at Mexicans in the mistaken belief their words are not understood. But many Mexicans do understand the words, and if not the words themselves, they understand the intent and disrespect underlying the words. As one street vendor Cisneros interviewed stated, the Breakers like to "humiliate" Mexicans and pick fights.

Since a peak year in 1990, the numbers of Spring Breakers coming to the area has tapered off slightly. This is believed to have been the twin effect of the Mark Kilroy murder and the growing popularity of Cancun, Mexico, as a rival Breaker destination. The bizarre nature of the Kilroy killing attracted unfavorable national and international media attention to the area. Mark Kilroy, a Breaker down from The University of Texas in Austin, drunk and disoriented, was abducted in March 1989 two blocks from the International Bridge. Shortly thereafter, following an extensive search, parts of his body, along with twelve other corpses, were located at Santa Elena Ranch west of Matamoros. Kilroy had been the human sacrifice of a drug-smuggling satanic cult based at the ranch that had specifically targeted a large, blonde, Anglo Spring Breaker. The young man had been castrated, and his heart and brain were removed. Some of his organs and bones were found in a pot. Needless to say, this frightful incident had at least a temporary chilling effect on Spring Break in Brownsville and South Padre Island.

Probably a greater long range challenge to the local Spring Break is the growing popularity among Breakers of Cancun and other Mexican tourist sites. Some of the Mexican resorts like Cancun, Cozumel, Mazatlan, and Acapulco have huge numbers of hotel rooms and, especially with the peso devaluation, very competitive air/hotel deals. With more campus publicity, were the Mexican tourist industry to actively target U.S. college students, there is no doubt they could siphon off even more of this market. However, there are already signs that the Mexicans find it difficult to stomach Breaker behavior, and some Cancun hotels will not accept Breakers. As Elizabeth Allen reported in a March 19, 1995, *Herald* article, Cancun officials no longer welcome the "rowdy young revellers," and that might translate into more business for the Island.

One wonders why Brownsville and South Padre Island should be any more welcoming. The profits they bring benefit a relatively small segment of the area population — beer distributors, condom sellers, obscene T-shirt store owners, hotel and condominium owners, and, admittedly, their numerous employees, but the social costs to the area seem hardly worth it. Not only is the local community prostituting itself to serve this rabble, but it is also placing its own young people at risk. BISD has its own Spring Break in March and, by hook or crook, many under-age high school students and even junior high school students make their way to the Island beaches and the Matamoros bars to join in. Moreover, in pandering to these Breakers in March and April — two of the most attractive months for tourists — wholesome vacationers are effectively driven off; they avoid the area in those months.

Years ago, Fort Lauderdale, West Palm Beach, Boca Raton, and other South Florida tourist meccas — the original home of the Spring Break phenomenon — realized their mistake in hosting and condoning Spring Break. Their city governments moved very effectively to discourage and end it. It's not difficult. Much of the Spring Breaker activity — the nudity, the under-age drinking, the public drunkenness, the obscene dress and language — is illegal. A full court press by the Brownsville and South Padre Island Police Departments, the Cameron County Sheriff's Department and the Texas Alcoholic Beverage Commission (TABC) could bring Spring Break to a screeching halt.

That, of course, will not happen until the Cameron County judge and the respective city commissions of Brownsville and South Padre Island order it. At present, there is no sign of that happening. On the contrary, Nick Reyna at the Brownsville Tourist Bureau, a city employee, says he is working "to stimulate the Spring Break industry in Brownsville" with even more campus flyers and other advertising — although in fairness, it must be said he'd like to attract a more "mature" Spring Breaker and thinks more organized activities, like, perhaps, a Spring Break Olympics, would be desirable. Nor is it likely that the SPI city council will alter matters. When Rev. Bruce Webb complained during Spring Break '94 of a new topless bar going in near his church, SPI Alderwoman T-Bird Sitgreaves (that's right) pooh-poohed the objection by reasoning you could see the same thing on the beach. An indisputable point.

On the opposite end of the decency spectrum would be the Winter Texans — the local subspecies of the snowbirds who flock to Southern Florida, Southern California, Arizona, and other sunny climes for the winter. Every fall they arrive in thousands to renew their seasonal romance with Valley residents. According to studies undertaken by Professor Vern Vincent, a statistician with the University of Texas-Pan American at Edinburg, about 100,000 Winter Texans now come to the Valley each year. His surveys show the typical Winter Texan is 68 years old, married, retired, lives in a recreational vehicle, and stays four and a half months. And what is most important from an economic standpoint, the typical Winter Texan household spends about $1,000 a month on living expenses while here, plus an average of $2,100 per stay for durable goods such as automobiles, appliances, furniture, and mobile homes.

Seventy percent of the Winter Texans come from the Midwest and the northern plains states, with thirty percent from Minnesota and Iowa alone. By no means do all these winter visitors stay in Brownsville. In fact, Mission, with seventy-three RV parks, is clearly the Winter Texan capital, but Brownsville's forty-two RV parks do get their share.

No doubt part of the mutual attraction Winter Texans and Valleyites have for one another has much to do with their respective demeanors. For the most part, Winter Texans have cheerful dispositions. They are not crotchety old people — the curmudgeons stay home in Minnesota. After all, the old people Brownsville and other Valley cities host have little reason to be cantankerous; they are the lucky ones. They still have their life mates; they are, by and large, still active and healthy (or, at least, not too badly decayed); and, as anyone who has ever priced a recreational vehicle knows, must be financially comfortable, if not actually affluent.

For their part, the overwhelmingly Hispanic population of the Valley offers the Winter Texans a warm and respectful welcome. Again and again Winter Texans remark upon the harmonious interpersonal relations they enjoy while in the Valley. This a result of a very real Hispanic social sensitivity in general, and a cultural deference to older people in particular. The "yes sirs" and *"si señoras"* Winter Texans can expect in the Valley are in marked contrast to the indifference, bare tolerance or even open hostility they often experience in the wintering grounds of Southern Florida and Southern California. As Mrs. Sheila Florence McDonough, a refined 80-year-old Christian lady, related, in Southern California she had her way on the sidewalk blocked by a hostile young black man in an African tribal smock and beanie who told her the sidewalks were reserved for blacks. "White trash walk in the gutter." Such incidents and, far more often, the fear of such incidents will continue to make the Valley a welcome winter refuge for the nation's elderly snowbirds.

A final, very important segment of Brownsville's tourist market would be the Mexican nationals. Unless the typical American has a map before them, their mind's eye tends to picture Mexico as a vaguely triangular mass extending southward below the southwest quadrant of the United States. There is little appreciation of exact distances and directions. Recourse to an Atlas will result in some revelations: Brownsville, at the extreme tip of South Texas, plunges more than 400 miles further south than such U.S.-Mexican border cities as San Diego-Tijuana and El Paso-Juarez. What is more, the Mexican "triangle" projects not southwards, but East-Southeast, so that Mexico City (the world's largest city with over 20 million people) lies almost directly south of Brownsville, and only 465 miles away "as the crow flies" (Dallas is more distant at 475 miles). Similarly, Americans, Brownsvillites included, usually regard San Antonio with its 1 million people as being the nearest big city to Brownsville. But they are wrong. Monterrey with its 3.5 million population lies just 175 miles due west — seventy miles nearer than San Antonio.

What this means is that Brownsville represents the closest U.S. destination for residents of Mexico City and the densely populated plateau which surrounds it and contains the bulk of the nation's 90 million population. Consequently, Brownsville and nearby South Padre Island attract many middle-class Mexicans from land-locked Monterrey and Mexico City who are looking to combine shopping with a seaside vacation. The recent peso devaluation has temporarily crimped this market, but Brownsville's geographical strengths are permanent and long-range prospects are good.

As for what there is to "do and see" in Brownsville, there is quite a lot. Brownsville is certainly no cultural mecca, and art, opera and ballet lovers will find very slim pickings here, but for the average American, Mexican, or foreign tourist, there is a wonderful natural setting, a delightful bi-national cultural blend, and more than adequate recreational and entertainment opportunities.

Beach activities at South Padre Island are popular with visitors of all ages and at all seasons of the year. People watchers and crowd lovers are happiest on the Gulf side of South Padre Island. The densest crowds will be found in front of the beach front hotels and on the Gulf side of Isla Blanca County Park. The waves here are often surfable, but both surfers and bathers have to be careful of treacherous riptides. There are some drownings in this area every year. Shark attacks are extremely rare, although any bather who swims out far enough — beyond the second sand bar — puts himself at some risk. Sharks are there. For families with young children, the Dolphins' Cove on the protected "Laguna" side of Isla Blanca Park is very suitable. This small beach has minimal waves, a very gradual, predictable seabed slope and no treacherous currents. Moreover, the Cove frequently does have the gregarious dolphins appear in it. This is well worth remembering, particularly for true-blue, deep-dyed cowards. To an untrained eye, the dorsal fin of a dolphin looks much like that of a shark. This can produce some truly remarkable displays in the Cove. Fathers with timid hearts who have gotten through life using bluff and bluster to conceal their condition from family and friends can see the work of a lifetime destroyed in an instant if they turn around in the water and see a foot-high dorsal ten feet away and closing. Daddies are sometimes first out of the water.

Andy Bowie County Park, which begins just north of the South Padre Island township and extends all the way north to the Madison Cut, is another fine island beach. Highway 100, the beach road, ends after three miles, and most bathers park in this stretch and hike over the dunes to the beach. Locals drive their cars and pickups right on to the beach and may be parked on the sand side-by-side for almost three solid miles on warm weekends. The more adventurous can continue beyond the beach road for nearly fifteen miles of unspoiled, virtually unvisited beaches, provided they have a 4-wheel drive vehicle or rent horses or dune buggies available in the town of South Padre Island.

SPI tourist brochures claim that beachcombers will find shell collecting rewarding and — a lucky few — might even find gold coins and flotsam from ancient Spanish galleons that shipwrecked off the coast. Neither of these claims should be taken seriously. Unlike some Florida beaches, there are no off-lying coral reefs in Texas waters and, hence, very few species of mollusks wash ashore. Clams and other bi-valve shells are in great abundance, and a few whelks and other gastropods may be found at the tide line after storms, but, on the whole, serious shell collectors will be disappointed with area beaches. As for finding Spanish "treasure," you'd have a better chance trying to find a sober priest in Ireland. A fool's errand.

One other popular local beach is the five-mile strip of sand that lies between the sea terminus of the Brownsville Ship Channel at Brazos Santiago Pass and the mouth of the Rio Grande. Known variously as Boca Chica Beach, Del Mar Beach, and Brazos Island (although it is a peninsula and not an island), this beach is reached by taking Highway 4 out of Brownsville. The beach is not as clean and well-maintained as the county-owned beaches, but it is especially favored by surf fishers.

Fishing, incidentally, in the Brownsville-South Padre Island area is excellent the year around. The surf fishing at Boca Chica Beach and on the Gulf side of Padre Island will render trout, redfish, whiting, croaker, drum, sheepshead, shark, and tarpon. Bay fishing in the Laguna Madre (whether from boats, piers, or by wading) will be productive of trout, redfish, snook, and flounder. Bank fishing along the Brownsville Ship Channel, the Arroyo Colorado, and at the mouth of the Rio Grande is often good for flounder, trout, redfish, snook and black drum. As for deep-sea fishing, the local area has the advantage of being closer to the one hundred fathom curve (the Continental Shelf) than any location on the Texas coast. This means the area's charter boats waste less time in reaching the deep waters where blue marlin, white marlin, Atlantic sailfish and other large predators roam. Some of the deep-sea charter vessels and party boats specialize in traveling to off-shore reefs where the highly-prized red snapper are abundant, and are pulled up from the depths on time-saving, electrically-powered reels. Regardless of the type of fishing done, it should be remembered that any-one who fishes in Texas waters must have a valid fishing license, except for persons younger than 17 or over 65.

Hunting is also popular in rural areas outside Brownsville, particularly in the drier range area north of the Valley. The more common animals taken are white-tailed deer, wild hogs, the collared pecary or javalina, wild turkey, quail and white wing dove. Because Texas has very little public land, hunting in Texas is largely a mat-ter of buying hunting rights on a rancher's land. These hunting leases are not cheap: a typical annual lease on, say, 3,000 acres might cost anywhere from $500 to $6,000 depending upon the quality of land and its abundance of wildlife. Serious hunters can also make ar-rangements through Brownsville travel agents and hunting guides to fly down to private hunting lodges in Mexico that offer plentiful wildlife and more exotic species.

One rapidly growing type of tourism in the area is birding. Surveys conducted by Nick Reyna and the Visitors Bureau show that 2% of Brownsville's 1995 tourists came to the area primarily for the purpose of bird watching. Two major flyways along which birds migrate between North America and tropical regions in Cen-tral and South America converge in the Lower Rio Grande Valley. These are the "Central Flyway" coming down from Canada and the Great Plains, and the "Mississippi Flyway." Both of these flyways are shaped like gigantic funnels with their spouts touching or con-verging at the Valley, from whence the birds are poured down the narrow isthmus connecting North and South America. The birds are poured down in the fall, and poured back up in the spring. The volume of the birds being poured back in the spring is greater — after all, the birds have had time to refreshen themselves in tropical climes, and the flocks are reinforced by hatchlings that have been rapidly fattened, and, newly air-worthy, are ready for their first northern migration. This makes spring the best time for Valley birding, but then that is also when Spring Breakers infest the area and most birders — decent, god-fearing people for the most part — wisely avoid the area. Instead, the birders mainly come in the fall. The birding is not quite so good, the flocks are depleted by natural attrition during the course of the year, and it is only the survivors heading south for the winter. Still, even the second-best fall season is quite good, and birders may be able to identify up to 370 migrating or native species, including many types of parrots, gulls, herons, pelicans, ducks, owls, parakeets, hummingbirds, hawks, sandpipers, orioles and, of course, the ubiquitous grackles. Birding guru Roger Tovy Peterson wrote, "Four of my record breaking attempts to set the North American record for the greatest number of birds seen in one day were done in Texas and all four attempts began in the Rio Grande Valley."

Recommended birding sites in the vicinity include the Sabal Palm Grove Sanctuary six miles southeast of Brownsville. This 172-acre palm jungle is run by the Audubon Society and was once the setting for a Tarzan movie. Green jays, buff-bellied hummingbirds, and tropical parulas exist under the tightly-meshed botanic canopy. The large 45,000-acre Laguna Atascosa National Wildlife Refuge thirty miles northeast of Brownsville offers two driving tours which loop through the refuge on single-lane roads. The refuge is home to alligators, ocelots, deer, mountain lions, raccoons, weasels, and other varmints — all of which do an excellent job of making themselves completely invisible. What *can* be seen is a great abundance of butterflies and birds, especially water fowl. Santa Ana National Wildlife Refuge is a smaller, 2,000-acre refuge on the north bank of the Rio Grande forty-five miles to the west of Brownsville. It harbors a great diversity of birds, some prizes being the chachalaca, green kingfisher, hook-billed kite, and the least grebe, plus 265 species of butterflies. The Audubon Society operates guided tram tours through the refuge during winter months. Non-squeamish birders should also visit the Brownsville garbage dump, euphemistically known as the Brownsville "Sanitary Landfill." Admission is free, and large numbers of scavengers of both the human and feathered variety can be seen picking through the garbage.

One other attraction for local and visiting nature lovers is the Gladys Porter Zoo. This zoo, which opened in 1971, was built, stocked, and given to the City of Brownsville by the Earl C. Sams Foundation. Sams was the friend and right-hand man of James Cash Penny, and served as President and Chairman of the Board of the J.C. Penney Company for many years. The zoo is named for Sams' daughter, Gladys Porter (1910-1980), who married a Texan, settled in Brownsville, and became the guiding light in the zoo's creation.

At some stage some authority listed the zoo as one of the ten best in the nation, and rarely is the Gladys Porter Zoo mentioned without some reiteration of this fact. What criterion was used in determining the ranking seems to have been forgotten. Certainly, it cannot have been based either on the physical size of the zoo (a compact thirty-one acres) or on the size of the zoo's collection (1,900 animals live there), but no one who has visited the zoo can dispute the fact that this zoo is beautifully designed and superbly maintained. It is a complete delight to the eye. Lovely paths, seldom crowded, wind through a tropical botanical garden and one comes upon each animal exhibit almost by surprise — monkeys on an island, panthers in a grotto, hippos in a pool. The layout is such that usually only one species is in view at a time, and this lends itself to a curious sense of intimacy between man and creature. All the typical animals one expects to find at a zoo are there, and many atypical ones as well: Jentink's Duiker, the rarest antelope in the world; the Gaur, largest member of the cattle family. The zoo also possesses a credible aviary, aquarium, and reptile house.

For those tourists who enjoy sight-seeing of an historical nature, there are several sites of interest. After all, Brownsville bills itself as, next to San Antonio, the most important historical city in Texas. To begin with, there is the Historic Brownsville Museum housed within the old Southern Pacific Depot. This is only a small museum with perhaps an hour's worth of exhibits, but the items and curiosities on display do give a newcomer some appreciation of Brownsville's founding and early years. The Stillman House Museum downtown is another small museum, this one housed in the 1850s home of Brownsville founder Charles Stillman. The home is filled with furnishings and artifacts of that era. Another possibility for visitors is a walking or trolley tour. The Brownsville Heritage Trail is a series of short walking tours each of which takes about ten to twenty minutes to complete. Each tour is organized to take the walker past Brownsville's most historic homes and buildings in different downtown neighborhoods, and markers with bilingual texts describe the significance of each location. The Heritage Trail Tour can also be undertaken aboard a replica of a turn-of-the-century trolley. The trolley tours are narrated and take about two hours to tour the historic downtown area, the buildings of old Fort Brown, and either the Stillman House or the Historic Brownsville Museum.

Two other points of interest are the Confederate Air Force Museum and Palo Alto Battlefield. The term "Confederate Air

Force" baffles many people, but what it is is a group of veterans and air buffs who continue to maintain and fly vintage military aircraft. The CAF has eighty-five chapters or "wings" around the nation and the world and the CAF's Rio Grande Valley Wing is based at a hangar at Brownsville-South Padre Island International Airport. About a dozen aircraft are on display in the hangar, while the adjacent museum houses World War II artifacts and mementos. Each October the Valley Wing hosts a four-day "Air Fiesta" that draws thousands of spectators. Dozens of vintage warplanes plus state-of-the-art fighters and bombers from the air force and navy fly in for the occasion to be put through their paces in mock battles, precision air drills, and acrobatic flying displays.

At present, the Palo Alto Battlefield is commemorated only by a stone marker and a cannon at a shabby roadside park a mile north of the city where Paredes Line Road intersects with FM 511. Considering the great attention and funding given to preserving Revolutionary War and Civil War battle sites, this neglect seems shameful. After all, this war (of which Palo Alto was the first full-fledged battle) had immense territorial consequences for both Mexico and the United States. Moreover, in purely human terms, this battle had more combatants engaged than most of the Revolutionary battles. Upward of 2,000 American soldiers and 5,000 Mexicans confronted each other in this hotly contested battle, and no less than three future presidents participated: Lt. Ulysses S. Grant, Gen. Zachary Taylor and Gen. Mariano Arista.

Efforts to correct this oversight and spur binational tourism in the area were set in motion in 1992 when Congress and President Bush approved legislation and funding to create a Palo Alto Battlefield National Historic Site as part of the National Park Service. This bill would permit a 3,400-acre park (on land to be purchased from nineteen different landholders), a tourist center, bilingual markers, and park guides. The intent would be to memorialize the soldiers of both countries. Since 1992, budget-slashing Congresses have carefully scrutinized the park's funding, but as of 1995 it appears the park itself is assured — albeit the generosity of the funding may be less than originally expected.

One area in which Brownsville is frankly lacking is in cultural activities — at least in what might be called "high-brow" cultural activities. This is naturally a reflection of Brownsville's population.

Brownsville's population is, after all, the nation's poorest, and most of the city's residents have very modest educational attainments. Their tastes do not run to art, opera, ballet, and serious music. This is "Selena Country"!

Still, no city the size of Brownsville can be totally lacking in culture, and Brownsville does have the Brownsville Art League and Museum that offers permanent and rotating exhibits, while The University of Texas at Brownsville's Patron of the Arts Program engages to bring in a number of nationally and internationally known artists and musicians each year. There is also the Camille Lightner Playhouse (named for another of Earl Sams' philanthropic daughters) which presents four or five plays and musicals each season. If this seems like meager fare for the culturally starved, at least be thankful that Brownsville doesn't have drag races and tractor pulls like Harlingen and McAllen.

A final attraction for (American) tourists is Mexico. Some visitors to Brownsville, taking note of the city's poverty, drifting trash, and good-natured indifference to barely checked chaos may think they're already in Mexico, but there's no substitute for the real thing. Matamoros must be seen.

Seriously, Matamoros does have much to offer. For instance, Matamoros has many good restaurants, even elegant ones, that provide dining at very reasonable prices. There are shopping bargains in Matamoros too — particularly for shoes, boots and leather goods, silver jewelry, pottery, dish and glass ware, onyx ornaments, hand-sewn or woven clothes, blankets and tablecloths, and pharmaceuticals. There is also cheap dental service to be had. Walk down any street in Matamoros and you'll swear ten percent of Mexicans must be dentists.

Best of all, American tourists will be pleasantly surprised to find that unlike peoples in so many countries of the world, Mexicans harbor no ill-will towards Americans. The people are friendly, most can be trusted, and robberies of Americans are rare. Certainly, any American urbanite walking about in Matamoros will feel safer, and probably be safer, than he or she would be in comparably-sized U.S. cities.

The only thing that takes some Americans a bit to get used to is the poverty of the country. Mexico's per capita income is only $3,600, about one-seventh that of the United States. And while

Mexico's PCI does not rank badly by world standards — indeed, Mexico ranks almost exactly midway when the world's 190 nations are ranked by wealth — the poverty is immediately apparent and may be troubling to untraveled American tourists. A small army of beggars, urchins, and street peddlers are present just on the other side of the bridge. This puts many tourists off in the first block. They'll dart into Garcia's for a meal and a drink, buy a trinket, and dash back to the American side. Eventually, they'll go home to Michigan or Minnesota or wherever and claim they've seen Mexico. That is unfortunate, and it is untrue. If they would only go deeper into Matamoros — visit the city square, the old market, the pedestrian mall — they'd find the city gets better, not worse. And they'd find that same theme played out on a grander scale if they approached the whole of Mexico the same way. The worst part of Matamoros is the gauntlet of hucksters one must run at the bridge, and in Mexico itself, it is the big Mexican border cities that are the least characteristic of their nation as a whole. The interior of Mexico has many beautiful, sophisticated, remarkably livable cities.

W.L.A.

The Twin Cities looking north. Matamoros is in the foreground. "Dense block after block" housing 500,000 people. Brownsville, across the Rio Grande and in the background, is much more sparsely settled. Its 125,000 inhabitants have more room and enjoy large yards, parks, and "green space."

Port Isabel lies 22 miles east-northeast of Brownsville. The alternating strips of land and channels in mid-photo are known as "The Fingers." In the background, the two-mile-long Port Isabel Causeway spans the Laguna Madre ("Mother Lagoon") to Padre Island ("Father Island"). The acred line of the causeway is an engineering stratagem to enhance the span's survivability during hurricanes.

The coastal barrier island of Padre Island sweeps north towards Corpus Christi: The Laguna Madre is to the west (left); the open waters of the Gulf of Mexico to the east (right). This photo shows the extreme southern tip of the island and the resort community of South Padre Island. The town's 2,000 permanent residents are joined by as many as 200,000 "Spring Breakers" each March. Brazos Santiago Pass in the immediate foreground provides access to the Port of Brownsville.

The 17-mile-long Brownsville Ship Channel connects Brownsville to the Gulf. The Port of Brownsville's turning basin is at top right. Industries along the Channel have the capacity to manufacture, modify, repair, and dismantle off-shore oil platforms. Three jack-up, jack-down platforms are shown here in jack-down position. The platform can quickly be ratcheted up when being readied for positioning in deep waters.

"The Brownsville-Port Isabel shrimping fleet, with 360 off-shore boats, is the nation's and the world's largest shrimping fleet by any measure used — total vessels, weight of catch, value of catch, whatever." This is the Port of Brownsville's shrimp basin. Over 200 shrimp boats dock here. Access to the Brownsville Ship Channel is at the extreme right.

The maquiladora or "Twin Plant" program allows American manufacturers to locate their labor intensive assembly operations in labor cheap Mexico. There are 111 maquiladoras in Matamoros employing 41,000 workers. Above is the General Motors complex (8,500 employees) at FINSA industrial park. This photo was taken some years ago before TRICO and other factories arrived to fill in this landscape.

"The low-rise, no-nonsense, functional factories of modern corporate America." These two factories are located at Brownsville's Airport Industrial Park. The Haggar plant (above) has 900 employees to cut and sew perma-press slacks. TRICO (below) is the world's leading maker of car windshield wiper assemblies. The plant shown has 515 employees, while its "twin" in Matamoros employs 3,000.

Off-shore shrimp boats at the Port of Brownsville shrimp basin — shown in "sweeps up" position. Once in open waters the sweeps are lowered to drag, usually four nets. The mouths of the nets are kept flared open by "doors" — the wooden rectangular devices shown resting on the sterns of the boats in these two photos. Crews vary in size, but a four member crew is the most common: a captain, a net rigger and two "headers" to decapitate the shrimp.

Brownsville bills itself as "The Crossroads of the Hemisphere" and trans-shipment activities are important. This photograph shows a concentration of warehouses and trucking firms in the north-eastern part of the city.

The center of Brownsville: City Hall at Market Square. Brownsville's municipal offices are located in this building — which reflects the heavy Spanish influence on Southwestern architecture. The structure was built between 1850 and 1852, and completely renovated in the 1980s. Originally the site of the city's main market, Market Square still lies at the heart of the downtown commercial district and serves as the hub of intra-city bus service.

(Above) The downtown campus of the University of Texas at Brownsville occupies land on the north side of the Fort Brown Resaca. Some of the old fort's refurbished buildings house classrooms and administrative offices. (Below) A stretch of Town Resaca beautifies backyards in Rio Viejo, Brownsville's premier residential neighborhood.

(Above) A view of Elizabeth Street taken just after dawn on a deserted Sunday morning. "Walking down Elizabeth Street one enters a time-warp commercial district reminiscent of downtowns across America during the 1950s. There is even a Woolworths."

(Left) "Running on an east-west axis through the center of the city is Boca Chica Boulevard . . . your usual urban stretch of burger joints, pizza franchises, Jiffy Lubes, Wal-marts, and strip malls. Hideous of course, but apparently essential and inevitable." This photo was taken at 8:00 on a Sunday morning while traffic was still light.

(Right) "Shopping in downtown Brownsville is fun. It is an experience. Virtually any item wished for, of any quality, can be obtained. Best of all, every store has its own ambience." This store sign reads: "Esmeralda's Herb Store. Amulets, charcoal, perfumeria, sprays, soaps, incense, powders, essences, perfumes. We legitimate ornaments with their guarantees." Esmeralda is evidently also a parapsychologist.

(Right) Ramirez' House. This versatile downtown store offers clothes, boxes, shoes, and toys. Retail and wholesale.

"*The* ropa usada *business is another unique feature of the Brownsville economy . . . but one that the Convention and Visitors Bureau chooses not to include in its list of attractions. Every city has some kind of second-hand or used clothing stores, but Brownsville has them in spades.*"

(Above) A row of ropas usadas on Adams Street.

(Left) The typical manner of displaying merchandise in a ropa usada. Just wade in. "Here one can find the finest in ties as wide as bibs and pastel polyester leisure suits . . . as well as stylish designer clothing if one has the time and stamina for the search."

(Above) The Aguilar corner grocery in the Lincoln Park area.
(Below) This store on 13th Street offers farm fresh fruit and vegetables.

(Above) Night life Brownsville style. Nearly two dozen bars and night clubs line a short stretch of 14th Street. Many of these gritty bars employ Honduran "Hostesses." In this photo are shown Papucho's Bar, Las Cabanitos Lounge and the JP Lounge.

(Below) A clump of Casas de Cambios (money changers) on International Boulevard three blocks from Gateway International Bridge. These businesses trade pesos and dollars for travelers and shoppers crossing the border in either direction.

Brownsville residences run the full spectrum in quality—from grand to quite basic. Here are two homes on the higher end of the scale. (Above) A residence on Palm Boulevard. The hurricane shutters and wrought-iron filigree work are reminiscent of the French colonial style, but are also characteristic of Spanish colonial style. (Left) This graceful, doric-columned home in toney Rio Viejo would not have been out of place in the ante-bellum South.

The residences on this page would represent the middle of the housing spectrum.

(Above) A three-bedroom home on a shady street in the Los Ebanos section of the city — an addition built during the Depression years of the 1930s, and now registered as a National Historic Neighborhood.

(Below) A pleasant, working class neighborhood in the Southmost area. With over 30,000 residents, Southmost is the city's largest single neighborhood.

"Any newcomer to Brownsville will quickly deduce that Brownsville is a high crime area. The evidence is everywhere . . . the barred windows on houses, and the prevalence in many city neighborhoods — unusual elsewhere in America — of homes having both their front and back yards enclosed by high chain-link fences and, as often as not, with watchdogs patrolling within."

(Above) A home in Southmost.

(Below) A home in Cameron Park.

Basic, but decently maintained, homes.

(Above) Two residences in Cameron Park. "This colonia *situated on the northern edge of Brownsville is a maze of unimproved dirt roads and 1600 mainly poorer homes housing 4000 people — many of whom are recent Mexican immigrants or illegals — which Brownsville's city government refuses to annex for fear of the drain it would be on the city resources."*

(Left) Two tiny homes fronting onto an alley a few blocks from the downtown area. Several small children who were playing on the porch of the first home shyly ducked inside just before the photograph was taken.

On a Shrimp Boat

It's 5:00 on a warm, September morning, and I'm creeping through Port Isabel in my car, following the directions I've been given and looking for my turnoff. Finally, I see it: "Franklin Trailer Camp." I turn left into the camp and follow the lane. Trailers are on either side. Not flashy Airstreams and Winnebagos — not tourist and Winter Texan trailers — but the real thing. Permanent trailers, working people's homes, shrimpers' homes. Many are rust-stained from long years of sitting in the salt air. At the end of the lane, the dock. Here lie the three bait shrimping boats owned by Gordon Williams. A man and his boy are about to get underway in one of them. I ask them where "El Gorupo's" boat is. The boy points to one and says, "He will come." Sure enough, a few minutes pass and another pair of headlights start down the lane. A car door slams and a moment later El Gorupo (which means "chicken lice") is on the dock shaking my hand. El Gorupo is fifty-two years old, and he has earned his living as a shrimper since he was seventeen years old. He has a lined, weary-looking face, but he is very fit — there are knots of muscles in his neck, shoulders, and tattooed arms. He is a serious, reserved man even though he wears a yellow T-shirt which informs me that Spuds Mackenzie is the original party animal.

We hop aboard. Lights are turned on so Gorupo can see what he's doing. It's a very humble craft. Maybe thirty feet long, ten or twelve feet wide. Wooden hulled and many years since its last painting. All the metal stanchions are eaten with rust. The boat's most prominent feature is the tall rectangular frame, guyed by several heavy chains running fore and aft, which bears the net.

Gorupo goes into the pilot house and turns the ignition. The big diesel, squarely in the middle of the boat to support its weight, erupts in noise. Talking will be impossible. Communication will be with shouts and hand gestures. We cast off.

We wind our way through channels and bays thick with shrimp boats: Texas Lady, Indigo, Henry C., Tabby. *Gorupo switches off the light in the pilot house so we can see better, and we chug along in the moonlight. Gorupo sits on a stool and steers. His cigarette glows orange. Gradually, the lights of the causeway and the South Padre Island hotels recede in the distance. We head up the broad Brownsville Ship Channel. Flashing red lights to starboard, flashing green lights to port mark off the channel fairway. Traffic picks up. We meet big Gulf shrimpers, sweeps held high, coming down. Another large Gulf shrimper overhauls us from the rear. It's the* Tiburon, *and with a wrist-thick steel cable it is towing a disabled sister ship — ironically named* Tag-A-Long.

At 6:40, with a hint of light in the east, stars begin to fade and blink out. Soon the eastern sky takes on an orchid hue, and the first seagulls begin to fly. It is now a half-hour before sunrise, and we can legally begin to shrimp. Gorupo slows the boat to a crawl, frees some knots, and begins heaving our net in wads over the side. The sea grabs it and it splays out behind us. The two heavy wooden "doors" are then wrestled into position on the stern platform. Once in the water, their job will be to hold the mouth of the net open and drag the "tickler" chain on the seabed. The tickler will rouse the shrimp from the mud and cause them to hop into our net. Once all is ready, Gorupo, in a fine display of agility, leaps to the pilot house and throttles up, steering with one hand and operating the winch with the other. He hoists the whole rig of net, chains, doors, and rope to the top of the frame, and then immediately reverses the winch and lowers the rig into the water. As soon as the doors take purchase the net pays out rapidly and the boat takes on a load. The stern is pulled down, the bow rises, and water runs over the transom and wets our shoes. The cables holding the net whine as they pay out through steel pulleys overhead. With the net now on the channel bed forty feet below us, we commence our first "drag" of the day. We proceed at a leisurely two or three knots to minimize damage to our catch. Gorupo can relax now. He lights a cigarette, sits on his stool and steers with one hand. We each have a cup of coffee from his thermos.

While we crawl along, other shrimp boats pass us by — some going up channel, some down. Miss Lorena, Little Romero. *Two top-heavy tugboats pass.* Little E *and* Bayou Lady. *Both wear skirts of car tires. A squadron of pelicans passes, their wing tips skim just above the water.*

After forty minutes our first drag is complete and Gorupo hauls in. The winch is engaged, and now the boat really takes on a load. Once again the bow goes up, the stern comes down, and more water rushes into the boat. The cables running through the overhead pulleys to the winch are now so taut they hum as they vibrate. Finally, the doors and net mouth come clear of the water and rise to the top of the frame. Gorupo idles the boat and pulls on a rope that hauls the tail of the net to the stern platform. You can now see a large clump of sealife fluttering in the net's tail. Gorupo lifts this writhing mass — it must weigh sixty or seventy pounds — and sets it on the edge of the holding tank. Immediately Gorupo ties the net tail back up, throws it overboard, and lowers the net and doors for the second drag. Once we are back to normal, slowly chugging along on our drag, Gorupo returns to the holding tank. The holding tank is divided into two parts. One section holds the catch, the other section is where the shrimp will go as they are sorted.

Gorupo starts sorting. He has a big wooden tray for this. Three sides of the tray are enclosed, and one side — leading overboard — is open. He takes a hand net like a sport fisherman would use and plunges it into the holding tank. He scoops out part of the catch and empties it onto the tray. It is a writhing mass. The first thing that happens is that the crabs get clear. They wiggle out of the tangle and arch themselves up in defense mode; claws up and opened. In an instant, most of them see the open end of the tray and the water beyond. Without any hesitation they make a sideways dash and plunge over. A few confused crabs run the wrong way and get piled up in the corners. Working with bare hands, Gorupo nudges the bigger ones in the right direction and flicks the smaller ones over himself. There is a stingray in the pile. This is scooted over the side. There is some sort of a silvery, eel-shaped fish with snapping jaws. Gorupo pulls it out by the tail and drops it over the side. He's actually quite gentle with all these creatures. Once the worst of the biters, spikers, and stingers are gone, he rapidly flicks the rest of the fish out — leaving a few dozen shrimp hopping like mad in the tray. These he gathers into a mass and tosses into the shrimp side of the holding tank. Then he gathers his net and scoops out another writhing mass and starts sorting again. He repeats the process five or six times — taking about ten minutes to work through the whole catch. While this is going on he's constantly watching other vessels and occasionally correcting our course. He is busy.

Meanwhile, a serious seagull problem is developing. We are infested. Sixty or seventy of them hover about us squawking and flapping, feeding on the crabs and trash fish going over the side. The more brazen gulls flutter a foot from Gorupo's face and snatch out fish and shrimp from the sorting tray. Others plunge their heads into the holding tank and make off with shrimp. Gorupo just tolerates them. He never lashes out at them. Perhaps they'd peck. They act like they would.

When the sorting is done, the gulls clear off. They are waiting for our next haul. Some perch in the rigging, others float in groups beside the boat. The more impatient fly off to join skirmishes in progress at nearby boats. The morning proceeds and we make a total of seven drags. Each time the same flurry of activity when the net is raised and lowered and the catch is sorted. In between times we drag at three miles an hour. Once we have to interrupt our drag when a huge cargo vessel moves up the fairway. Shrimp boats scurry from its path as it comes on surprisingly swiftly. Completely empty, it's very high in the water. Its bulbous bow foot is actually clear of the water. It gives us a warning blast with its horn and passes very close by. Crew members at the rail high above us stare indifferently down. No one waves. The vessel passes. Its stern reads: "Conorar, Limassol (Cyprus)."

The net goes back in, and we continue to drag. Two porpoises pass us going down channel. Pelicans fish. They dive into the water with wings in graceful swept-back position, then struggle back up out of the water and lumber clumsily aloft. The bluffs of the channel banks are dun colored. Atop them Spanish sabers and yuccas stand in silhouette against the sky. I wonder if Gorupo has shrimped these waters so long that he is immune to the loveliness of the setting. I watch his eyes following a pelican patrol for long seconds. Perhaps not.

By 11:00 we have completed our final drag and head back towards Port Isabel. Back through the winding channels and bays. We pass the sea cottages. We pass the Southpoint Marina. The pleasure yachts of the rich tied up at the marina bear names with more of a tang than those of the mundane shrimp boats. I see Second Wind, Class Act, *and* French Kiss.

Tied up back at our dock, Gorupo shuts the engine off. He removes the lid from over the holding tank. Hundreds of bug-eyed shrimp swim about trailing their long antennae. Gorupo begins to unload the shrimp from his boat's holding tank into a second holding tank on the dock. Gorupo transfers net after net from tank to tank. He estimates that we have between fourteen to eighteen quarts of shrimp, and each quart will be sold for $10.50 at Gordon's Bait & Tackle on Highway 48.

While Gorupo is scooping, I ask him if he likes his work. He immediately stops what he is doing and looks up at me. "Yes. Yes. I like my work." I ask him if there is anything about the job that he doesn't like. He thinks a moment and then says that the only thing he doesn't like is that the state no longer allows him to shrimp at night. Before he could make $22,000 a year, but now he makes only $14,000 to $15,000. I ask him if he has a family. Yes, he has a wife, three daughters, and a son. He smiles.

We shake hands and I leave. Back in my car, I start the engine and I'm about to go when I realize I don't know Gorupo's real name. I shut off the engine and walk back to the dock. I call out to him: "What is your real name?"

"My real name is Dolores Dominguez — but they call me 'El Gorupo.'"

W.L.A.

The Shrimp Industry

Shrimp, the most abundant and active of the decapods (an order of 10-footed crustaceans that also includes prawns, crawfish, and lobsters), are spawned in the Gulf of Mexico throughout the year, but with a noticeable peak in February and March. The fertilized eggs float in the water and pass through five larval stages before molting into a segmented form. They then pass through six further stages, known as "mysis," in which they grow a hard shell or "carapace" and take on recognizable shrimp form. They are now "juveniles." They are tiny; they are nearly transparent; but they are clearly shrimp. This whole process from newly shed egg to juvenile takes a minimum of fifteen days. The juvenile shrimp now seek out in-shore waters. Using their fan-shaped tails to propel themselves backwards through the water, they seek out the coast, then the large inland bays (like the Laguna Madre), and finally smaller, more protected bays and river estuaries like South Bay and the Arroyo Colorado. Here, in these so-called "nursery" areas, the juveniles begin to grow rapidly, feeding by night on mud, sand, algae, fish larva, fish wastes, and other organic matter found on the sea bed. By day, the animals burrow into the sand and mud and sleep. So averse and sensitive to light are these creatures that shrimping on nights with a full moon will be significantly less profitable than on darker nights. As the animals grow and put on weight, they reach "adolescence" and at that time may move from the nursery areas to larger, more exposed bays and lagoons. Finally, when they are four or five months old and approaching maturity, they migrate back to the waters of the Gulf, where they may live three to four years if not caught. It is, of course, the job of the Brownsville-Port Isabel shrimp fleet to catch them.

The Brownsville-Port Isabel shrimping fleet, with 360 off-shore boats, is the nation's and the world's largest shrimping fleet by any measure used — total vessels, weight of catch, value of catch, whatever. In fact, Brownsville-Port Isabel (officially regarded as a single port for statistical purposes) is, overall, the fourth most important fishing port in America. The value of its 1994 catch was exceeded only by Unalaska-Dutch Harbor, Alaska ($224 million); Kodiak, Alaska ($108 million); and New Bedford, Massachusetts

($82 million). The Brownsville-Port Isabel catch had a value of $64 million, and 98% of that was attributed to shrimp, whereas the Alaskan catches consisted almost entirely of fish and crabs, and the Massachusetts catch of fish and lobsters. In shrimping, Brownsville-Port Isabel's closest rival is Palacios, Texas, up the coast on Matagorda Bay. But even though Palacios has 300 boats, its 1994 catch was valued at only $25 million.

Of the 360 vessels of the Brownsville-Port Isabel fleet, just over 200 are docked at the recently modernized Port of Brownsville shrimp basin, while the remainder are tied up along the myriad bays and channels of Port Isabel. It should be remembered, however, that in addition to the local area's 360 big off-shore Gulf shrimpers, there are scores of smaller bay and bait shrimp boats.

The three varieties of shrimp boats (bait, bay, and off-shore) are designed, naturally, to harvest the shrimp in the various stages of their development. Accordingly, there are three distinct types of shrimping practiced in Texas: bait shrimping, bay shrimping, and off-shore shrimping. Each type requires a different license and each type is subject to different regulations and restrictions.

The tightest restrictions are placed on bait shrimpers. Because they are targeting juveniles and adolescents, their shrimping efforts have been intentionally handicapped in order to insure most of the shrimp will reach maturity and migrate back to the Gulf — to reproduce and/or be caught by the more numerous and politically powerful off-shore shrimpers. As a result, bait shrimpers are only allowed to carry one small net, and they are no longer allowed to shrimp at night when the shrimp are active. They can only drag in clearly designated areas (like the Brownsville Ship Channel), and they can only do that from half an hour before sunrise to half an hour after sunset between August 15 and March 31, and from half an hour before sunrise to 2:00 P.M. between April 1 and August 14.

These new restrictions, particularly the ban on night shrimping, have seriously eroded the bait shrimpers' standard of living. At least one local official (who wished to remain anonymous) said he believed the restrictions were unnecessarily harsh and another example of government "overregulation." Certainly, the bait fishermen themselves think so. Gordon Williams, the proprietor of Gordon's Bait & Tackle on Highway 48 and owner of three Port Isabel bait shrimping boats, claims the current live shrimp catch is no longer sufficient to meet the large local demand of sports fishermen and charter fishing boats, and that large numbers of fishing tourists have foresaken the area. Instead, he says, these tourists are stopping at fishing havens further north on the coast where live bait is always available. Williams thinks the night shrimping ban on bait shrimping is hurting the local economy more than it is helping it.

All thirty to forty of the area's bay shrimping boats tie up at Port Isabel, but they are no longer shrimping. These boats — intermediate in size between the small bait boats and the big Gulf shrimpers — no longer even apply for bay licenses. This is because of the ban on night fishing coupled with the redesignation of the Laguna Madre as a bait shrimping area. Perhaps because of the shallowness of the Laguna and the relative scarcity of rivers emptying into it suffusing it with fresh water, there are insufficient numbers of adolescent and nearly mature shrimp to make it profitable as a daytime shrimping ground for bay shrimpers who are limited to two nets (a try net and a trawl net) with mesh sizes that allow smaller shrimp to escape. Hence, the Laguna is now open to bait shrimping only. On the other hand, because the only big bays where day shrimping is still permitted and profitable (Corpus Christi, Aransas, San Antonio, Matagorda, and Galveston Bays) are so far north, the local boats cannot make the long two-way trip and return with a profit — since the lucrative night shrimping is banned in those bays also. Only shrimp boats home ported in the immediate vicinity of those bays can go out for the day and return to port at night with a catch sufficient to meet their operating expenses.

The Texas Department of Parks and Wildlife places the fewest restrictions on the big shrimping boats that trawl in the Gulf. There are a number of restrictions on shrimping in waters shallower than seven fathoms (42 feet), but in deeper waters — all the way out to the nine-mile seaward limit where Texas' legal control ends — day and night shrimping are permitted throughout the year except for the period May 15th to July 15th, known as the "Summer Closed Season," and the six weeks between December 16 and February 1, known as the "Winter Closed Season." But otherwise, the Gulf shrimpers may operate as many nets as they like (usually four), and there are no limits to the number or size of shrimp they can take. Should they encounter poor shrimping or a closed season, they are free to cut across the Gulf to Louisiana, Mississippi, Alabama, or

Florida waters and try their luck there provided they acquire the appropriate licenses. There is, of course, nothing to prevent them from traveling in international waters either, but very few shrimp are found in such deep waters so far from shore.

Generally, when the Gulf boats do put to sea from Brownsville-Port Isabel, they stay out from anywhere between fifteen to forty-five days. Those going out for the shorter fifteen-day stays are usually the older "ice boats." Lacking refrigeration, these boats carry block ice which is shattered and laid over the shrimp as they are caught. Layer after layer of shrimp, ice, shrimp, ice is built up in the hold, but after about fifteen days there is the risk of the ice melting and the shrimp spoiling. On the other hand, the more modern and expensive "freezer boats" can stay out much longer. Preserving their catch is not a problem. However, they too need to return to port after 30-45 days if they are not to exhaust their food, fuel, or crew's endurance. Once back in port, they unload the catch, clean, replenish and refuel the boat, and after a few days, the refreshed crew returns to sea.

The crew of a Gulf shrimping boat may have two to six members. The average is four: a captain, a rigger and two headers. The captain commands and pilots the boat, and seeks out trawling areas he believes will yield the most shrimp. The rigger is responsible for handling the sweeps and nets. He also, by tradition, usually takes care of the cooking. And since the boat is moving twenty-four hours a day, he occasionally has to relieve the captain at the wheel to allow him to get some rest. It is possible for the rigger to perform these additional tasks since the boat trawls for many hours at a time without lifting the nets. Both the captain and rigger have complex, demanding jobs, but for sheer hard work, the worst position on board ship is that of the headers. The headers must decapitate the shrimp as soon as possible to prevent them from spoiling. This is hard, unglamorous work. As soon as a net is hauled inboard and the catch is dumped on the deck, the headers must wade into the pile and discard the trash fish overboard — and the trash fish in these big Gulf nets will include such dangerous animals as sharks, barracuda, stingrays, moray eels and extremely toxic varieties of jellyfish. Once these have been swept, dragged or kicked overboard, the headers, sitting on low stools or in cross-legged Indian fashion, will begin taking the heads off the shrimp — like snapping string beans. Really adept headers can use both hands and do two at a time: pop, pop. But when the shrimping is good, even the best headers find it difficult to get through the pile before the next net load is brought aboard. At such times, the boat may have to be idled (and the catch and profits reduced), while the captain and rigger leave their other duties and pitch in with the heading.

One of the most acute problems facing the local shrimping fleet is the difficulty in securing experienced, proficient headers. The work is hard and does not pay very well — usually $20 per hundred pound box of deheaded shrimp, plus free food and accommodation while on board. As a result, header help wanted ads that run regularly in local newspapers usually go unanswered — and this in a county with a persistent 12-13% unemployment rate. To solve the problem shrimp boat captains have had to resort to hiring Mexican headers who are eager for the work and, to them, high wages. There are many willing, experienced headers in Matamoros who learned their trade on shrimpers operating out of La Pesca, Tampico, Veracruz, and other Mexican ports.

To be hired, however, the Mexican headers must first obtain an H-2B permit — this is a six-month non-agricultural worker's visa available at the U.S. Consulate in Matamoros. You would think this would be an easy matter. After all, the Matamoros headers desperately want the work, and the Brownsville-Port Isabel owners and captains desperately need the headers. But it is not. In order to be granted an H-2B the header must first prove that he has "strong ties" to Mexico which will insure he will return there and not simply lose himself in the American population and become just one more of the innumerable illegal aliens adrift in America. For the zealous officials at the U.S. Consulate, "proof" is evidence of having a family and owning property in Mexico. This is a standard of proof headers can seldom meet. The nature of their work is such that usually they are single men without families, and they are too poor to own real estate. This dilemma reached crisis proportions in the summer of 1994 when the Brownsville-Port Isabel shrimp fleet was short nearly 900 headers. As reported by the *Brownsville Herald,* Israel Linarte, an agent for alien labor certification in Port Isabel, accused one particular U.S. official (Janet Jacobs) at the Matamoros consulate of being either "prejudiced" or "pro-environmentalist" and responsible for blocking the permits. Fortunately,

Linarte had the wit to bus some of the rejected Mexican headers to the U.S. Consulate in Mexico City where the officials proved more flexible and granted the visas. Meanwhile, Father Joe O'Brien, the much revered parish priest at Port Isabel, brought his very considerable weight to bear. He contacted U.S. Attorney General Janet Reno's office and called a press conference to alert the broader community to the severity of the problem being faced by his shrimp families. He did not mince words. As the *Herald* reported, he said: "The shrimping industry in Port Isabel has a dock value of $500 million, and it's been severely damaged due to one woman . . . and that is Janet Jacobs."

In the end, the Mexican headers got their permits thanks to Father O'Brien and Israel Linarte. As for Ms. Jacobs, her work complete, she left the Matamoros consulate in July 1994 for assignment elsewhere. According to Father O'Brien, "Not one tear was shed when she left."

Whether or not Israel Linarte was accurate in labeling Janet Jacobs an "environmentalist" is debatable, but it is indisputable that environmentalists do pose a threat, and a serious one at that, to the local shrimp industry. Their current efforts center around endangered sea turtles. Since 1987, Gulf shrimpers have been required to fit all their trawl nets with TED's — an acronym for Turtle Extruder Devices or, more popularly (albeit inaccurately), Turtle Excluder Devices — which are trap doors designed to allow entrapped, air-breathing turtles to escape shrimp nets before they drown. The TEDs allow a portion of the shrimp to escape too, but obviously there is no accurate method of determining how substantial the losses are. All estimates are purely speculative. Environmentalists say the losses are insignificant; but many shrimpers believe the losses are quite significant. In fact, some shrimpers try to shrimp without them, or sew their TEDs shut. But in just two weeks in July 1994 vessels of the Coast Guard and Texas Department of Parks and Wildlife boarded 188 shrimp boats, found 24 TED violations, and seized the catches of seven vessels. Yet even though most shrimpers have been forced into grudging compliance with TED laws, some sea turtles continue to die. In 1994, 550 turtles were found dead on Texas beaches, and environmentalists believed shrimp boats were to blame. In 1994 they filed a federal suit demanding that shrimping be completly banned in the Gulf of

Mexico. Wilma Anderson, president of the Texas Shrimp Association, and Deyaun Boudreaux, a TSA spokeswoman, suggested many of the turtle deaths could be attributed to natural causes, ships' propellers and sports fishermen and that shrimpers shouldn't be given all the blame. Be that as it may, there is no question that there is a very high correlation between turtle beachings and periods of high shrimping activity. Still, one wonders whether preserving the lives of a few hundred turtles should be given the same moral weight as preserving the livelihoods of the 30,000 Texas shrimping families dependent on this industry. One's first instinct might be to think surely not — and surely the federal government will never impose a shrimping ban. But, then again, nobody thought a handful of lawyers, environmentalists and spotted owls could have been successful in their efforts to introduce 30,000 proud logging families in the American northwest to a world of welfare and food stamps — but they were.

One relatively recent development in the local shrimp industry has been the introduction of shrimp farming. In the late 1980s three Taiwanese-owned operations (Chung Mei Shrimp Farm, Southern Star-Hung Shrimp Farm and Harlingen Shrimp Farms, Incorporated) began raising shrimp in artificial ponds — two next to the Arroyo Colorado at Arroyo City and one at Bayview. These three farms, with a total pond acreage of 770 acres, produced 2.3 million pounds of shrimp in 1994 with a value of $8 million. The ponds carry between 50,000 to 200,000 head of shrimp per acre. The shrimp raised in the ponds are not the native brown shrimp *(Penaeus aztecus)* which make up 98% of the catch landed by the local shrimp fleet, but an Asian exotic species *(Penaeus vannamei)*. Unfortunately, Taura virus, a virus named after an Ecuadorean river where this shrimp disease first appeared, had been working its way northward through shrimp farms in Central America and Mexico, and reached South Texas in March 1995. The exotic shrimp at all three of the Taiwanese farms caught the disease, their tails turned pinkish red, and the entire stock, valued at $11 million, was lost — along with 108 permanent jobs. Naturally, local shrimpers are very concerned that the virus might spread to the native brown shrimp in the area's bays and the Gulf itself. As of September 1995 the answer seems to be no. Laboratory tests show brown shrimp to be immune to the virus. White shrimp, however, which make up one percent of the local catch, do appear somewhat susceptible to the disease in their juvenile stage, and local bait shrimpers have reported catching some white shrimp with pinkish-red tails. Ominously, the *Valley Morning Star,* in July 1995, reported that Harry Goette, while shrimping in the Brownsville Ship Channel, pulled up some dead brown shrimp with the symptomatic pinkish-red tails.

Needless to say, local shrimpers are greatly perturbed by the Taiwanese shrimp farms. Not only do they see the Taiwanese as cutting into their market and lowering shrimp prices, but now they blame the Taiwanese — rightly or wrongly — for introducing the Taura virus to the area and jeopardizing the entire industry. For their part, the Taiwanese did all they could to contain the spread of the virus and placed their farms under self-quarantine and stopped all effluent discharges as soon as the disease was noticed. Nevertheless, even before the extent of the problem was recognized, seagulls were observed plucking dead and dying shrimp from the ponds and flying off.

A final component of the local shrimping industry is the host of businesses that service the fleet and handle the catch. These include fuel suppliers, ship repairers, net makers, shrimp processors and packers, shrimp brokers, and cold storage operators. One of the most important of these firms is Emilio Sanchez' Tex-Mex cold storage located on Brownsville's 14th Street. The bulk of this three-million-cubic-foot warehouse is not involved in the shrimping industry, but instead is a mammoth refrigerator maintained at -10° Farenheit containing endless, ceiling high rows of strawberries, okra, broccoli, carrots and other vegetables that have come up from Mexico, especially from Durango and Sinaloa states. This produce is destined for the American market and major grocery chains like H.E.B. and Kroger's. Also stored in the cold storage are American products headed for the Mexican market — principally beef and chicken. Perhaps the most arresting sights in the building are the huge vats filled with frozen cows' heads. Because the heads are glazed with ice and are cut off sheer behind the ears, they are not immediately recognizable — they are just strange, oblong shapes. One has to get close and study them to realize what they are. And even then, one wonders what they are for. But, of course, with a little thought the answer is obvious. Whereas cows' heads have little value in America other than for bone meal and pulverized fertilizer, those same heads are much in demand in Mexico and Central America where *"barbacoa"* (the flesh of cow's face) is something of a delicacy. At any rate, streams of semi-trailers depart Tex-Mex daily speeding south with the much prized faces.

The shrimp processing side of Tex-Mex's operations is under the management of Emilio's thirty-year-old son, Robert Sanchez. Tex-Mex has processing lines where shrimp are graded by size (the larger the size, the higher the per-pound value), veined, and custom packed for scores of shrimp wholesalers and retailers. About one hundred permanent employees do the processing, and these may be supplemented by as many as two hundred temporary employees during hectic periods. Such periods do not necessarily coincide with the local shrimp fleet's activities, because Tex-Mex also processes shrimp for the Taiwanese shrimp farms and shrimp arriving in refrigerated trucks from Veracruz and Campeche Bay on Mexico's East Coast, and from Oaxaca and Guerrero states on Mexico's West Coast.

If there is one thing that stands out in touring Tex-Mex's shrimp processsing facilities, it is the care taken with each individual shrimp. Ten million pounds of shrimp a year pass through Tex-Mex's employees' hands, and the uninformed might imagine such quantities must inevitably be sorted and handled in a rough, offhand manner. Maybe shovels are used. Not so. Quality control is applied to each shrimp — discolored or torn specimens are discarded. When the shrimp are veined, they are then delicately placed on trays in perfect, symmetrical rows, each crescent faced in the same direction. They are now ready for packaging in boxes with brand names intended to appetize: "Trade Winds," "Ocean Glow," "Ocean Star," "Campeche Treasure," "Texas Bay," "Gulf-Pearl," "Island Time," and "Texas Best." Another Brownsville product is ready for shipment.

W.L.A.

CHAPTER 9

Northbound on the Grain Train

The four of us come out of the crew lounge in our big, lace-up, steel-capped work boots and clump across the tracks towards the locomotives. It's a hot and gritty Saturday afternoon, and we all wear dark sunglasses. Engineer Pat Metzler has our train warrant in his hand: we're "GEBVCV 13" (Grain Empties Brownsville, Texas to Coffeyville, Kansas, April 13, 1996). The warrant further details that we will be pulling ninety-nine grain cars of a total length of 5,816 feet and weighing 3,073 tons. The warrant stipulates to the minute times we must enter and clear different sections of the track because much of the time we will be on single-track line (with intermittent spurs and sidings) bearing both north and southbound traffic.

While conductor Ramon Pena and brakeman Evan Norman work in the yard locating our grain cars and throwing switches, Pat and I see to the locomotives. About eight or nine locomotives are in the yard, all painted in Union Pacific's yellow-orange — the same colors pencil manufacturers for some reason favor. The locomotives hum with electric power and each of their twelve-drive wheels go "pop, pop, pop" as their air brakes interminably vent excess pressure. Pat and I climb up the ladder and enter through a door in the locomotive's nose, go past the toilet and up a few stairs into the cab. Big, comfortable cab in this late *model locomotive: four swivel seats, air conditioning, sound insulation. Unfortunately, this is not the locomotive we'll make the journey in. We're just using this one to shuffle around different locomotive units to different tracks. After half an hour we finally have our A and B units linked in tandem on a clear track. Each unit is rated at 3,000 horsepower. (General Motors diesel-electric powerplants harnessed to traction motors, with wheels in 0-6-6-0 configuration.) I follow Pat around each unit as he releases safety brakes, checks electric circuit panels, reads the gauges on the four saddle-bag fuel tanks (each tank holding 5,000 gallons of diesel) and looks into the sand bunker. (A maze of hoses clamped under the locomotive units ends in nozzles positioned just in front of each of the drive wheels, and they will spray sand between the wheels and the rails whenever we need extra traction: starting off; encountering inclines; during rain.)*

We're all set, and now we're ready to build our train. Ramon and Evan, on the ground with hand-held radios, direct us to different sidings as we couple cars. Forward and back; forward and back. The train grows longer and longer: four blocks long, six blocks long, eight blocks long, twelve blocks long. Each time we pull ourselves forward, crossing gates drop and we block off many intersections. We can't see the tail end of the train, which is by now more than a mile behind us, but Evan is way back there with his radio telling us to back six-car lengths, two-car lengths, one-car length, two feet. Clunk. The cars in the long, long line each shiver in turn as they accordion up.

Finally, we have all ninety-nine cars and we're ready to go. Pat sits on the right side of the cab behind a control panel that forms a semicircle around him. He slides the throttle lever to the left and the electric hum takes on a deeper growl. We commence our pull. Slowly, slowly. Ramon, hot and sweaty, hops aboard and comes through the door by the nose to join us. Evan, though, is so far behind, we'll have to leave him. A Union Pacific pickup truck will rush him up to Harlingen and he can hop on there as we come through.

The train snakes through West Brownsville. From our lofty seats, we look over fences and down into people's backyards: a lady pinning clothes to a clothesline; a watch dog barking at us; kids splashing in a blue, plastic wading pool; adults sitting in

*lawn chairs sipping beer at a Saturday barbecue. Kids wave,
adults wave. I say, "Everybody waves." But Ramon remarks,
"Not everybody. Some of them flip you the finger or throw rocks."*

*As the train crawls through the western stretches of the city,
the speedometer registers ten miles per hour. The law allows us to
go twenty, but Pat feels more comfortable at ten to twelve miles
per hour within urban areas. Trackside signs are frequent. Every
quarter-mile of the line is noted by a sign so that we always know
(and can radio) our exact location. There are also endless small
white signs marked with blacks "Xs." These advise Pat of approaching crossings, and he must employ the mournful, piercing
whistle at every crossing, whether it has drop gates or not. His left
hand rests permanently on the steel whistle lever, and he wears
ear plugs that are attached to a blue rubber cord that droops across
the back of his neck.*

*Once clear of the city, we pass a large yellow "V" sign that
marks the end of both the twenty mph speed zone and the
Brownsville depot's authority. The cab's radio receiver squawks.
It's the Brownsville dispatcher. He says, "Good-bye. Good luck
grain train."*

*Now we begin to build our speed. Pat slides the throttle all
the way to the left, and the ever-present electric growl grows
deeper still. The cab's steel walls, floor, and ceiling vibrate. We
slowly, almost imperceptibly, at first, begin adding speed in tiny
increments, pulling harder and harder on that mile-long train.
The speedometer reaches twenty mph; a few minutes later twenty-five; more minutes pass and we're at thirty, then thirty-five,
creeping ever upwards. Ramon opens the heavy, steel-front cab
door and while slouched in his swivel chair holds the door open
with his booted foot. This at last gets us some real air into our sti-
fling compartment. Ramon pulls a small, plastic water bottle out
of our styrofoam ice chest and begins sipping on that. Meanwhile,
Pat zips open his duffel bag and takes out a large, economy-size
sack of sunflower seeds. He nibbles on these while he "drives" —
spitting the shells into a cup his right hand holds poised at his chin.
His left hand's always on that whistle.*

*We're moving right along, passing through country crossings.
At each of these road/rail intersections the rails rise slightly, just
as the road does for cars. But unlike the cars, the train can't slow*

down and lofts over these rises and settles on the other side, giving me that funny, queasy feeling in my stomach. A metal plate attached to the cab wall says our "A" locomotive weighs 392,000 pounds, and the "B" unit weighs the same. But the suspension system is truly superb. You glide up and over the crossings and settle ever so gently on the other side with only the slightest side-to-side rocking. Beautiful ride. Cushion ride.

These country crossings are, of course, mostly gateless, and we are now passing through them very briskly. I ask Pat, who has been driving trains for sixteen years, how many cars he's hit. Pat looks over at me. It's impossible to read his eyes behind the dark sunglasses. After a moment or so he replies, "Twenty-plus." I ask him if the people ever survive. He stares at me for another moment. "Occasionally."

Three days earlier, I had read in the newspaper of two illegal aliens having been killed on this same Union Pacific run in the dry chaparral country between Raymondville and Kingsville. They had apparently been traveling through ranchland on foot at night, trying to skirt around the Border Patrol's Sarita highway checkpoint. The illegals went to sleep on the tracks.

I ask Pat about this and he tells me that exhausted illegals crossing the chaparral often crawl onto the tracks at night to sleep, thinking that if they stay in the space between the rails the snakes won't get them. But Pat says this is a big mistake. Snakes are actually attracted to the rails. The sun heats up the steel rails during the day, and they'll retain much of their heat during the early part of the night. The cold-blooded snakes like to stretch themselves out either on or alongside the rails to get warm. So the illegals face the danger of the snakes and, of course, the danger of the trains. Pat says he killed one illegal last year and one the year before as well — both had been sleeping on the track. I ask how this can happen. Can't they hear and see the train coming? But Pat says that most of these people are so exhausted, so fatigued by their hike across the ranchlands that they fall very deeply asleep on the tracks. When he spots them in the locomotive's light beam, jams on the brakes, blows the whistle, they're too tired and groggy to react quickly enough: "They're asleep. Then they're awake. They see a brilliant light. They hear an enormous noise. For a moment they don't know where they are. They don't know what's hap-

*pening. And then it's too late. The train's on them. (Long pause.)
It rips them apart."*

*By now we're moving along at a pretty good clip. The speed-
ometer's at forty-five and still climbing. Another crossing up
ahead. Three little Mexican-American girls stand beside it with
their fingers stuck in their ears and their faces squinched up in
pleasure. Pat, with the hint of a smile beneath his dark glasses,
gives them an extra long, strong blast of the whistle. We sail up
and over the crossing: the three girls a blur of bare feet, cheap
smocks, and toothless smiles. Our two units settle in ever so soft-
ly on the other side. Really smooth. Dyn-O-Glide.*

Building speed.

Heading north.

W.L.A.

Transportation

Brownsville christened itself "Crossroads of the Hemisphere"
back in the 1970s, owing to the fact that numerous transport routes
converged or terminated at Brownsville. And, although there is
more than a dash of typical Chamber of Commerce hyperbole and
"boosterism" in the "Crossroads" claim, it is not complete balder-
dash. Brownsville does have an impressive transportation infrastructure with all modes of transport represented: sea transport,
barge transport, air transport, railroads, and automobile roads.

The centerpiece of the local transportation network is the Port
of Brownsville. As Ralph Vela pointed out in his unpublished 1995
study, "An Analysis of the History of the Port of Brownsville," as
early as 1854 U.S. government engineers realized that a harbor utilizing Brazos Santiago Pass would be ideally situated "to control the
trade not only of the Rio Grande Valley, but of a large part of
Northern Mexico." This vision was finally resolutely acted upon in
1928 when the Brownsville Navigation District was created. Two
years later, President Herbert Hoover signed legislation authoriz-
ing the creation of a deep water port at Brownsville, the dredging of
a 25-foot deep shipping channel, and the laying of the massive gran-

ite and limestone jetties that would protect the port's mouth from tidal erosion. The Army Corps of Engineers performed the bulk of this work between 1934 and 1936, and the port opened for business in May of 1936.

Today the Port of Brownsville occupies a 40,000-acre tract of land adjacent to the seventeen-mile long Brownsville Ship Channel. This channel, running southwest from Brazos Santiago Pass and Port Isabel to the eastern outskirts of Brownsville, passes through undeveloped "wetlands" (which, ironically, are bone dry most of the year). Industrial development and docking facilities — the actual "port" — are located at the Brownsville end of the channel which terminates in a turning basin where ships of up to 875 feet (soon to be 1,000 feet) may pivot and head back down the channel to the sea.

At first glance, the five-mile-long port area strikes the observer as a nondescript jumble of ships, cranes, and storage tanks, but a more careful examination of the more prominent features lends some semblance of order to the scene.

There is the shrimp basin that leads off the main channel in a single inlet and then divides into three prongs. Over two hundred shrimpboats dock there, and dockside sheds and buildings house owners' offices, packing facilities, fuel, ice and net suppliers, repair facilities, and so forth.

There is the AMFELS (Allison-McDermid Far East Levingston Shipbuilding) shipyard. This yard has a huge welding shed, administrative and design offices, a forest of cranes, and the seven-story, 32,000-ton capacity Solomon P. Ortiz Floating Drydock — the largest drydock in Texas. AMFELS, with its thousand-man workforce, specializes in constructing, modifying, and repairing ships, barges, floating power plants and off-shore drilling platforms.

There are four ship "breaking" yards. These yards, inevitably rather slovenly looking, buy old ships, dismantle and cut them into convenient two- or three-foot-long metal chunks that are then trucked or railed to the steel mills of Monterrey, Mexico, for recycling. In March 1996 the four yards were engaged in collectively chewing up six ships, one barge, and an oil drilling platform. Five of the ships were U.S. Navy vessels — including a guided missile cruiser and a submarine tender — that had become victims of the government's decision to "build down" the fleet to fewer than four hundred ships in the post-Cold War era. Within six months the

Assault Carrier *Iwo Jima* was expected to arrive at one of these maritime knacker's yards.

Tank farms are another prominent port feature. The largest tank farm operator at the port is Statia Terminals, Inc., which has sixty-six tanks holding vegetable oils, gasoline, and various chemicals. In the main, they are storing vegetable oils from Canada for delivery to Mexico, and receiving Mexican fuels and chemicals for further delivery to Canada. The Port of Brownsville is the exchange point for this two-way traffic. Other tank farm operators are Petro Liquids (twenty-one tanks), ITAPCO, Western Terminals and Citgo. Most consumers don't realize it, but Citgo is the distributor of virtually all gasoline and diesel fuels in Cameron County, regardless of the brand names on gas station signs. The fuel is barged down from the Citgo refinery in Houston, and tanker trucks fill up at Citgo's port terminal and make their rounds of the individual stations.

Another "stand out" at the port is the grain handling facility. This includes the main elevator, two smaller elevators and three "crackers." The crackers take mainly American-grown whole kernel corn and crack each kernel into about ten pieces (as opposed to milling it into finer corn meal). This cracked corn is destined to feed animals — chickens, pigs, cattle — in Mexico. Domestic Mexican grain production is virtually sufficient to meet the needs of Mexico's human population, but not its animal population as well. The grain terminal's dock can load outbound vessels expeditiously, but unloading an incoming grain ship may take a week or longer. Besides corn, the grain facility handles barley, soybeans, and other grains.

Aside from the grain dock, the port has five oil docks, a liquid cargo dock, ten general cargo docks, and an express dock. All of these docks and indeed the whole of the built-up port area are served by the port's own railroad — the BRG (Brownsville & Rio Grande International Railroad). The BRG's thirty-three miles of port trackage converge in the northwest corner of the port at facetiously named "Bedlam Yard" where the BRG system ties in with Union Pacific trackage.

Some of the most arresting sights around the port area are the dockside sheds and concrete "patios" stacked with steel — steel pipes, steel beams, steel plate, and, most conspicuously, rolled steel coils. Over the decades of its life, the Port of Brownsville has been, in turn, primarily a vegetable port, a cotton port, a banana and pineapple port, and a fuels port, but in the nineties, the Port of Brownsville has become predominantly a steel port. In the early nineties most of the steel was inbound — American and European steel destined for the industrial, but land-locked, powerhouse of Monterrey, Mexico, 215 road miles to the west of Brownsville. Monterrey firms do make some use of the Mexican ports of Tampico and Veracruz, but those ports are more distant than Brownsville and notably less expeditious in cargo handling. Consequently, Brownsville is Monterrey's port of choice. In the early nineties steel was moving in both directions. Semi-finished steel was coming out of Monterrey mills in big spools of rolled steel weighing up to fifteen and even twenty tons apiece. These spools or coils would be exported to the U.S. and Europe. Loading this out-bound steel onto ships at the port might take a week or more since each mighty coil had to be laboriously blocked and chained down in the cargo hold to prevent shifting while at sea. This Mexican export steel could be readily identified at the port or on trucks or trains rolling through Brownsville because it was never covered, and being exposed to the elements, always had a visible layer of rust. But of nearly equal volume and far greater value was steel being imported into Mexico via the Port of Brownsville from U.S. and European mills (mainly in Britain and Germany). This was finished steel, rolled much thinner, destined for automobile and household appli-ance plants in the Monterrey-Saltillo area. This finer steel could also be easily identified. The spools were invariably carefully protected from the elements by plastic coverings or galvanized encasements while in transit. While at the port, the spools would always be stored indoors in sheds. The storage sheds themselves were always kept in the most orderly fashion, and the shed floors were meticu-lously swept. Were a spool to be set down on, for instance, a nail, the first ten layers of sheeting on the spool would be ruined.

Whereas this two-way trade in steel moved in roughly equal volume (albeit not equal value) in the early nineties, there has been no such balance since the peso devaluation of December 1994. The 50% drop in the peso's value has made Mexican steel the cheapest in the world — cheaper even than Russian and Ukranian steel — and Mexico is trying to recoup its financial stability with an export-led recovery. Steel is pouring out of Monterrey and piling up at the Port of Brownsville's docks. Truck transport to the port remains heavy, understandably so, since to load or unload a vessel with 20,000 tons of steel coils requires, according to the Port of Brownsville's Sidney Beckwith, seven to eight hundred trucks.

There is no question that the Port of Brownsville does much to add to the international flavor of Brownsville. In 1995, 195 ships, many of them foreign-flagged and foreign-crewed, called at the port. When this author visited the port on March 4, 1996, aside from six vessels, mainly U.S. Navy vessels, undergoing or awaiting dismemberment in the "breaking" yards, there were four barges loading or unloading fuels, plus four foreign ships. These were the Ukraine's 463-foot *Titan II*, in for hull repairs; St. Vincente and the Grenadines' 635-foot *Rossel Current* loading steel pipes; Liberia's 496-foot *Dzintari* loading safflower oil; and Greece's 415-foot *San Pedro* unloading monoethylene glycol (antifreeze). Within the next twenty-four hours, three additional foreigners were expected: Liberia's *Stolt Jade* and China's *Zing Yang* and *Hai Wang Xing.*

Under the vigorous leadership of its current board and director James Kruse, activity at the port is palpable. Some of the changes recently wrought or currently underway are altering both the face and the character of the port. In 1994 the board invited a third stevedoring company to operate at the port. This was Houston-based Gulf Stream Marine, a non-union outfit. Gulf Stream immediately began to offer competition to the port's two existing stevedores: Dix Shipping Company and Shaefer Stevedoring — both of which employ union workers of the International Longshoremen's Association. This had the effect, as chagrined union officials reported to the *Brownsville Herald* (December 14, 1995), of forcing Dix and Shaefer to reduce wages from $16.50 an hour to $12.50 an hour, bringing hardship to scores of longshoremen and their families. Another effect, however, was to hone the Port of Brownsville's competitive edge *vis-a-vis* other Gulf ports.

The Brownsville Navigation District is also deeply involved in the railroad relocation project designed to reduce intracity traffic congestion by re-routing port-generated rail traffic around the city rather than through the city. Likewise, plans for a future international road/rail bridge in the port vicinity should help minimize truck and train traffic in the city of Brownsville, and have the added benefit of linking the port directly to the mushrooming industrial parks on Matamoros' eastern outskirts. Since roughly 90% of the cargo handled by the Port of Brownsville either originates in, or is destined for, Mexico, this new road/rail bridge makes eminently good sense.

Director Kruse and the Brownsville Navigation District's board have also been making efforts to heighten the community's awareness of, and appreciation of, the port. In September 1995 the board approved and initiated trolley tours of the port in conjunction with the Brownsville Convention and Visitors Bureau. Moreover, there was talk of setting aside some sections of the port for recreational fishermen eager to take advantage of the port's exceptional angling opportunities — where else can non-boat owning fishermen cast into forty-foot waters? The possibility of a port museum and/or acquiring decommissioned U.S. Navy warships to attract tourists are other ideas gaining momentum.

Of ongoing concern, too, is future widening and deepening of the port and the shipping channel. Since the day in 1936 when the port was opened with a depth of twenty-five feet, the channel has had to be deepened and widened at intervals to keep up with the trend in world shipping — and that trend never changes: ships get larger. The larger ships are, the more they can haul, and the cheaper they can haul it; a simple matter of economies of scale. In 1995 the port completed its most recent dredging project and was deepened to forty-two feet over a breadth of 250 feet along the channel fairway to within about one mile of the turning basin, which is thirty-six feet deep. (This means heavy-laden ships must be unloaded before entering the basin for turning.) Further deepening must now be considered, and something, too, will have to be done about the tugboat situation. There are, at present, just two boats. The eighty-one-year-old *Warsaw* and, what is known as "the new boat," the fifty-nine-year-old *Sturgeon*. Port officials, pilots, and ship captains all name this as an urgent issue: the turning basin is 1,200 feet wide and would comfortably allow for pivoting 1,000-foot vessels, but the underpowered, antique tugs are, according to Sidney Beckwith and pilot Jim Franceschi, effectively limited to ships of 700 feet.

One of the more controversial issues the Port of Brownsville is caught up in concerns the intercoastal waterways in the region. In response to heavy losses of oil tankers and other coast-borne shipping to German U-boats in World Ward II, the U.S. government undertook the construction of the Gulf Intercoastal Waterway System — whereby shipping (i.e., barge traffic) could move in dredged channels behind the sandy barrier islands, such as Padre Island, that lie just off the U.S. mainland along most of the Gulf Coast. The system was not completed until after the war, in 1949, but ever since then it has been used by barge traffic moving anywhere within the 1,300-mile extent of the system which runs all the way from Brownsville to St. Marks in the Florida panhandle — connecting Brownsville to Corpus Christi, Houston, New Orleans, and thereby, to the whole Mississippi basin river network. The primary use for Brownsvillle is to barge petroleum products to and from Corpus Christi and Houston.

The Army Corps of Engineers is responsible for waterway maintenance, and federal directives call for a minimum dredged depth of 12 feet over a breadth of 125 feet. Naturally, erosion and silting necessitate periodic Corps of Engineering dredging to maintain the channel at the correct dimensions. The problem that arises is what to do with the dredged seabed material known as "spoil." The easiest and cheapest disposal method is simply to dump the spoil in the adjacent lagoon area — between Corpus Christi and Brownsville this would be the Laguna Madre. But as environmental groups point out, and the Corps of Engineers readily admits, this disposal method covers up some Laguna sea grasses which are the habitat of some shallow water marine and bird species.

Adopting the typical be-damned-to-the-economy attitude that is increasingly the hallmark of environmental groups, some of these activists want the entire system closed down, even though this would almost certainly drive up Cameron County fuel prices and lead to significantly increased traffic congestion in the area as more expensive truck and train transportation would be needed to haul the cargoes formerly moved by the frugal barges. As of 1996, the Corps of Engineers was studying the problem and expected to announce its decision in 1998. One of the possibilities the Corps was considering was to use the spoil to create ecologically-enhancing artificial islands in the Laguna which would have the twin benefit of increasing the Laguna's overall shoreline area (a popular wildlife habitat) and, being islands, offer eggs, birds, and smaller animals protection from large mainland predators.

Another waterway concern of far-ranging consequence is the 1995 decision by the state of Tamaulipas, Mexico, to build a 260-mile-long intercoastal waterway from Tampico to Matamoros and tie the waterway/canal into the U.S. system at the Port of Brownsville. The Mexican system would interface perfectly with the U.S. system — both would have the same 12-foot depth and 125-foot minimum channel breadth — and the Port of Brownsville's administrators have already allocated a "transportation corridor" for the final three miles of the canal's journey where it would cut through U.S. land between the Rio Grande and its confluence with the Brownsville Ship Channel. As the *Brownsville Herald* reported on September 25, 1995, some of the more vociferous environmentalists, including Mike Farmer of the National Audubon Society, would like the U.S. to effectively nix the project by denying the Mexicans the right to traverse those final, vital three miles. But as Port director Jim Kruse said in the same *Herald* article, "What [Farmer] has to realize is that they [the Mexicans] are doing this. It's going to happen whether he thinks it's an issue or not. This is reality."

At any rate, the Tamaulipas Waterway/Canal, which is scheduled for completion in 1998, should result in additional trade and traffic at the Port of Brownsville. This should be virtually guaranteed since, as Sidney Beckwith reports, there is a codicil written into the joint agreement that requires Mexico to use the Port of Brownsville's existing barge facilities and not attempt to build a competing barge port in Matamoros.

Another major transport mode represented in Brownsville is air transport. Brownsville International Airport (now Brownsville-South Padre Island International Airport) was built in 1928, the same year the Brownsville Navigation District was founded, and for basically the same reason: to take advantage of the locale's border setting as an entrepôt into Mexico. In those days of limited airplane size and fuel capacity truly long distant flights were impossible; short-legged flights with frequent refueling stops were the rule — and, hence, Brownsville, at the extreme southern tip of Texas, was ideally situated to serve as a hub for air traffic moving into and out of Mexico and Latin America. Pan American Airways immediately realized the Brownsville airfield's potential and in 1929 took over control of the airport's operations when Pan Am secured the U.S.

Post Office's New York-Mexico City mail contract. As local historian Bruce Aiken related to Anthony Gray in a September 10, 1995, *Brownsville Herald* interview: Brownsville International Airport "grew to be the top international airport in the country." That assessment might be a trifle overblown, but Bruce was relating facts when he stated that it was at Brownsville Airport that Amelia Earhart trained for her pilot's license, at Brownsville Airport that Charles "Lucky" Lindbergh refueled when he initiated the Mexico City-New York mail route, and at Brownsville Airport that aviation giant and movie mogul Howard Hughes (in his pre-dementia days) used to stop frequently on air jaunts into Mexico and Latin America. Brownsville Airport also played a significant role in World War II. It was the airport from which the Panama Canal Zone was serviced and supplied, and the airport at which Mexico's famous 201st Fighter Squadron was trained before being sent into combat in the skies over the Philippines.

But the "glory days" of Brownsville's airport are long gone. In this era when 747s can circumnavigate half the globe without refueling, Brownsville's utility as a stopover for air traffic moving into and out of Mexico and Latin America has evaporated. The only airplanes that come to the Rio Grande Valley these days are planes that actually have passengers or cargo to embark or disembark in the Valley. However, whereas the Lower Rio Grande Valley represents a conurbation of over a million people and thus warrants a medium-sized metropolitan airport, the problem is that there are three rival airports in place — one in McAllen, one in Harlingen, and the one in Brownsville. Keeping all three airports viable is a struggle. Harlingen, the middle city in the conurbation, is geographically best sited to serve as the region's air center since both Brownsville and McAllen residents are within an easy thirty-minute commute of Harlingen's Valley International Airport. Apparently, that is the logic the airlines themselves employ, because American, Southwestern, and Continental all offer several daily flights to and from Harlingen's airport, while McAllen and Brownsville have been left in the dust. In fact, there were times in the seventies and eighties when no carrier would service Brownsville. Since September 1993 Continental Airlines has served Brownsville with several daily flights to and from their Houston hub, but they were only enticed to do so when the City of Brownsville agreed to subsidize the flights to the tune of about $50,000 per month over the three- year life of the agreement — an agreement that expired in September 1996.

The question: Can Brownsville-South Padre Island International Airport continue to survive and operate a passenger service when the controversial subsidy is dropped? As for the first part of the question there is really no doubt. The airport will survive.

The airport is, after all, far more than just a passenger terminal, and, as airport director Dan Weber relates, many of its other operations are doing very well — thriving. For instance, the airfield's cargo handling function is booming — mainly due to GM and other *maquiladoras* with high priority shipments. As a result, Brownsville-SPI International is the Valley's largest cargo handling airport — moving 49% of the Valley's air freight, as compared to Harlingen airport's 43% and McAllen airport's paltry 7%. Director Weber says he expects 11% annual absolute growth in Brownsville-SPI air freight for the foreseeable future, and believes the airport will at least maintain its market share relative to Harlingen and McAllen airports. Part of the reason is Brownsville-SPI International is fortunate in serving as a base not only for UPS but also for Burlington and Emory, the Valley's heavy cargo specialists, whereas Harlingen's Valley International has Fed Ex and Airborne Expressway which are primarily small package carriers. A substantial portion of Brownsville-SPI's air freight is generated by six firms (Delco Leaseway, AT&T, Panasonic, Sunbeam-Oster, Alps Electronics, and El Faro) that lease hangar-style buildings at the eastern edge of the airport, next to the cargo terminal and within FTZ 62 (actually a remote site of the Port of Brownsville's Foreign Trade Zone No. 62). Brownsville-SPI also serves as home for 151 light aircraft. Fifty of these planes belong to Southwind Aviation, primarily a flight training company, that is growing by leaps and bounds. As of 1995-1996, Southwind had won contracts and was conducting initial pilot training for both Indonesia's Garuda Airlines and South Korea's Asiana Airlines, and was negotiating similar contracts with airlines of Singapore and Saudi Arabia. (An added bonus conferred by Southwind's contracts with foreign airlines is that the pilot trainees are sent to learn English, the requisite language of the airways at the University of Texas at Brownsville, and thereby contribute to the multicultural atmosphere of that campus.)

As for the second part of the original question — whether or not Brownsville-South Padre Island can sustain a passenger service once the controversial subsidy is dropped — the answer may be less certain, but director Dan Weber is convinced it can. He feels the three-year subsidy was, at the time, "absolutely necessary" to re-establish passenger service to the city, but believes it has done its job and can now be dropped. "I understand the subsidy is controversial with the public," and think the airport is now generating sufficient passengers to attract another carrier should Continental abandon the city once the subsidy lapses.

As for the idea of Brownsville just concentrating on fostering its air freight business and getting out of passenger service altogether — gracefully conceding to Harlingen's Valley International — Weber will have none of it: "Why? Why should we? Brownsville has a large investment in this airport."

A glance from Weber's second floor office window in the terminal building serves to support his point. The viewer takes in the sweep of the airport: the main 7,200-foot lighted runway capable of landing any aircraft, including 747s, that is aligned northwest to southeast to take advantage of the prevailing southeasterly winds; the 6,000-foot secondary "crosswind" runway; and the 3,000-foot "general aviation" strip used by the light aircraft. These runways, along with their attendant ramps and taxiways, present a vast expanse of concrete. And then there are the hangars, the storage and maintenance buildings, the facilities of the National Weather Bureau, the parking lots, the Confederate Air Force Museum, the dominating ten-story, 130-foot-high air control tower. Seeing all this, one is inclined to accept Weber's argument: let market forces determine the airport's passenger service fate. If, as Weber is convinced, the airport has established a sufficient customer base to sustain itself without a subsidy it is evidently providing a desirable service and should continue to do so. If not, so be it. Let passenger service die.

Before Brownsville had either its airport or port, it had the railroad. Brownsville was first linked into the American railroad system with a line (the St. Louis, Brownsville, and Mexico Railroad) laid down from Sinton, near Corpus Christi. This track was opened in 1904, and six years later, with the completion of the Brownsville and Matamoros (B&M) Bridge, interfaced with the identically gauged Mexican national railroad system.

Today Brownsville is served by both the Omaha-based Union Pacific and Denver-based Southern Pacific railroads. The Union Pacific operations in Brownsville are the more extensive of the two. The UP railyard near downtown Brownsville has a 350-railcar capacity and is serviced by three switching locomotives that help break up incoming trains and assemble outbound trains. The yard handles three northbound (Houston, Fort Worth, and Coffeyville, Kansas) trains a day, and three southbound trains a day going into Mexico. The Union Pacific Railroad is the owner of the B&M road/rail bridge. The UP also has a spur that runs across town to the Port of Brownsville. This spur interfaces with both the Southern Pacific line and the Port's BRG (Brownsville & Rio Grande International Railroad). According to Roy Weaver, the Union Pacific's manager in Brownsville, the northbound trains will be pulled by two or three locomotives of up to 4,000 horsepower each, and the trains typically are 5,500 to 6,000 feet in length (in other words about a mile long) and composed of about one hundred cars. Those northbound cars are principally hauling automobile parts, paper, Mexican beer, chemicals, sulfuric acid, chlorine, and lubricants. Southbound trains are carrying principally sulfur, scrap metal, corn, soybeans, and other grains destined for Matamoros, Monterrey, and the interior of Mexico.

The smaller, 150-car capacity Southern Pacific Railyard is situated near the geographical center of the city and stretches six blocks, sandwiched between Sixth and Seventh streets which run parallel to it on either side. A train, mainly of empties to be forwarded into Mexico, arrives from Harlingen each night around midnight, while a northbound train carrying mainly autoparts and chemicals departs at 8:00 A.M. each morning for Harlingen and, ultimately, the Victoria, Texas, switching yard where the train is broken up. The manager of the Brownsville SP yard is Wally Gonzalez.

Currently, the railroad scene in Brownsville is in great flux. For nearly twenty years, city leaders have been trying to better locate the railyards — to get them away from the center of the city where the scores of level crossings exacerbate traffic congestion and motorist frustration. This is particularly true when the mile-long departing trains are being "built" or arriving trains are being "broken." There is seemingly endless advancing, backing, and switching of trains at several critical crossings. There is a city ordinance forbidding trains to sit idle, blocking traffic arteries, for longer than five minutes between 6:00 A.M. and 9:00 A.M. and between 4:00 P.M. and 6:00 P.M., or for more than twelve minutes at any other time. However, so long as the train is in motion, advancing and backing and so forth, the time limits do not apply. Car and truck traffic may get backed up for blocks. There is also a degree of hazard associated with the trains' chemical cargoes and with the scores of level crossings. This latter hazard received renewed attention in 1995 as a result of a Union Pacific train's collision with a speeding Channel 5 newsvan, a collision which killed Roy Pena, one of the local media's most popular reporters. A final drawback of the two railyards' central locations is the annoyance they cause at night to people trying to sleep in the densely populated neighborhoods adjacent to both railyards. Locomotives rumble back and forth and slam the chains of freight cars about during coupling and de-coupling. Then, when the night trains finally pull out, they blow their piercing whistles at every level crossing, waking up half the city in their progress across town.

To alleviate these problems a $42 million railroad relocation project (funded mainly by the federal and state governments, but in part by the two railroad companies and local entities as well) is in the final stages of implementation. The project calls for the Southern Pacific Railyard to relocate closer to the port at a 300-car capacity facility and for an expanded, 600-car capacity Union Pacific Railyard to be sited north of the city alongside the 77/83 Expressway. Ten miles of new track will be laid to arc around the northern edge of the city tying both UP and SP lines much more directly to the port. This will allow for both of the old yards and much of their attendant trackage to be removed from the city center — eliminating over eighty level crossings in the process, and freeing up some very desirable real estate for parks, urban development or what have you. The Union Pacific line that connects with the B & M Bridge will of course have to remain, but trains on this line will be routed directly through the city and will not be sitting idle at crossings while conducting switching operations. The project may be completed by 1998 or soon thereafter.

Another change on the horizon for Brownsville railroads is the prospective merger of the Union Pacific and Southern Pacific

Railroads. Financially strong Union Pacific has applied to the U.S. Department of Transportation to buy financially strapped Southern Pacific for $5.4 billion. As Lisa Marie Gomez reported in a January 11, 1996, *Herald* story, local politicians have mixed feelings regarding the possible merger, and the Port of Brownsville's director and board members are especially skeptical. They fear if the port and city are served by only a single rail company competition is eliminated and rail rates will inevitably rise. For its part, to assuage such worries, the UP ran full-page ads in Texas newspapers (one appeared in the March 20, 1996, edition of the *Herald*) assuring residents that rate competition would be preserved since a merged Union Pacific and Southern Pacific Railroad would grant trackage rights to 3,800 miles of their Texas lines to the similarly recently merged Burlington Northern and Santa Fe Railroad.

Highways make up the final component of Brownsville's transport network. Aside from a number of state and county highways and roads, no less than three national highways originate or (depending upon your viewpoint) terminate in Brownsville. These are U.S. 77 with its northern terminus in South Sioux City, Nebraska, and U.S. 83 and U.S. 281 with terminal points seventy miles apart on the U.S.-Canadian border in North Dakota. Regrettably, however, neither Brownsville nor any other city of the Lower Rio Grande Valley was included in the Interstate Highway System — the nation's premier highway system — which so facilitates traffic, especially truck traffic, by virtue of its roadways being "limited access" and having no traffic signals, no roadside buildings, no obstructions of any kind. This situation may, in the aftermath of NAFTA, finally be corrected. The U.S. Department of Transportation is planning to take the currently existing Interstate-69 (which runs only from Port Huron, Michigan on the U.S.-Canadian border to Indianapolis), and extend it all the way to the Mexican border at Laredo, running it south via Memphis, Shreveport, Houston, and Victoria, Texas. As the *Herald*'s Anthony Gray reported on March 24, 1996, Brownsville's political and commercial leaders have joined "Alliance for I-69 Texas" and have lobbied, apparently successfully, for the DOT to consider running one or even two spurs down to the Lower Valley from Victoria, Texas. If two I-69 spurs are accepted, one would probably go to Brownsville, the other to McAllen. This proposal, although it has yet to be funded by Congress and, even then, would take about fifteen years to be completely constructed, would definitely enhance Brownsville's prospects of capitalizing on expanded Mexican-American trade. Especially if Mexican and Tamaulipas authorities honor pledges to improve the highways between Matamoros and Tampico, and between Matamoros and Ciudad Victoria and even beyond — over the Sierra Madre Oriental to San Luis Potosi and the Mexican heartland. This would place Brownsville squarely on the most direct highway artery linking Mexico's industrial core with America's Midwestern industrial centers and the province of Ontario, Canada's, manufacturing powerhouse.

In a similar effort to facilitate NAFTA trade in the Lower Rio Grande Valley conurbation, in March of 1996 the Texas Department of Transportation approved six-laning the current four-lane, and increasingly congested, U.S. 83, the main intra-Valley artery. The "widening" project would extend all the way from Brownsville to McAllen and cost $560 million, or $8 million per mile over the seventy-mile stretch. Construction was slated to begin in 1997.

Brownsville city traffic is another area that needs urgent attention. Part of the problem stems from the inordinate amount of truck traffic in the city: a host of trucking and "forwarding" companies operate out of the city; trucks shuttle across the border between the *maquiladora* twin plants; goods arrive on trucks out of the interior of Mexico; and Mexican trucks are forever running back and forth to the Port of Brownsville to load or discharge as the case may be. And, bear in mind, it takes 700 to 800 semi-trailers (18 and 22-wheelers) to load or unload a single vessel with 20,000 tons of steel coils.

But despite heavy inter-city traffic between Brownsville and Matamoros, only two bridges link the two cities: the Brownsville & Matamoros (B&M) Bridge which opened in 1910 (referred to by locals as "the old bridge"), and Gateway International Bridge, which opened in 1928 (and which is referred to without any sense of irony as "the new bridge"). Since that time, the twin cities have grown many fold in population (and cross-border trade has grown correspondingly), but still, Brownsville and Matamoros have only those same two bridges. The result, not surprisingly, is that car and truck traffic gets backed up for blocks and blocks in both cities during peak hours — and drivers may have to wait one to two hours or even more for their turn to get through the toll and inspection booths.

Finally, in the 1990s, action is being taken. In 1993 a four-lane Free Trade Bridge opened at Los Indios, spanning the Rio Grande in a rural area nineteen miles northwest of Brownsville. This county-owned bridge was designed to assist cross-border trade for Harlingen and San Benito and to provide an alternative route for trucks moving between Brownsville and Matamoros that wished to avoid the long delays at Gateway and B&M. So far, however, relatively few trucks are diverting to Los Indios — they choose to idle and inch along in line for an hour or two in Brownsville for their turn at Gateway or B&M rather than dashing out to Los Indios and crossing there. The reason, according to Cameron County International Bridge System Director Jose Galvan, is that the legal weight limit for trucks in Texas and the United States is 80,000 pounds, but that most of the Mexican trucks typically overload to 140,000 pounds — very nearly twice the legal limit. These trucks — real street busters — will wait at the Port of Brownsville or at city loading docks and then head for B&M or Gateway during the evening rush hours and try to cross between 5:00 P.M. to 8:00 P.M. It is the truckers' belief, Galvan says, that that is a high crime time and a heavy traffic accident time and that Brownsville police are so fully engaged they don't have time to be fooling around with portable scales and citing trucks for weight violations. These truckers fear that if they try to make the quicker but longer run out to Los Indios they'll be "more exposed" to ticketing by county and state law enforcement officials. So they wait in line in Brownsville. Nevertheless, Joe Galvan's statistics reveal that traffic at the Los Indios Free Trade Bridge is gradually increasing.

Also alleviating the bridge crossing situation will be the expansion of the B&M rail and road bridge. Four additional vehicular lanes were being built for that bridge, scheduled to open to traffic in 1997. Well along in the planning and permit stage (always a complex problem since international bridges necessarily involve approval and funding by both Mexican and American government entities) are the Los Tomates and Port bridges. The Los Tomates International Bridge (four road lanes) will be built one and a half miles east of Gateway and become the new terminating point of an extended 77/83 Expressway. The Port Bridge — a combined road/rail bridge with four road lanes — will span the Rio Grande three miles south of the Port of Brownsville and should go a long way towards ridding central Brownsville of much of its truck traffic. More distant on the horizon is a proposed Flor de Mayo Bridge which would be sited four miles west of the B&M Bridge and serve to link the northern and western neighborhoods of Brownsville with the GM plants and other *maquiladoras* at Matamoros' Finsa Industrial Park.

Seeking to address Brownsville's traffic problems at both the micro and macro levels, seeking a coherent solution to the problem as a whole, is Mark Lund, the City of Brownsville's transportation planner. A big job, but then at 6´6, Mark is a big man. In his third floor office of the El Tapiz Building opposite City Hall, he sits amid a blizzard of maps, traffic flow charts, and file folders and attempts to cope with the problem. Seven-lane Boca Chica Boulevard is too congested. Can it be eleven-laned? No: land acquisition too expensive; FM 802 will have to bear more traffic. Six-laning the Expressway, can it be done? Yes: already own sufficient right of way. Need for hazardous cargo corridor for trucks? Working on it. He unveils his master guide: "1995-2015 Brownsville Transportation Thoroughfare Plan" which entails 128 separate projects from widening various roads to four, six or eight lanes; building overpasses; reconstructing interchanges. The completed plan shows seven "Primary Arterial" roads radiating from the center of the city: West Loop, Central Boulevard, 77/83 Expressway, Paredes Line Road, International Boulevard/Highway 48, Highway 4, and the East Loop. These spokes are then tied together with increasingly distant concentric "Primary Arterial" roads: Boca Chica Boulevard, FM 802, Tejon Road/FM 3248, and FM 511. Most of these roads exist, at least in part, but much of the East Loop and West Loop exist only on the planning map — and, of course, they need to be built before the city grows much larger and land acquisition costs become prohibitive.

W. L. A.

CHAPTER 10

At the Ropas Usadas

As you exit the front entrance of City Hall at Market Square, turn left and walk up the short block to Adams Street. Turn left again, and you are in the very heart of ropa usada *country. For the next two blocks the entire northeast side of the street is a continuous procession of these used clothing establishments, bearing such names as Los Elizondo's, LaurAziz, and L&S Boutique. Some have well-lighted, attractive interiors with the clothing organized on racks, in buildings ranging from utilitarian to historic. Here one can find the finest in ties as wide as bibs and pastel polyester leisure suits . . . as well as stylish designer clothing if one has the time and stamina for the search.*

My destination, however, is the ropas usadas *with no names. Across from the Central Fire Station are three of the six stores owned by Jim Johnson, though there is nothing to indicate either purpose or ownership. Those who would have business at these stores apparently know what and where they are. Each of Johnson's stores has a plain but neat exterior in good repair. The brick logo on one betrays its original incarnation as a Chevrolet dealership.*

As I enter one of the stores, no one attempts to greet me, although I stand looking about for several minutes — either you know what you want or you don't! An inquiry leads me to the *manager, Sonia Guerra, who responds pleasantly to my questions. She has been in the business many years and knows both merchandise and customers well. The interior of the store is poorly lighted and cavernous, cooled only by a single fan. Clothing is everywhere, in piles, bundles, and bales of various sizes. Ms. Guerra informs me that the small wire and plastic-wrapped bales near the front of the store are for customers who cannot afford the large bales. The small ones sell for $55. Items in the huge pile of denim garments go for $5, while other assorted clothing (ropa mixta) sells for a dollar (adult) or fifty cents (children).*

The peso devaluation of late 1994 struck hard at the ropa usada *industry. Many Mexican customers can no longer buy as much American clothing as in the past, and Ms. Guerra's store has only a handful of customers. The manager also claims that her customers face more difficulties in getting their purchases past Mexican customs authorities. When clothing does not sell in Ms. Guerra's store it is moved to another Johnson store and replaced by newly-acquired goods. Ultimately, some clothing is returned to Johnson's* bodega (warehouse), *where it is cut apart and recycled. Other stores sometimes deposit such items in the dumpsters in the alleys, where scavengers pick through them.*

The ropa usada *business is another unique feature of the Brownsville economy . . . but one that the Convention and Visitors Bureau chooses not to include in its list of local attractions. Every city has some kind of second-hand or used clothing stores, but Brownsville has them in spades, many located only a block or two from the heart of the downtown business center, Elizabeth Street. It's not an image that the downtown merchants like to project, and over the years there have been several calls for "doing something about the* ropas usadas."

The dominant figure in the ropa usada *business is Jim Johnson. Johnson is not in the least intimidated by what others think of his business, pointing out that he is engaged in free enterprise and that there is nothing morally reprehensible about this activity. He is, after all, engaged in the highly fashionable practice of recycling. Johnson also notes that his businesses provide a $4 million payroll each year, and that the total for the* ropa usada *industry may be double that amount.*

Jim Johnson moved to Brownsville from East Texas in 1964

and bought a store on Adams Street for $400. A former associate began shipping him used clothing from Houston in bulk. Today, he has six trucks constantly bringing in loads from Alabama, Mississippi, Louisiana, and Texas. Hidden away behind the Golden Corral restaurant on Boca Chica Boulevard are a series of gray, warehouse-style structures. Through the open doors (a necessity due to lack of air-conditioning) dozens of workers can be seen, standing at tables, sorting clothing. The clothing arrives in bundles resembling cotton bales of no prescribed size and are known locally as "pacas." The better quality clothing is then delivered to Johnson's six outlets downtown. Johnson even supplies goods to several of his downtown competitors as well as his two outlets in Laredo.

Approximately 80% of the business of Johnson International Materials, Inc., involves export of what remains after the pacas *are sorted: lower grade clothing and wiping rags, often sent to third world countries more impoverished than Mexico. Obviously, the whole enterprise has been profitable for Jim Johnson, who declares that he has no intention of ever retiring — a disturbing notion to the upscale merchants of downtown. However, one comes away with the impression that Johnson continues in business primarily because he enjoys what he does.*

A.K.K.

Commerce

Walking down Elizabeth Street one enters a time-warp commercial district reminiscent of "downtowns" across America during the 1950s. There is even a Woolworth's. Brownsville's downtown district maintained its viability over the past forty years by focusing attention on Mexican customers, particularly those crossing Gateway Bridge on foot. Even in Brownsville, however, changes have come with the displacement of department stores and pharmacies and the closing of movie theaters.

Elizabeth Street and its neighbors, Levee and Washington Streets, cater to a diverse clientele, overwhelmingly Mexican. Some

Americans, particularly Anglos, complain that they are ignored by clerks who are unable or unwilling to communicate in English. Stores vary from those selling very cheap items often imported from the Orient to high fashion boutiques and jewelry stores purveying Rolex watches.

The dependency on the Mexican trade has created a boom-or-bust economic environment during the era of peso devaluations. Joe Calapa established J&O Men's Wear on Elizabeth over forty years ago. The casual visitor to his store, hoping to strike up a conversation, might greet him with a casual "How's it going?" "Not good," Joe would growl in reply and proceed to express his frustrations over the results of the December 1994 peso devaluation.

After the devaluations of the early eighties, Joe Calapa and other concerned merchants created the Downtown Development Corporation to create a more appealing environment. Jeweler and former city commissioner Bobby Lackner is president of the D. D. C., which has a membership of approximately one hundred. According to Lackner, the hundreds of downtown businesses provide up to 25% of city revenue as well as serving as a major employer. Downtown is the banking center, as well as the historic core of the city. Besides the retail business *(menudeo)*, Brownsville also serves as a wholesale *(mayoreo)* center for clothing, costume jewelry, and other inexpensive items bought in quantity by Mexican importers *(chiveras)*.

Bobby Lackner claims that the effect of the recent peso devaluation has been more devastating than those of the early eighties ... and he expects the effects to linger for years. Lackner's gloomy observations were confirmed by a spring 1995 survey of downtown businesses conducted by the city and a follow-up analysis by Impact Data Sources, an economic forecasting service. The survey and analysis projections showed that nearly 70% of downtown customers came from Mexico and that their loss of purchasing power would result in a $200 million decline in annual sales and the loss of nearly 400 jobs throughout the city. The reduction in sales downtown was estimated at over 60% for the year. The analysis noted the likelihood of downtown's continued dependency on the Mexican economy and projected additional, though more moderate, economic losses in Brownsville businesses for the next two years.

The downtown merchants continue to be buffeted by fluctuations in peso value and Mexican importation policies. After months of rumors that the $50 limit on free importation of U.S. goods by Mexicans was to be raised to $400, the government confirmed the rumor, but soon announced that the $400 figure applied only to Mexicans living on the border. Disillusioned merchants claim they cannot depend on any consistency in Mexican government policy or practice.

While conditions downtown have been severe if not catastrophic since the peso devaluation, other indicators, such as building permits, point to a more positive scenario for Brownsville as a whole. Bobby Lackner attributes the diminished impact of this devaluation outside of downtown to the extensive influence of government employment and spending, ranging from education to food stamps.

The extent of the impact of public assistance on the Brownsville economy may not be completely quantifiable, but it is abundantly evident in another major retail enterprise — food stores. In Brownsville such stores range from tiny *tendajos* located on the corners, or even in the middle, of otherwise residential blocks in various *barrios* to the more generally recognizable gas-and-food chains such as Circle K, Get-and-Go, and Maverick Mart, to the apparently dominant H.E.B. supermarkets.

A distinctive entry in the Brownsville sustenance sweepstakes is the Lopez Food Stores operation. The Lopez family has been in the food business for many years: Felipe R. Lopez established the original store at 14th and Ringgold in 1941, and his father operated a tiny store still earlier. A brother branched off to establish Lopez Wholesale Meats & Poultry. Today there are nine stores operating under the Lopez name and the president of Lopez Food Stores is Mike Lopez. It continues to be a family operation, but has been undergoing reorganization since the death of Mrs. Lopez, Felipe's widow, in 1944. Over the years family members have disagreed over how stores should be operated, and now the business seems to be in partial devolution as family members claim ownership of individual stores. Each store continues to be supplied by Lopez Food Stores, which deals with the wholesalers, and thus continues to benefit from economies of scale.

Mike Lopez appears untroubled by the inclination of his relatives to run their own stores; in fact, he was an originator of the concept, having operated the M. A. Lopez Supermarket independently for many years — Mike claims that a major factor in the success of the Lopez stores has been the "hands-on" approach of the owner/operator, who focuses on the needs of the neighborhood and community. The Lopez family stresses community involvement through participation in activities ranging from Little Miss Kickball to Brownsville Crippled Children. Each store "adopts" a school, and Joey Lopez is a prominent member of the BISD Board of Trustees. And the Lopez family can fairly claim that their profits remain in the community.

How can Lopez compete with the H.E.B. behemoth? Several years after Lopez opened the first supermarket in the Southmost area H.E.B. plunked a giant new store down directly across the street from Lopez. Mike Lopez does not see it as a case of direct competition. The Lopez operation is not seeking to dominate the grocery business in Brownsville; instead, they have sought a segment of the market and believe they have achieved success. Mike acknowledges that the Lopez stores try to create an environment congenial to Mexican-American customers providing traditional cultural foods and personal relationships. He notes the success of the Fiesta Supermarket chain in Houston in reaching this same clientele. For many working-class Mexican-Americans, grocery shopping is a family event, and Lopez encourages this activity. For Mike Lopez the success of his family's business is due to intangibles of style which H.E.B. cannot emulate.

Although H.E.B. has a downtown store which does compete with a Lopez store for the Mexican trade crossing the bridge on foot, the two major H.E.B. stores are both located on Boca Chica Boulevard, which has supplanted Elizabeth Street as the major commercial artery of Brownsville. Nearly every major fast-food chain has a representative on Boca Chica, along with the newest and most fashionable of eateries for members of widely varied social sets. Palm Court caters to a well-dressed cosmopolitan and Junior League clientele, while the venerable Vermillion provides a laid-back environment for the beer-drinking and burger crowd. Miguel's provides Mexican food with a touch of class, while El Torito offers Tex-Mex with few frills. Applebee's offers the illusion of a yuppie urban dining experience. Nacho Mama's is a recent entrant in the latest fad of chic outdoor taco restaurants. Neither Boca Chica nor

Brownsville serves as a gourmet Mecca-on-the-Rio Grande, but the situation has improved with the growth of recent years.

Boca Chica Boulevard is also home to such mass-merchandisers as Wal-Mart, Builders Square, and a new Target. Almost in their shadows, however, lurk the "recyclers" of a low-income community: the ubiquitous pawn-shops. Even this ancient enterprise has been modernized by corporations which try to create an up-scale atmosphere in clean, well-organized, and brightly lit interiors.

In this day and age, any city worthy of the name must be able to claim a shopping mall as part of its retail establishment, and Brownsville is no exception. Amigoland was constructed near the border to take advantage of Mexican trade during the seventies, and its fortunes have waxed and waned with the fluctuations of the peso. Sunrise Mall on the freeway on the north edge of the city has been somewhat less affected by the peso. Neither mall is particularly distinctive and neither offers much in the way of local "color."

A.K.K.

Inside a Maquiladora

We are in the visitors' waiting room at Lauro Villar 378 in Matamoros — Eaton Corporation's CONDURA I plant. While we wait, we look at a showcase displaying the goods the plant manufactures: electro-mechanical controls for household appliances. These are the obscure devices you'd find if you ripped apart your refrigerator, stove, or washing machine: odd-shaped bits of plastic, rubber, and metal with wires sticking out of them. A thermostat for a refrigerator, the spark mechanism for a gas range, the valves to flood a washing machine basin. Boring stuff. Stuff the average person never thinks or cares about. Hopefully, our visit will be brief. A quick breeze through the plant, gather a few impressions, and we'll be out the door.

But this is not to be. Our host arrives. He is Manuel Alcocer, a fifty-two-year-old Mexican engineer who is the Staff Manager and one of a triumvirate of executives who oversees Eaton's local operations: a distribution center at Brownsville's Airport Industrial Park and three large Matamoros assembly plants — CONDURA I, CONDURA II and CONTROLAM. It soon becomes apparent that the combination of Manuel's Latin manners and his engineer's mind (which assumes even social scientists share his passion to know exactly how everything works) will conspire to keep us at Eaton the whole of the day. We will visit all three plants; we will pace eight acres of assembly lines; we will see everything!

Before we begin, Manuel fills us in on the basics. Eaton Corporation is a Fortune 500 firm based in Cleveland. It produces electro-mechanical controls and other devices for America's household appliance manufacturers (Maytag, Whirlpool, etc.) and the Big Three automakers. "CONDURA," we learn, is not Spanish for some South American bird, as I vaguely thought, but an acronym for "consumer durables." CONDURA I, which was one of the first area maquiladoras, was established in 1970 and manufactures devices for household appliances; CONDURA II was set up in 1990 and specializes in automobile controls; and CONTROLAM (Controlos Latin America) was set up in 1995 to produce both in the facility formerly occupied by the now defunct Fischer-Price toy factory. The firm employs just over 2,000 workers locally, only seventy of whom are American, and a mere eleven of whom work at the Brownsville distribution facility — which gives some idea of the imbalance in the "twin-plant" misnomer.

Virtually all the parts and materials needed for the manufacturing are trucked over from the Brownsville distribution center and are then fed into Eaton's Matamoros plants in meticulously labeled boxes that identify exactly which one of the scores of assembly lines they are intended for. They are then unpacked and distributed along the line. Timing is paramount. The whole process of receiving materials, assembling, and delivering the completed product to the customers (appliance and car manufacturers in the Midwest) is carefully orchestrated to comply with the "just-in-time" principle of modern manufacturing which keeps inventories, warehousing and, therefore, costs, to a minimum.

On the CONDURA I plant floor one's first impressions: vast, clean, efficient, so young! The building is even larger on the inside than it appeared on the outside. Hundreds of people are working here. Each person is working fairly quickly, but there is no sense of franticness. The tasks are being done at a steady, rational pace. The factory is clean, cool, well-lit. During the debate that went on prior to NAFTA, American labor union leaders tried to convince the American public that the maquiladoras were gloomy, inhuman sweatshops. Sheer bunk. This factory is about as bearable as any American factory, or any factory anywhere, is likely to get.

But the strongest impression of all is made by the youth of the work force. Even for middle-aged college professors who spend their lives among young people, these workers seem young. Kids. "How old?" we ask Manuel. "They must have turned sixteen." To be sure, many are older than this — late teens, twenties, some thirties. We even see one or two antiques in their forties tottering about. But they are true rarities. The median age seems to be about 18 or 19. And, of course, most are women — girls. We ask Manuel about this, and he explains that the girls' smaller, nimbler hands are useful on many of the lines; and that they prove a more stable work-force than males — have less turnover than males. We ask Manuel if another reason is that the girls are more docile than men. He replies: "Yes. They are more docile." He adds that there has never been a strike at any of Eaton's Matamoros plants. The disparity in male-female numbers is being lessened somewhat, however, with the introduction of twenty-four-hour, round-the-clock operations at one of the plants. Many women are shunning the night shifts in order to look after husbands and children. Consequently, more men are being hired.

We walk the lines: youths tending industrial machines of marvelous intricacy, performing at prodigious speeds. Machines that bend, cut, drill, mold, inject, insert, heat, cool, spin, twist, splice, weld, solder, pound. One notices that all the more dangerous looking machines have two activating buttons on either side of the machine. The operator must push the buttons simultaneously (thus ensuring both hands are free of the machine) before it cuts, pounds, or does whatever it does. In the future, Manuel informs us, the buttons will not even have to be pushed. Sensors will indicate the hands are free — a further preventive measure against carpal wrist syndrome — a hazard to anyone who continuously strains their wrists.

Moving along an assembly line that is forging and constructing washing machine valves, Manuel snatches the gizmo out of the line at several stages to show us exactly what each operator's contribution is. Always he greets the operator; always he thanks them as we move on. Impeccable manners. Workers further down the line see us coming and stiffen ever so slightly. Whatever they do, they are going to do it just a little bit better, a little bit quicker, as we pass.

At CONDURA II, where the workforce is somewhat older and more experienced, we again walk the lines. On one line thirty-six workers sitting at thirty-six different machines carry out thirty-six separate processes to make and test an up-down switch — just the switch mind you — for a Chrysler passenger-side automatic car window. Several nearby assembly lines are doing almost the same thing — but doing it for different makes, different years. At the end of each line is the line supervisor's desk: tablets, pads, pocket calculators, and a big two foot by three foot scoreboard. At the top of one board it says '96 Chrysler window switch model number something or another. Below, there is a chart breaking down a target quota of 341,000 units. This is then broken down into weekly, daily, and hourly quotas. The chart shows that 520 switches is the quota for each hour of this day. One o'clock comes, and the supervisor stands up and writes in "520 actual." He sits down.

We go into an ultra-clean, climate-controlled, work area. Here, the workers are wearing hair nets and they have velcro wristbands with plastic-coated wires running out of them to sockets on the workbenches before them or on the floor beneath them. These are to prevent their bodies' static electricity from contaminating the circuit boards they are handling. Eaton has stolen a march on their competitors. They are producing automotive controls for 1996 that, with a squeeze of a car's remote-control unlock button, customize control settings for a car's various drivers. For example, a family buys one of these new cars. The husband programs himself as "Driver 1." As he approaches the car, he unlocks it by pushing "Driver 1." Immediately, the door unlocks, the circuit board adjusts the driver's seat to his height, rear-view mirrors plane themselves at his eye level, the radio switches to his favorite station and his preferred volume, the air conditioning sets itself to his individual comfort zone. Later in the day, the wife wishes to use the car and punches "Driver 2." A complete re-alignment to her needs is made. To produce the sophisticated circuit board needed for these customized controls, Eaton relies on a pair of million dollar computerized robots that can solder 440 circuits on each of the boards in eighty-six seconds. Wizard machines. They operate almost faster than the eye can follow. John Willett, a soft-spoken, middle-aged engineer, strolled over to us and told us he was confident his team could make

*some adjustments and shave ten seconds off the time. Get the 440
circuits soldered in seventy-six seconds. He also told Manuel they
were going to need a third machine if they were going to keep up
with demand.*

This was Eaton Corporation.

W.L.A.

Manufacturing and the *Maquiladoras*

The Brownsville area has ten industrial parks, and among these
two stand out: the Port of Brownsville and the Airport Industrial
Park. These two sites have not only obvious transportation advan-
tages, but the added inducement of being part of U.S. Foreign
Trade Zone Number 62, the nation's largest general service Foreign
Trade Zone (FTZ), and the FTZ that in some years does the
greatest amount of business, save only that of the New York/New
Jersey Port Authority FTZ. The FTZ consists of 2,000 acres that
can be spot allocated anywhere within the Port's vast 40,000-acre
tract, plus 300 acres at Brownsville/South Padre Island
International Airport that incorporates part of the Airport
Industrial Park. (A further 320 acres of FTZ No. 62 is located at
Harlingen's Airport Industrial Park.) Industries which lease or own
facilities within these zones have substantial advantages over their
competitors by minimizing customs hassles and receiving various
breaks on duties and taxes. Nor have these advantages become irrel-
evant with NAFTA's implementation, since NAFTA affects tariff
duties solely between the U.S., Canada, and Mexico, whereas FTZ
advantages apply to all international trade.

As of 1995, over 240 enterprises leased sites at the Port of
Brownsville — some within the 2,000 acres of the FTZ, some without.
By no means were all of these *manufacturing* enterprises. In fact, the
great majority were not manufacturers, but such miscellaneous users
as warehouse and storage tank operators, grain handlers, trucking
concerns, shrimpers, and even ranchers (grazing leases), the Cameron
County Sheriff's Department (pistol and rifle range), and the City of

Brownsville (landfill and Fire Department training). However, there were a number of manufacturers at the Port making everything from ships and off-shore drilling equipment to paper bags and kitty litter.

The largest manufacturing concern at the Port is AMFELS (Allison-McDermid Far East Levingston Shipbuilding), a subsidiary of Singapore's FELS company — one of the world's largest shipbuilders, and the only company in the world still constructing off-shore oil drilling platforms. Singaporean Y.Y. Chow is the president of the local AMFELS subsidiary, and since his arrival in Brownsville two years ago, the firm has added employees and shifts to allow for twenty-four-hour, around-the-clock operations. About one hundred engineers, draftsmen, accountants, and other salaried employees plus 728 non-unionized welders and other hourly wage earners work at the yard.

The company constructs specialty vessels of up to about 25,000 tons (primarily for the oil business) and repairs, modifies, and extends the legs of jack-up oil drilling platforms. Most of the customers are foreign (especially Norway, Denmark, and other nations adjacent to the North Sea oil fields), but American customers are served as well. The company also hopes to capitalize on its location within easy towing distance of Mexico's Gulf and Campeche Bay off-shore oil fields. In August 1995 the Mexican government began its long awaited divestment of the giant, state-owned, oil monopoly PEMEX. Private companies that buy up PEMEX's off-shore platforms will be required to make extensive modifications to those platforms to bring them into compliance with international standards before they can be insured. If AMFELS can secure a portion of this business, the company and the Brownsville economy would enjoy the benefits for years to come.

Another sign of AMFEL's health and vigor is their recent acquisition of a large-capacity floating dry dock and a huge floating crane. The dry dock was purchased from the U.S. Navy by the Port of Brownsville for $5 million, and AMFELS is the initial leasee. The dry dock was towed down in sections from Norfolk, Virginia, in 1995 and gives AMFELS the capacity to repair ships of up to 600 feet in length. Also arriving from Norfolk was "The Atlantic Giant," a floating crane with a 700-ton lift capacity. Previously, AMFELS' most powerful lifters were two 150-ton capacity cranes.

According to Project Manager Leland Salinger, one of the

greatest attributes of AMFELS is its largely Hispanic workforce. Salinger says that the Hispanic worker is "tool wise" and knows how to use hammers, pliers, and screwdrivers at a very early age. Consequently, they prove to be quick learners and highly adaptable in the skills of welding and metal fabrication: "Absolutely first rate. Absolutely the best."

The principal raw material used in AMFELS' operations is, of course, steel, and that is purchased from whoever can supply it most cheaply. Currently they are purchasing mainly from U.S. firms, such as Bethlehem Steel, and from the Republic of Ukraine. Ironically, even cheaper steel — and in exactly the forms AMFELS wishes to buy — is piled up all around the Port of Brownsville. This is Mexican steel manufactured in Monterrey. Unfortunately, AMFELS cannot buy this steel because an anti-dumping suit brought by U.S. steel makers has led to strict quotas on Mexican-made steel.

Another major manufacturer located at the Port is the Duro Paper Bag Company. The local Duro plant was established in 1969 when Charles Shor, an entrepreneur from Cincinnati, Ohio, was visiting his daughter who was vacationing on South Padre Island. Mr. Shor, delighted with the area, decided on the spot to establish a Brownsville branch factory of his Duro Paper Bag Company and soon obtained an old cotton bale warehouse at the Port for his operation. The company is headquartered across the Ohio River from Cincinnati in Ludlow, Kentucky, and today has eight plants, most of which are located in the northeast quadrant of the United States, although the company's newest and largest plant is in Rio Bravo, Mexico. Charles Shor died in the late 1980s, and the company is now wholely owned by his son, David Shor. The Brownsville plant has about 200 non-unionized employees, still working in the original, non-air-conditioned warehouse. The plant operates twenty-four hours a day, seven days a week, and its thirty-two bag-making machines churn out an astounding 96 million bags a day. The local plant supplies 75% of the Texas bag market, and also a significant portion of the market in the eastern half of the United States. The Duro Bag Company is the exclusive provider of paper grocery bags for H.E.B., Safeway, and Kroger and also smaller bags for the fast-food chains of McDonald's, Burger King, What-a-Burger, Wendy's, Taco Bell, and others. Fred Perez, the local plant's very affable purchasing director, says that the increasing use of plastic bags by the grocery chains has prevented rapid growth of the paper bag industry but that Duro is holding its own and even growing slightly.

Twenty-five railcars per week arrive at the factory with the raw materials — in this case mainly huge, one-ton spools of varying widths of brown and white paper. Inside the factory the thirty-two bag-making machines of different sizes cut, fold, glue, stamp, count, and stack the bags. The glue for the bottom and side seams of the bags is made in a separate building from corn starch and water. Overhead pipes take the glue to the main building and continuously feed the bag-making machines. The glue is itself safely edible — an important consideration since it will be in contact with groceries and fast foods. Even the dyes used to stamp and print company logos on the bags are produced at the plant, and they too are edible — being made from natural vegetables (corn oil, linseed oil, etc.).

About 90% of the paper used at the local plant comes from U.S. suppliers (Georgia-Pacific, James River) and 5% each from Mexico and Canada. The company is moving aggressively to use more recycled paper and, in fact, some of its customers (McDonald's and Wendy's to name but two) are insisting upon it. As recently as 1993 the local plant used only 5% recycled paper. That grew to 40% in 1995, and is slated to reach 90% by the end of 1996.

Although for a time Duro used ships to import bag handles from China, there is no real reason for the local plant to be sited at the Port other than the easy access to road and rail transport. The paper comes in by rail, and trucks (twenty per day) haul the mountains of bags to the customers.

The newest manufacturer to arrive at the Port is Columbia Western Clay Company. This mining company recently discovered sodium bentonite clay deposits near Terlingua in the Big Bend area of West Texas and needed a coastal processing site for the clays. The local operations manager, Jaime Martinez, said Brownsville was chosen because it offered both cheap ocean transport for the finished product and proximity to Mexico. The company eventually intends to also use Mexican clays in its various clay blends.

Columbia Western brings the materials to the Port by rail, and then crushes and mills the clay into powder, granules, or lumps. Depending on grade and composition, the clays are used for oil field drilling mud, the binder in cattle feed pellets, or kitty litter. Columbia Western's Brownsville plant is the only processor of sodium bentonite on the whole of the Gulf Coast, and the plant, which just started up in June of 1994, hopes to employ twenty-five Brownsvillites once fully underway.

The second major concentration of industry in Brownsville is at the Airport Industrial Park. On the drive to the airport along Billy Mitchell Boulevard, one confronts the low-rise, no-nonsense, functional factories of modern corporate America. The faces of these factories are blank and indifferent — revealing nothing of what goes on within them. A sweep of lawn, the inevitable flag poles, the rectangle of the factory. And, of course, a sign. Not a sign shouting for customers like some car dealership or fast-food store, but an understated sign bearing the corporate name. Sometimes, the name is a self-explanatory household word like Haggar or Levi's, but more often the name is as abstruse as the building itself: TRICO, MagneTek.

The average Brownsvillite will never enter these factories, never know of the activity that goes on within them. But these are the industries that will likely make or break Brownsville's economic future. These are the assembly industries and the *maquiladoras*.

Haggar Apparel Company and Levi Strauss and Co., two of the larger factories at the Airport Industrial Park, are not *maquiladoras* and do not have factory twins "across." The reason for this is that prior to NAFTA, the U.S. had a very strict quota on cotton to protect American cotton growers, and finished, manufactured denim cotton jeans were technically regarded as "cotton" for U.S. customs purposes. Hence, customs duties effectively prohibited U.S. importation of jeans. However, by locating near to the border, but on the U.S. side, both Haggar and Levi's could take advantage of the plentiful, and (compared to elsewhere in the United States) relatively low-cost labor force. The fact that their area plants are far from the main U.S. markets is not an important liability. Their products have such a high value per weight ratio ($30 to $40 for a pair of slacks or jeans weighing a few ounces) that transportation costs are not overly burdensome. A fully-loaded Levi's truck leaving an area plant will typically be hauling $900,000 worth of jeans. The ancillary costs for the truck, driver, and diesel fuel are fairly inconsequential expenses.

Levi Strauss and Co. is the world's largest clothing manufacturer. It was founded by and named for the enterprising Jewish businessman who originally thought he would make his fortune selling denim tents to prospectors during the 1849 California gold rush. He struck it rich when he realized what the "Forty-niners" really needed was extra tough trousers for sloshing around in riverbeds and scrambling up and down mountainsides. Soon, he was cutting up his denim tents and turning them into durable jeans with his trademark double-stitched seams and rust-proof, copper-riveted pockets able to hold heavy nuggets and ore samples.

Today this privately-owned, San Francisco-based company has factories all over the world. There are twenty-eight production plants in the U.S. — with the largest concentrations being in the El Paso area and the Lower Rio Grande Valley. The bolts of denim are trucked in from textile mills in the Carolinas and then are cut up and sewn into jeans and other articles in the local plants. Brownsville's plant employs 550 workers to produce children's jeans; San Benito's plant employs 400 workers to produce men's and women's jeans; Harlingen's 400 workers make denim shirts and shorts and other specialty goods; while the largest area factory, in McAllen, has about 800 workers who specialize in making short-legged, slim-waisted, teeny-bottomed jeans for the Japanese market. The Valley plants are unionized (Amalgamated Clothing Workers Union), but the union is considered "reasonable." The Brownsville plant completes about 20,000 pairs of jeans a day.

The other major apparel factory in Brownsville, Haggar, is owned by a Lebanese-American family of that same name in Dallas. The local plant makes men's slacks from a cotton denim and chemical blend that produces a "permanent pressed" material requiring no subsequent ironing. Unlike the Levi Strauss Co. whose world-wide advertising campaigns have succeeded in cultivating significant brand loyalty among a more youthful market — a market which often "insists" on Levis — Haggar's is catering to adult males whose main criteria for buying includes both quality and price. Haggar's customers are extremely sensitive to even marginal price differences of competing brands. As a result, Haggar's has had a real struggle in recent years. They had to close the bulk of their production facilities (eight plants in Oklahoma and Texas) and relocate to cheaper factories in the Dominican Republic. Fortunately, Haggar's non-unionized Valley plants in Weslaco, Edinburg, and Brownsville escaped the closings.

In other respects, too, Haggar's Valley plants face more diffi-cult manufacturing challenges than Levi's. For one thing, Haggar's must change the "weight" of their slacks to conform to the various seasons of the year. For another thing, Haggar's does not maintain warehouses like Levi's. Instead, Haggar's operates on the just-in-time principle and supplies their slacks directly to retailers. If, for instance, a New York department chain puts in a large order for Haggar slacks, the Valley plants may have to put on extra shifts to meet that demand and then truck the goods directly to New York. Under such conditions, a certain ongoing crisis atmosphere is un-avoidable at Haggar's plants.

The Haggar plant in Brownsville employs 900 people. It rivals AMFELS as the city's largest manufacturing concern.

To appreciate the diversity of the city's manufacturing and assembly industries, a roll call of some of the other companies oper-ating within Brownsville (whether at the Port, airport or any of the eight other industrial zones) would be useful. That list would include: Alps Automotive Division (electronic automobile compo-nents); Becker Manufacturing (plastics); Carlingswitch (electronic components); Chem Pruf Door Company (fiberglass doors); Crest Packaging (corrugated boxes); Dixie Tool Company (tools); Donie Chair Company (chairs and furniture); Eagle Coach (buses); International Stainless Steel Company (steel shelving); Johnson International Materials (wiping materials); Kearfott Guidance and Navigation (communication and navigation systems); MagneTek Universal Manufacturing (fluorescent light ballasts); Norton Company (abrasives); Rio Grande Tool Company (tools); Rio Plastics (spas and automotive fiberglass); Sunbeam (mechanical and electronic controls); Transforma Marine Corporation (ship build-ing and dismantling); Therma-Tru Corporation (door transoms); Unique Molded Products (plastic injection molds); United Technology Motor Systems (small motors); Valley Rio Enterprises (apparel); and Young Dental Manufacturing Company (dental products). But while Brownsville offers its own particular advan-tages as a manufacturing site, its long-term economic health is also reliant on its ability to maintain, and, if possible, attract even more *maquiladoras* or "twin plants."

The *maquila* program was initiated by Mexican-American agreement in 1965, and in 1967 Teccor, a division of Ranco Corporation, opened the first Matamoros *maquila* plant. By the end of 1967, three *maquilas* were established in Matamoros. By 1975 that number had grown to fourteen; by 1985 to thirty-seven; and by 1995 there were 111 *maquilas* in Matamoros employing 41,000 persons. Those numbers make Matamoros the third most important *maquila* site in Mexico, exceeded only by Ciudad Juarez (opposite El Paso) with 100,000 employees and Tijuana (opposite San Diego) with 82,000 employees. Reynosa (opposite McAllen) with 34,000 *maquila* workers trailed Matamoros and was fourth in ranking. All told, Mexico now has over 2,000 *maquiladoras* employing approximately 500,000 workers — and while the bulk of the plants are in cities and states adjacent to the U.S. border, *maquilas* are springing up in Mexico City, Guadalajara, Guanajuato, and even the Yucatan. In fact, anywhere cheap labor can be found — and it can be found anywhere in Mexico — *maquilas* may prove profitable, particularly in such labor-intensive industries as electronics, apparel, and textiles. Already over 300 of America's Fortune 500 companies are operating Mexican *maquilas* in an effort to keep their competitive edge in the international market. The economies *maquilas* offer are difficult to argue against: in 1993 the average hourly wage of a production worker in the U.S. was $16.79, in Japan it was $19.20, but in Mexico it was just $2.65. This was only about half the cost of production workers in such typically low wage manufacturing nations as South Korea, Taiwan, and Hong Kong. And that was in 1993. The December 1994 peso devaluation further enhanced the competitiveness of the Mexican worker. When the peso plunged from three to the dollar to six to the dollar in a few weeks, the effect was to cut *maquila* owners' labor costs in half. Naturally, the financial bonanza enjoyed by the corporations will be short lived since almost immediately the devaluation was accompanied by workers' demands for wages to at least inch up (within Mexican government cap limits) while the *maquilas*' corporate customers insisted that the savings be passed along to them. Nevertheless, the Mexican *maquilas* maintain a very strong international position at present.

In some ways, TRICO is as good a model of a *maquiladora* as any. TRICO (short for Tricontinental Corporation, in reference to their manufacturing and marketing facilities in North America, Australia, and Europe) is a division of the publicly-traded Stant Corporation. TRICO is the world's largest manufacturer of windshield wiper assemblies. The company was founded in 1917 by John Oishei, a Buffalo, New York, theater owner. Driving one rainy New York night in that pre-windshield wiper era, he knocked down and injured a bike rider. The very next day he set to work on the problem and soon came up with his patented "Rain Rubber." Aggressive marketing (including the neat inspiration of installing a free sample on Henry Ford's personal car) and a rapid succession of innovative modifications helped build this company into the industry leader. Today TRICO makes 83% of the wiper arms and 80% of the wiper blades used in America, and it has a substantial share of the world market as well.

By the 1970s, however, according to Brownsville Vice President and General Manager Martin Kennedy, TRICO's main manufacturing facility in Buffalo was facing typical "Rust Belt" America problems: obsolete, multi-storied "vertical" factory buildings that greatly complicated movement of materials during the manufacturing process; high labor costs; and an inflexible, unionized work force that refused to perform any tasks not specifically spelled out in a contract. All three problems were solved when the company relocated its manufacturing to Brownsville-Matamoros twin plants.

The two ultra-efficient new plants each have 360,000 square feet occupying a single floor for ease of material movement. The Brownsville plant has 515 non-unionized, highly-flexible, willing workers. All are paid above minimum wage, and the most highly-paid toolmakers receive $16.50 per hour. The Brownsville plant manufactures the components of wiper blades, wiper arms, linkages, and wiper motors, while the more labor intensive assembly is carried out by 3,000 workers at the Matamoros plant. Employees at both plants participate in TRICO'S *Kaizen* program. This is a technique borrowed from Japanese industry whereby employees are divided into small units or "teams" and encouraged to brainstorm solutions to production and ergonomic problems they encounter.

The world's largest corporation, General Motors, is both the largest manufacturer and largest *maquiladora* in the Brownsville-Matamoros area. GM has about 8,560 employees in the twin cities — a mere sixty contract employees in Brownsville warehouses, and about 8,500 actual GM employees at three plants at Matamoros' FINSA industrial park. Recently, the Matamoros plants underwent a realignment. The former GM Inland and GM Fisher Guide divisions have been combined and are now known as GM Delphi. GM Delphi operates two of the Matamoros plants. One has 3,300 mainly male employees making instrument panels (dashboards) and steering wheels, while the other has 800 mainly male employees making side molding trim and rubber bumpers. GM Delco Electronics retains its former name, and its plant continues to make car radios using 4,400 mainly female employees. Together, these three manufactories supply a large portion of the parts needed to construct cars and trucks (Chevrolet, Pontiac, Saturn, Oldsmobile, Buick, and Cadillac) for GM's American market. They produce about 30% of the bumpers, 65% of the side moldings, 80% of the radios, and 90% of the steering wheels.

Most of the finished parts are trucked to GM assembly plants in California, Tennessee, Ohio, and Michigan. The heavier and bulkier dashboards and bumpers are sent by rail. From ten to twenty boxcars a day will cross over the B & M bridge to commence an eight- or nine-day journey to the midwestern and California assembly plants. The logistics of the operation, particularly in the case of the bumpers, is impressive. GM operates on the just-in-time principle and, of course, the bumpers must arrive at the assembly plant just in time. Moreover, the bumpers are "sequenced," that is, the pre-painted bumpers en route from Matamoros are in racks in the railcar in a specific order — say twenty-four green bumpers, ten white bumpers and twelve maroon bumpers, and so forth. These are to match up with makes and models scheduled to come down a GM assembly line in that identical sequence nine days from the time the train crosses the B&M bridge. However, this particular logistical nightmare will phase out during the course of 1996. GM's Delphi bumper plant will gradually cease making bumpers and convert to air bag manufacturing.

The *maquiladora* plants all along the U.S.-Mexican border have been the topic of considerable heated debate within the United States. Critics of the *maquilas*, particularly U.S. labor unions, environmental groups, and the press, argue that the *maquiladora* program is exporting American jobs while simultaneously exploiting the Mexican laborer. *Maquilas* are accused of being heedless environmental polluters who enthusiastically despoil the Rio Grande, belch chemicals and carbon monoxide into the border air, and callously order their cowed workers to handle poisonous and carcino-genic materials. Using highly selective photojournalism, the stereo-typical *maquiladora* image that magazine articles and television news stories have successfully implanted in many American minds is a gleaming American factory enclosed by a barbed wire fence (presumably to protect it from the hostile local inhabitants). Beyond the fence are stagnant pools of chemical wastes and a sea of squalid workers' shanties — suggesting a straight-forward relation-ship of cause (the American factory) and effect (shanty towns and hazardous wastes).

The sole point of truth in this argument and in this image is, yes, the *maquiladora* program is exporting some American jobs. But the hard economic reality is that these are American jobs that would be lost anyway. What are the alternatives, after all? Any way the situation is looked at, only three alternatives present themselves. One would be for the U.S. to retreat from the global economy, erect absolutely pro-hibitive tariff walls to keep out foreign-made goods and, in so doing, almost certainly precipitate an international trade war and world-wide depression. This is exactly the kind of response taken with the Fordney-McCumber Tariff Act (1922) and Hawley-Smoot Tariff Act (1930) that plunged the world into the Great Depression of the 1930s. A second option would be to remain committed to free trade and complacently watch American manufacturing further erode while Asian corporations (or multinationals operating within Asia) contin-ue their relentless advance. The third alternative, the alternative of the *maquiladoras*, would appear the best course for America to follow. At least this alternative has something of the nature of a compromise. In locating on the Mexican border, at least some jobs, usually the more highly skilled and better paying, are kept on the American side. Moreover, the less highly skilled jobs that are exported are going to Mexico, our closest neighbor (along with Canada), and the nation whose economic health most directly impacts upon the United States — socially, politically, and economically. If America is inevitably going to lose many less-skilled manufacturing jobs, wouldn't we pre-fer to see those jobs go to Mexicans, particularly border Mexicans, rather than to anyone else — from Asia, Africa, or another country?

As for charges that the *maquiladora* industry is exploiting Mexican workers, one wonders from what possible perspective these charges could come. Certainly not from the Mexican government. In 1994 the *maquiladora* industry eclipsed Petroleos Mexicanos (PEMEX) to become the nation's primary source of foreign income. Tourism was a distant third. The Mexican government is doing all it can to attract even more *maquiladoras*, not only from America, but also from Japan, Taiwan, and other nations of the Pacific Rim. Do the charges come from Mexican unions? No, at least not anymore. When *maquila* growth began to stagnate in the late 1980s and then to actually decline between 1991 and 1994 as a result of excessive demands by labor unions in Matamoros and its state, Tamaulipas (considered the most strike-prone and truculent unions in all of Mexico), the local union leaders quickly backed off, realizing they were about to kill the golden goose and drive the *maquilas* off — to Juarez or Tijuana or deeper into the interior of Mexico. Led by Agapito Gonzalez Cavazos, the Matamoros head of the giant Union of Day Laborers and Industrial Workers (SJOI), union bosses and Matamoros business and *maquiladora* leaders signed a "No Strike Pact" on November 5, 1994, with Manuel Cavazos, Governor of Tamaulipas, and Fidel Velazquez, national leader of Mexican labor unions, witnessing the signatures.

Nor do the charges of exploitation stem from the *maquila* workers themselves. As an August 29, 1995, *Brownsville Herald* article put it: "The *maquiladora* industry is the single biggest inducement that brings people from the interior of Mexico to the country's northern border." On a typical day, 300 hopeful workers will show up at the Matamoros SJOI union hall to compete for 50 *maquila* openings. According to the Brownsville Economic Development Council (February 1995), lowest level assembly workers in Matamoros *maquilas* average $228 in monthly wages. That translates into $2,736 per year. That same source cites average yearly *maquila* wages of $3,545 for security guards; $4,050 for welders; $4,565 for receptionists. Certainly, these are pitiful wages from an American standpoint where per capita income averaged $22,470 in 1994. But these wages are not so pitiful in Mexico, where PCI was $3,200 in that same year, or in Matamoros, where an elementary teacher starts at $3,984.

Accusations that the *maquiladoras*, as an industry, are polluters would not seem to bear up under scrutiny. Certainly, all the larger *maquilas* like Eaton or TRICO give every appearance of being good environmental citizens, taking exceptional care with even low-level hazardous wastes. By-products of the industrial process are recycled, sold for scrap, or safely disposed of in accordance with strict Mexican environmental codes. Most wastes, in fact, have to be returned to the U.S. side for disposal. The idea of trucks sneaking out of *maquila* plants at night to dump their hazardous wastes in ditches is ludicrous. These are high-tech factories with the most sophisticated management — and their high visibility inclines them to obey both the letter and the spirit of the law. Furthermore, most *maquiladoras* draw their power from the electrical grid — they are not generating their own power and belching smoke into the atmosphere.

But despite their good environmental records, there was a lawsuit brought against the *maquiladoras* following a spate of anencephalic births in the early 1990s. A few dozen children were born in Matamoros and in Cameron County with partial brains or no brains at all. A lawsuit filed in March 1993 named thirty Matamoros *maquilas* as defendants, along with the Brownsville Public Utilities Board. (The Brownsville PUB was named, presumably, to allow the case to be heard on the U.S. side where dollar settlements are higher.) According to Dr. Dennis Perrotta, chief of the Bureau of Epidemology for the Texas Department of Health, the cause of the anencephalic births has not been found. On August 23, 1995, the *Brownsville Herald* quoted him as saying: "We've taken steps to answer the question as best as science can, but for all that we've done, it's still a mystery." Nevertheless, the cynical shotgun approach to lawyering paid off for the lawyers and their clients. In the end, to spare themselves the costs and risks of defending themselves in court, all thirty *maquilas* settled out of court for sums ranging from $100,000 to $2 million. One wonders how many similar legal shakedowns the *maquilas* will tolerate before they choose to move elsewhere.

W.L.A.

CHAPTER 12

The Search for the Ultimate Pachanga

My adventuresome colleague and co-author has ridden with a police patrol, panhandled on Brownsville thoroughfares, and hopped a freighter in the Gulf heading into our port. But I had been relegated the most fearsome task of all: confronting the wiley border politician in his lair. Since it was election time (as it often is in Brownsville), I chose to visit the beast in his natural habitat during the campaign season — the pachanga. *The local interpretation of the term is "a big party," and can apply to parties of all kinds, but normally not including "dress-up" affairs. Most often the term is used to promote a political campaign rally involving music, plates of food, beer, and (inevitably) political pitches. Political* pachangas *have been an essential part of South Texas politics since the nineteenth century.*

Although I had been to several pachangas *in the past and had a basic grasp of what they were all about, I decided to research the topic by interviewing* pachanga *"experts" Pete Benavides and his wife Sofie, old friends. Pete was well into his second term as a Brownsville city commissioner when he opted to challenge incumbent Lucino Rosenbaum for his Cameron County Commission seat.*

Meeting at the offices of the Benavides Driving School, I asked Pete what the purpose of pachangas *was. He replied that, contrary to some perceptions, it was not fund-raising. Pachangas lose money even if there is an admission charge. Rather, pachangas provide a "show of strength," an opportunity to meet new people, and a means of motivating supporters. Pete also used an up-scale pachanga to announce his candidacy for reelection to the city commission in a successful attempt to scare off potential challengers.*

Organizing a pachanga is an art as well as a science. Sofie and political ally Butch Barbosa do the organizing, but Pete is involved in the major decisions. Location is one of those, because it is essential to find a place "where people will feel comfortable." Its size should not exceed the likely attendance or it might appear that the candidate lacks support. Despite a very cold Sunday in February, Pete managed to attract 1,200 people to a pachanga that filled every table at the pre-fab, metal Convention Center.

Some pachangas are free, but this tempts "spongers," who hang around the beer keg all afternoon, and "leavers," who grab the food and run. Pete opts to sell tickets (typically $5.00), then induces more affluent supporters to buy them in batches and give them to friends, which in turn increases the likelihood that uncommitted voters will show up and decide to vote for Pete. The Benavides campaign advertises pachangas in the newspaper three times before the event.

To keep costs down, volunteers are recruited to decorate the pachanga site. Even the music may be cost-free, as local bands will offer their services for recognition. Pete has a dependable source of entertainment in his brothers' band, Nosotroz. The big expense is in food, where attendees expect rice and beans, jalapeños, onions, and other trimmings, and of course, meat. Fajitas or chicken, the usual entrees, are costly and time-consuming in preparation. Pete expected to obtain a 500-pound pig for an upcoming pachanga and was contemplating an asado de puerco in an effort to provide something "a little different."

Candidates and local luminaries are expected "to say a few words" at any pachanga. Typically, candidates for other offices will show up as well to "work the crowd." Pete will introduce all who show up, but the opposition is not welcome at any pachanga. However, opponents do appear at those pachangas sponsored by political parties before primaries. Most pachangas *are family affairs, but some are "men only" events.*

Bolstered by my new knowledge of the working of pachangas, *I decide to make a trial run at an invitation reception for district attorney candidate Eddie Medrano, then involved in a hard-fought campaign against the incumbent. Sponsored by former D. A. Rey Cantu and his wife, UTB professor Ethel, the reception was the antithesis of a pachanga. It occurred at Cantu's law office (which he shares with Medrano) located in a restored historic building. Although canned beer was available, most of the small crowd sipped wine and nibbled* hors d'oeuvres *while making "small talk" with the candidate and each other. No band, no mob, no other candidates, and no speeches (while I was there). A steam table attended by uniformed servers was dispensing a meal from several trays as I departed. Suburban Americans from anywhere would have felt comfortable at the Medrano reception.*

As the weeks of the election season roll by, my search for an authentic pachanga *is becoming a matter of some concern. Advertisements in the* Herald *invite attendance at "An Easter Egg Hunt & Pachanga" at the Rosenbaum Flower Shop for Lucino Rosenbaum's reelection and a fund-raiser to reelect school board member Joe Colunga (a colleague) at Frank's Round-up Restaurant. Colunga's opponent, "Coach" Gus Zavaletta, is holding a "Campaign Kick-off" at the Fort Brown-Holiday Inn. None of these sound like quite what I am looking for, and I'm reduced to depending on rumors of a real* pachanga *for Eddie Medrano and perhaps Pete Benavides on the coming Easter weekend.*

The weather turns cold and wet as the weekend approaches and evidence of the rumored pachangas *fails to materialize. Easter Sunday, however, dawns crisp and clear. The Rosenbaum Flower Shop confirms that the event is still on, and, in fact, is already underway. I'm on my way.*

The Rosenbaum Flower Shop is located in the heart of Southmost, a 30,000-inhabitant barrio of poor and working-class Mexican-Americans somewhat isolated from and little-known to the rest of Brownsville. The pachanga *has been set-up on a vacant lot next to the flower shop and conveniently adjacent to a city*

park. We arrive to the sound of ranchera *(Mexican "country")
music performed by* La Broma *(the joke), which advertises
"Musica para Todo Evento Social." The band's decrepit school
bus is parked immediately behind the musicians, its robin's egg
blue paint fading and peeling away. A keg of beer is available
near the bus and a dozen long tables with plastic cloths and folding chairs are half occupied. A brown and white bunny in a large
box is the center of attention for children.*

*Not surprisingly, I am the only Anglo in attendance, a cir-
cumstance that years ago made me ill at ease, but which I now
regard as a curiosity. I search for possible acquaintances and happen upon Walter Esparza, member of the Junior Chamber of
Commerce, who is video-taping the event on speculation of selling copies to the candidate or his followers. Walter has attended a
number of* pachangas *for this purpose, including the most recent
for Pete Benavides, Rosenbaum's opponent. Walter introduces
me to his father, a former haberdasher known as "Mr. Capi," and
an inveterate* pachanga *attendee.*

*The candidate had greeted his supporters prior to my arrival
and disappeared on some errand, but he now again appears near
the band. The "Lion of Southmost" is a short and slight figure,
dressed neatly but casually. I offer a greeting to Rosenbaum and
immediately find him an engaging and personable individual
despite his obvious difficulty with English grammatical structure.
I ask whether* pachangas *are still a viable technique of election-
eering. Rosenbaum responds obliquely that while he attempts to
raise funds and rally his supporters at some* pachangas, *this one is
"for the community," at no charge, for the holiday. He sees it as a
family style get-together and intends to make no political
speeches. Sincere or not, it's easy to understand his popularity.*

*Promptly at 3:00 P.M. huge pots of food appear on a row of
tables and a line forms to be served. Servings begin with* cilantro-
spiced beans ladled from a giant *olla (claypot) in a nod to tradition. Rice, potato salad,* carne guisada *(beef stew), and bread
round out this standard* pachanga *meal. Nearly every seat at the
tables is taken, and we estimate the crowd at about one hundred
at this point in the afternoon. People come and go, but most do
Rosenbaum the courtesy of eating before they depart. The great
majority are making an afternoon of it. The candidate strolls by*

and urges us to join the food line. As we sit to eat at a table, a woman emerges from the flower shop with a box of sliced cake, which is then distributed to each table.

Over by the cars parked on the field, Rosenbaum talks with various men who loosely gather around. His cellular phone is often in use. He introduces me to his office manager, a retired army sergeant, and casually discusses his background growing up in the Southmost barrio and as a businessman and manager. He is clearly a homeboy who made good. And he betrays no evidence of the extremely tight reelection race he is engaged in. As I depart, I regret only the lack of other politicos and the low-key political atmosphere of this otherwise very traditional pachanga.

The effectiveness of pachangas and other traditional Valley political techniques continues to be debated. Ralph Cowen, used car dealer and former mayoral candidate, organizes pachangas for others. Asked whether pachangas are effective, Cowen replied that "the old-fashioned political pachanga, where the beer and meat were given out by the gallons and pounds, does not work anymore. The way people used to waste money throwing parties for hundreds of individuals is no longer effective to get votes." But Cowen is convinced that "pachangas are not going away, simply because they are a strategy used to give the opposition the impression that a candidate enjoys great support, and are an old standing tradition in the Valley."

The Tuesday following the pachanga in Southmost Lucino Rosenbaum was defeated by Pete Benavides by a margin of two percent.

A. K. K.

Government and Politics

The close of the U.S.-Mexican War and the Treaty of Guadalupe Hidalgo in 1848 gave the U.S. and Texas full legal possession of the north bank of the Rio Grande. The formation of small populations opposite Matamoros, largely due to the presence of Fort Brown, made the establishment of local government essential. On February 12, 1848, even prior to the signing of the treaty, the Texas legislature had created Cameron County, named in honor of one of the Texas martyrs of the famous "black bean" episode. Texas Ranger Capt. Ewen Cameron was a Scot who was executed by the Mexicans after a Texan expedition against Mexico fell apart in 1842.

When the U.S.-Mexican War began, a number of Anglos fled Matamoros and established a tiny community on the north bank of the river on land left available by a southward shift of the riverbed. Named Santa Rita, this community became the first county seat. Elections were held on August 7, 1848, and Israel Bigelow was chosen to become the first chief justice ("county judge" today). The county court held its first session on September 11 and was primarily concerned with the business of issuing licenses for ferries.

The tendency of the river to flood Santa Rita inspired a competition among land developers to establish a dominant population center opposite Matamoros. Charles Stillman, who had spent twenty years as a successful merchant in Matamoros, gained the upper hand thanks to his ability to obtain information on the relocation of Fort Brown. Stillman and partners bought nearly 5,000 acres from Spanish land grants adjacent to the new site and set up the Brownsville Town Company to promote land sales.

Even at this early point political factionalism dating back twenty years in Matamoros mercantile competition first made its appearance on the north bank. Opponents of Stillman, temporarily including Israel Bigelow, applied to the State of Texas for permission to incorporate Brownsville as a city in order to block Stillman's claim to the land. Since the state was claiming title to all "undocumented" land, and many Spanish land grants had not yet been confirmed, incorporation would grant the city ownership of all state lands within its boundaries. The first city charter was issued by the state legislature on January 24, 1850. The Cameron County seat had been transferred to Brownsville a year earlier, as Santa Rita sank into oblivion.

Israel Bigelow resigned his county office to become Brownsville's first mayor. Switching his allegiance to the Stillman faction, Bigelow frustrated efforts of the city council to get into the land business through vetoes and refusal to call meetings. Bigelow attempted to run the city from his law office, but the council finally managed to oust him as mayor in September. The whole unsavory episode can still be read today in the original minutes of the council preserved at city hall, which was originally constructed in 1852 as the city market.

Deprived of the mayor's office, Israel Bigelow achieved election to the state legislature, where he and his Stillman allies managed to have the city charter revoked. A new city charter was issued in 1855 and a new government constituted under the auspices of the Stillman faction. Political factionalism meant competition for votes, and the impoverished Mexican-Americans of Brownsville could vote. The competing factions identified themselves by color, red or blue, in lieu of party names for the convenience of the illiterates whose votes they hoped to "corral." Corraling voters involved providing an all-night *pachanga* for supporters with free food, mescal, and whiskey. The following morning each party marched the beneficiaries to the polls.

The Red Club was the party of Stillman, Richard King, Mifflin Kenedy, Francisco Yturria, and their prosperous merchant allies. The competing Blue Club was organized by William Neale, Stephen Powers, James G. Browne, and the smaller merchants and professionals. Both groups made extravagant promises to their Mexican-American adherents; rarely were those promises kept. Elections were little more than "a combination of force, fraud, and farce," in the view of Texas historian T. R. Fehrenbach.

Thus, the dominant Anglo minority and their elite Mexican-American allies used the forms of democracy to further their political and economic goals. This system, in which the Mexican-American underclass remained politically impotent, became a lasting feature of Valley life. Prominent Texas historian T. R. Fehrenbach has concluded that this "was a logical outcome to centuries of Hispanic-Mexican tradition, in which the Indian and *mestizo* base were allowed no function in politics, and in which even the Spanish landed elite possessed no initiative beyond being permitted to sit on local municipal councils."

Civil War sympathies were reflected in local partisanship. Blue Club leaders labeled as Unionists found it expedient to relocate to Matamoros when Confederates took control of Brownsville, but when Union forces captured the city in 1863, Red Club notables were obliged to seek a similar exile. A reconciliation government with Israel Bigelow again serving as county judge was ended by a reconstruction military government. Brownsville's Edmund J. Davis took office as governor of Texas in 1870 under Radical Republican Reconstruction.

In 1872 Democrats, now firmly associated with the Blue Club, regained control of local government under Stephen Powers, a former county judge newly elected to the legislature, and ex-Confederate Rip Ford, who became mayor in 1873 and later served as state senator. Charles Stillman had already left the area, but his economic interests remained and soon found influence in the Blue Club.

Local Republicans, bolstered by federal patronage appointments, formed the Red Club to further their electoral interests. Robert B. Rentfro, a customs collector and already a Republican activist by the time of his arrival in Brownsville in 1879, soon dominated the Red Club organization. Political competition between the two clubs was intense and often degenerated into public brawling. Club color was especially significant because citizens voted by selecting a ballot of the color of their preference.

Although increasingly powerful, Stephen Powers was unable to consolidate control over Cameron County politics prior to his death in 1882. During his last years, however, he was in a position to prepare a successor who would establish boss rule in South Texas. Impressed by the performance of a young lawyer, James B. Wells, Jr., in a land suit, Powers invited Wells to form a partnership in 1878. Gaining Powers' confidence and marrying into the family, Wells soon joined the inner circle of the Blue Club. After Powers' death, Wells took control of the Blue Club and extended his domination across South Texas. Wells continued to exercise power as chairman of the Cameron County Democratic Party until 1920, although he rarely held public office himself.

Jim Wells' power was enhanced by support from the press and the prestigious. Thomas Carson, an Irishman who became mayor in 1879 and served through much of this era, was the local representative of the Stillman interests as well as an ally of Wells. Carson, who resided in what is now the Stillman House Museum, aided Wells in his quest for a dependable Democratic newspaper. Wells and Carson persuaded experienced journalist Jesse Wheeler to relocate from Victoria and transform an existing local newspaper into the *Brownsville Herald.* The first issue appeared on July 4, 1892.

Supported by the *Herald,* the Blue Club was Wells' vehicle for winning elections for his allies, who then took their orders from Wells. Such a well-organized operation for winning elections and controlling governments came to be called a "machine" during this era. The success of Wells' political machine, as was the case in many boss-ridden urban areas of the time, depended on providing basic services to disparate groups or interests. To maintain the support of area ranchers and Brownsville merchants, Wells used his influence to promote favorable state legislation and railroad development, helped hold down property taxes, and secured deployment of Texas Rangers and army troops to keep order along the border.

A crucial component of Wells' constituency, and ultimately the source of his power through their votes, was the population majority of working class Mexican-Americans. Wells relied on his merchant and rancher allies to turn out the vote of those dependent on them, claiming that the Mexican "naturally inherited from his ancestors from Spanish rule, the idea of looking to the head of the ranch — the place where he lived and got his living — for guidance and direction."

Both Red and Blue political factions exploited the votes of Mexican-Americans . . . and Mexicans, many of whom were "imported" at election time. In the 1884 election 100% of qualified voters cast ballots. Brownsville elections had little to do with policy issues and everything to do with personal relationships. Under attack at the end of his career for manipulation of Mexican-American votes, Jim Wells defended his behavior by saying, "So far as I being a boss, if I exercise any influence among these people it is because in the 41 years I have lived among them I have tried to so conduct myself as to show them that I was their friend and they could trust me. I take no advantage of them or their ignorance. I buried many a one of them with my money and married many a one of them. It wasn't two or three days before the election, but through the years around, and they have always been true to me." Wells obviously engaged in the same kind of paternalistic activity that characterized the operations of big-city machines by providing his own informal welfare system. Wells used the power of the ballot to benefit himself and his allies financially and to enable him to wield state and even national political influence. And he enjoyed the exercise of power.

Jim Wells contributed significantly to the economic revitalization of the area in helping to bring a railroad to Brownsville. The Cameron County boss solicited funds, conducted negotiations, and contributed his own money to several unsuccessful projects, but finally succeeded when the St. Louis, Brownsville, and Mexico Railway came to Brownsville.

In advancing the interests of his constituents (while pursuing personal profit) Wells was planting the seeds of his own political destruction. The railroad revitalized the economy of the county, creating the socioeconomic revolution that eventually would reshape the political environment. Almost immediately, developers began to subdivide ranchland into small tracts irrigated by the Rio Grande. Promotional campaigns and railroad excursions brought thousands of buyers from the Midwest, bringing the Anglo population to a sizable proportion for the first time. The new residents, plus Mexicans fleeing the violence of the Mexican Revolution, could not be manipulated as under the old system, because the adhesive of personal relationships and paternalism did not exist for them.

The challenge to Wells' dominance began with the formation of the Independence Party, an amalgam of Republicans and dissident Democrats. Rentfro B. Creager, nephew of the former Republican leader R. B. Rentfro, used his influence as a federal collector of customs to consolidate his control over the Independents. Backing Benjamin Kowalski for mayor, Creager and the Independents swept to victory in the Brownsville city elections of 1910.

The Wells machine was unwilling to surrender Brownsville without a fight. There were charges and countercharges of corruption. Amidst voter fraud and gunplay on the streets, the Texas Rangers were brought to the Valley, limiting the effectiveness of Wells' machine technique. Seizing the reform issues of nonpartisan elections and the restructuring of city government, Independents led by A. A. Browne secured the adoption, by a margin of ten to one, of a new city charter. The new charter, incorporating a city manager plan of government, opened a new era in Brownsville politics. Veterans of the Independent Party rebellion against Wells dominated city government for many years: A. A. Browne served as mayor until 1919 when he was succeeded by A. B. Cole, who was in turn succeeded by R. B. Rentfro, Jr., in 1929, with Rentfro serving until 1939. The new Brownsville leadership represented the Anglo and educated Hispanic elites of the community and comprised a small group interrelated through marriage and businesses and partnerships and usually descended from the early Anglo entrepreneurs and Spanish/Mexican land grantees.

The struggle between Jim Wells and the Independents for control of Cameron County lasted until 1920, when Wells had to relinquish his chairmanship of the county Democratic party, in part due to ill health. Shortly afterwards, Wells admitted that Cameron County was, "Anybody's and Everybody's County," a condition which Wells attributed to the influence of "Snow-Diggers," as he referred to Anglos from the Midwest. Deprived of his "corralled" Mexican vote by the Texas Rangers and deserted by several former lieutenants and allies, Wells' political demise was inevitable.

The ouster of the Wells machine in Cameron County saw the inauguration of an outstanding political career. Oscar Dancy, born in a log cabin in North Carolina, was elected county judge in 1920 and held the office for the next fifty years with one brief interruption. A staunch Democrat, Dancy avoided intra-party factionalism, concentrated on infrastructure development, and demonstrated his liking for and personal generosity to the common people. In his last term Dancy was transported to the county commission meetings from a nursing home.

The Depression of the 1930s and the tax burden necessitated by bonded indebtedness gave rise to a serious challenge to Brownsville's political establishment beginning in 1935. Ironically, the challenge was initiated by a member of the elite, Fausto Yturria, descendant of a wealthy pioneer family. Yturria was unsuccessful in his bid for the mayoralty, but one of the city commission candidates from his team, Robert Runyon, a photographer and botanist, would constitute the major threat to Brownsville's elite establishment for the next twenty years.

In 1937 Robert Runyon and other opponents of Brownsville city administration organized a Greater Brownsville Party to challenge the incumbents on the basis that the incumbents were Republicans who had meddled in Democratic Party elections and that they had been in office too long. Runyon lost his race against Mayor Rentfro by a scant thirty-three votes, but the rest of his ticket was elected, and they hired Runyon as city manager.

Principled but temperamental, Robert Runyon became embroiled in a lawsuit against the *Brownsville Herald* and political disputes with his erstwhile allies on the city commission. When the city commission fired Runyon, he promptly filed for election as mayor. Running on a program of improvements for city parks, Runyon and his entire slate won by sizable margins in the 1941 elections. By mid-1942 the new mayor was in court, accused of ballot fraud. A hostile *Brownsville Herald* called for "the eventual permanent elimination of the Runyon political ring from our community." The continuing controversies led to a thorough defeat for Runyon and his allies in 1943.

Despite the bitterness of the political struggles in Brownsville in the early 1940s, the issues were the traditional issues of local government: taxes, debt, public services, and patronage. Robert Runyon's challenge to the elite establishment was not a proletarian revolution but an attempt by bourgeois entrepreneurs and businessmen to wrest power from an entrenched establishment. The bi-ethnic nature of Brownsville's political factions also became evident during this era, although Mexican-Americans, who had held numerous local offices during the early years, had nearly disappeared from such positions by the turn of the century. The economic influence as well as the social position of the Mexican-American elite was too strong for that element to be permanently excluded.

For three terms during the 1940s, Mexican-Americans constituted the majority on the city commission in Brownsville. This phenomenon, which clearly predated the civil rights movement, provoked concern from *Herald* editors when the Mexican-Americans produced circulars printed only in Spanish. The *Herald* asserted that "some politicians are attempting to inject the racial issue." The Mexican-Americans who caused this concern were all in the early stages of professional careers and long service to the community: lawyer O. B. Garcia, historian A. A. Champion, Dr. Vidal Longoria, and lawyer Reynaldo Garza.

Son of an old Brownsville family, Reynaldo Garza received his legal training at The University of Texas and then returned home to practice law. In 1961 President Kennedy appointed Garza to the federal district court as the first Mexican-American to hold federal judicial office. Garza was named to the Fifth Circuit Court of Appeals in 1979, and currently holds senior status. It was no accident that a Brownsville Mexican-American could achieve such positions. Despite subtle (and sometimes overt) ethnic discrimination by Anglos, a distinction existed between "poor Mexicans" and educated, economically successful, and socially prominent Mexican-Americans such as Garza and his city commission colleagues. The "other side of the tracks" attitude that existed in other Valley towns, founded primarily by Anglos in the early twentieth century, never developed in Brownsville.

The challenge to the political establishment mounted by Robert Runyon had been crushed in the early forties. The traditional business elite supported the regime of Mayor Herbert L. Stokely, who held that office for a decade beginning in 1945. Stokely was the immediate past president of the Chamber of Commerce, so it was not surprising that his administration would focus on such projects as a new civic center. Favoritism toward the elite in a transfer of parkland was the issue which sparked the rise of a new challenge to the establishment. Margal M. Vicars, a laundry operator, was encouraged to run against Stokely in 1955 by other civic-minded young businessmen and Robert Runyon, who became Vicars' political mentor and close friend.

Given little chance of success by the *Brownsville Herald,* Vicars waged a Populist-style campaign, charging the Stokely administration with excessive tax and utility rates, reflecting Runyon's original attack on the establishment in 1937. When Vicars appeared to have achieved a razor-thin victory, the *Herald* noted "a sort of numb shock" among supporters of Stokely, who feared "that an enormous tragedy had overtaken Brownsville, the sort of political calamity one would assert, if, say, Liberace had been elected President." Vicars' triumph, however, was diminished by the defeat of most of his allies, including commission candidate Robert Runyon. Even Vicars' narrow victory was in dispute, and his election was overturned 17 months later in a lawsuit that reached the Texas Supreme Court.

Vicars sought and achieved vindication in the next election; not only was he narrowly elected, but the other members of his ticket won a commission majority. Vicars' team won by carrying the heavily Mexican working class precincts while losing the well-to-do Anglo neighborhoods in an election which brought out seventy-five percent of the registered voters. In the process, Vicars had made promises to fund new projects while reducing taxes and public utility rates. In trying to fulfill these promises, the inexperienced commission majority ran up a large deficit, causing the city's auditors to recommend reduction in spending and "drastic steps to cut personnel costs." Vicars saw his commission majority crumble and then suffered a stunning rejection at the polls when he sought reelection. The fifties ended with the elite establishment again in firm control of Brownsville's city government.

The ethnic transformation in local United States office-holding beginning in the 1960s was particularly evident in the Lower Rio Grande Valley. In Cameron County the fifty-year tenure of County Judge Oscar Dancy terminated with his retirement in 1970. Dancy's chosen successor was a Mexican-American, Ray Ramon. By 1986, nearly 80% of the county commissioners, constables, and justices of the peace were Mexican-Americans. A recent development has been the reemergence of partisan competition in Cameron County politics, resulting in the election of Republican lawyer Antonio Garza as county judge in 1988. A second Republican was elected to the county commission in 1992. After his election as governor in 1994, George Bush appointed Garza as Texas' secretary of state.

The city of Brownsville has had a long history of Mexican-American participation in its government, although normally in a numerically inferior position. The 1940s saw a Mexican-American majority on the city commission, but politics and government underwent little change. When populist Mayor M. M. Vicars was defeated in 1959, Antonio (Tony) Gonzalez was a member of the victorious establishment commission slate. Gonzalez was elected mayor in 1963, the first Mexican-American to hold that office, and was reelected three times. As commissioner and mayor, Gonzalez focused on the creation and operation of the Public Utilities Board, which provided electricity and water to city residents.

Mayor Gonzalez' preoccupation with nuts-and-bolts government activity during the era of national civil rights activism was indicative of the low level of ethnic conflict in Brownsville. Elections reflected class divisions to much greater extent than ethnic divisions. Both Anglo and Mexican-American candidates on an establishment slate received strong support in prosperous neighborhoods and low totals in poorer areas. Nevertheless, the power and influence of the predominant Anglo wealth in the community throughout its history should not be underestimated.

Even the success of an anti-elite candidate in the tradition of Robert Runyon and Vicars did little to change the status quo. Emilio Hernandez, whose family had backed Vicars in the fifties, was elected mayor in 1979 by promising to represent "all the people," which was a slogan aimed at lower class Mexican-Americans. Hernandez may have had the interests of the poor in his heart, but he and his associates had become successful businessmen with little interest in socioeconomic upheaval. After two terms, Mayor Hernandez left office under a cloud of investigations into possible corruption at city hall. Hernandez' subsequent exoneration seemed to confirm the suspicions of his supporters that he was the victim of an elite plot, and his political influence continued to be felt in later elections.

Hernandez was succeeded as mayor by Ygnacio "Nacho" Garza, son of Reynaldo Garza, senior federal appeals court judge and one of the Mexican-American city commission majority in the forties. Garza's election seemed to signal a return to elite control of the government, but the political situation proved to be much too fluid. During the latter half of his term, Garza faced a non-elite commission majority known as "The Three Amigos" in an ironic reference to the cinema comedy by the same name. The trio, which included Pete Benavides, received support from former Mayor Hernandez' organization. Mayor Garza, who became a successful spokesman for the city, did not seek reelection, and Brownsville faced the nineties with divided leadership and no clear sense of direction. An anonymous, humorous tract on local history and politics asserted that "The great majority of citizens simply want harmony and would like to see an amicable compromise by which the five city fathers would be tarred and feathered, rode out of town on a rail, their homes razed and salt spread on their land."

Some urban government analysts are of the opinion that when a city achieves a population of 100,000, it is no longer possible for a unified elite power structure to maintain control. By the nineties Brownsville had attained that population level and began to be subjected to modern political campaigning techniques designed to reach the uninvolved majority. Pat Ahumada, a virtual unknown, was the first to take advantage by running a high-dollar television campaign which boosted him into the mayor's office over Commissioner Tony Zavaleta, a Garza ally and fellow member of the "St.

Joe Mafia" — a reference to the presumed elite relationship among graduates of the private academy.

The inexperienced and erratic Ahumada was frequently at odds with the commissioners; the city budget was $1 million in the red; and by the end of 1992 the city manager had been fired. The *Herald* reported that city politics were "just as fractious and low-down as ever." Ahumada resigned before the end of his term, and Commissioner Henry Gonzalez was elected to succeed him in a duel with another commissioner. Gonzalez, owner of a popular restaurant, was reelected for a full term, against a little-known candidate who proposed erecting a statue of *Tejano*-music idol Selena.

Cognizant of Ahumada's problems, Mayor Gonzalez promised effective communication with the city commissioners, claiming that he knew "how to talk to people." As his top priority, Gonzalez zeroed in on a city-wide cleanup plan largely dependent on volunteers. "It's going to be a community effort," Gonzalez said, "because the city of Brownsville does not have the money or personnel in order to accomplish that." Left unanswered was the question of how the mayor hoped to inspire such volunteer activity.

Mayor Gonzalez was unable to quell dissent on the city commission as his former mayoral opponent, Ernie Hernandez, regained a seat on the commission. The mayor himself had been noted for his "volatile personality." Commissioners continued to pursue their own agendas, ephemeral alliances surfaced and disappeared, and the cleanup plan seemed to make little headway.

According to Gerry McHale, owner, manager, and janitor of *El Rocinante,* a sporadic "alternative" tabloid of political commentary, the cities of McAllen and Harlingen have "love affairs" with their mayors, Othal Brand, a twenty-year veteran, and Bill Card. Brownsville, in contrast, destroys its mayors. "This masochistic tendency has inflicted deep wounds in the community," McHale asserted. In the case of Gonzalez, he claimed, certain "fanatics will go to any extremes to ruin the mayor because they are filled with a righteous anger." Allowing for a degree of hyperbole, McHale's comments indicate the deleterious effects of continued factionalism in city politics.

The problem of factionalism continues to be the subject of much discussion by concerned citizens. Marcelino Gonzalez, perceptive editorialist for the *Herald*, has observed the "petty politicking that seems to have no end" in Brownsville. "A result of that has been a semiparalysis of decision making. The city's problems have been put on the back burner for too long time, and city leaders' vision has been blurred many times."

Conspiracy theories have appeared in an effort to explain Brownsville's failure to match the progress occurring in other Valley cities. Former *Herald* City Editor Rey Guevara-Vazquez noted claims by "People in Authority" that "our city is the victim of a highly manipulative cabal whose select members secretly get together and make the Big Picture decisions. . . . There are never any names, just references to an amorphous group of people . . . plotting to keep Brownsville down." Unable to confirm or disprove the existence of such a "secret clique," Guevara-Vazquez focused on the widespread credibility given such theories by prominent citizens, including at least one city commissioner.

Conspiracy theorists can point justifiably to history for partial confirmation of their suspicions: the Stillman influence, Boss Jim Wells' rule, and the rarely-threatened control by an elite establishment during most of this century. The inability of city leaders to cope with problems, however, may well be due to a lack of political cohesion reflecting a diffusion of wealth and influence beyond the confines of a traditional elite. Nevertheless, there remains a strong temptation to attribute a dearth of progress to a clique of wealthy families which, having "got theirs," has no interest in developments that might threaten the status quo and their domination of the community.

When factionalism rules, the structure of the local government can magnify problems. Policy-making in Brownsville is the function of the five-member city commission, one of whom is elected as mayor, a largely ceremonial office since his power does not exceed that of the other commissioners. The commissioners are paid $50 per month and are allocated neither office space in city hall nor personal staff to handle paperwork. Commissioners estimate that they spend thirty hours per week on city affairs, including an often lengthy commission meeting on one evening and attendance at various workshops and committee meetings. The commission appoints a variety of boards and committees ranging from the Citizens Advisory Committee, which makes recommendations for the allocation of federal block grant funds, to the Planning and Zoning

Commission to the Public Utilities Board, which supervises the management and operation of the electrical, water, and sewage systems owned by the city. These entities and many others advise the city commission and in some cases have direct policy-making power. The commission enacts ordinances, adopts a budget, and sets a tax rate.

A group of semi-autonomous entities receives at least partial city funding for the purpose of promoting the development of Brownsville in various ways. The Greater Brownsville Incentives Corporation (GBIC) acts as a clearing house to disperse receipts from one-half cent of sales tax specially authorized under state law. The Brownsville Economic Development Corporation (BEDC) promotes employment growth by attracting new business and industry to the city, often through subsidies involving GBIC funds. The Chamber of Commerce works with BEDC to foster economic development to the mutual advantage of local businesses and the city. The Convention and Visitors Bureau receives funds from the hotel/motel tax to attract conventions and promote tourism. The overlapping functions of these organizations create territorial jealousies and inhibit their ability to work in concert.

Brownsville's form of government is known as "strong city manager/weak mayor." The highest ranking full-time city employee, the city manager, supervises the day-to-day operations of the city government through the various departments, ranging from police and fire to health and the bus system. The present city manager, Andy Vega, is a former Brownsville police chief who is paid $90,000 and serves at the pleasure of the city commission. He was appointed in 1992.

Andy Vega says he loves his job, even though he doesn't expect to be doing it a year hence. Dark and heavy set, Vega can display the demeanor expected in his former position as police chief, but leavens his comments on city affairs with candor and an almost impish laugh. He claims that the financial problems of the city are being alleviated by economic growth and that the city now has the highest general fund balance in recent history. This has been accomplished despite the obligation to fund previous bond authorizations and the problem of meeting unfunded federal mandates. At the same time, the city property tax rate has been reduced from seventy-five cents to sixty-five cents per one hundred dollars of valuation.

A severely limiting factor in the successful operation of the city government has been an insufficiency of funds. Brownsville derives much of its revenue from the sales tax, a source undercut by the peso devaluation in December 1994. Other significant sources include property taxes, the public utilities, fines, fees, and state grants. Even before the peso crisis, the city found it necessary to borrow over $9 million in order to balance a $42 million budget for 1994-95. An analyst for Moody's Investor Service warned that Brownsville is "noted for having very high debt."

"No new debt" was the theme for 1995-96, the city having already accumulated $270 million in debt (including Public Utilities Board obligations). In the end, however, commissioners approved $4 million in additional debt to fund the Los Tomates International Bridge Project. As justification for the new debt, the commissioners noted that the new bridge would be revenue-producing for the city.

The city manager hopes to avoid extending the debt problem by setting aside the funds now to cope with future maintenance needs. He intends to keep expenditures under control by sticking to an "action plan" and working to coordinate large projects with other local governmental and private sector entities. Vega acknowledges the non-progressive image of the city, but attributes it to a lack of aggressive leadership in previous administrations. Perhaps this explains Vega's choice for most important success as city manager: inducing the city commissioners to work together as a team. A city manager can be effective only if the commissioners perform as professional policy-makers.

Despite the restraints of the budget and debt problems, the city has been able to make progress on several important, if unspectacular, fronts. A new and impressive public library has been established. A controversial subsidy to Continental Airlines has provided regular passenger service to the city. Street paving and repairing has kept pace with basic infrastructure needs, and preliminary work is underway on a proposed loop to relieve traffic congestion. Still, some wags claim to be able to spot a city work crew in action: one man with a shovel and a half dozen others giving advice.

Probably the most dramatic development in recent years has been the agreement by the city to join TSC, the county, and other governmental entities in constructing a convention center. Having a center is essential to Brownsville's identity as a modern city, but years of dithering, politics, and argument over location stood in the way of action. Particularly encouraging is the willingness of civic leaders to join forces for the good of the community. Perhaps Brownsville is beginning to cope with the leadership issue.

Cooperation among local government entities is increasingly important as issues and problems become more complex and inter-related. One observer has used the analogy of "a patchwork quilt" with "many quilts on top of each other in an overlapping fashion" to explain the relationship of these entities. Many citizens know little about the plethora of special districts whose functions affect the Brownsville community. Special districts have the authority to provide specific services within a defined area, and include not only the school district, the navigation district (the port), and the college district, but also such exotica as the Cameron County Emergency Communications District and an irrigation and drainage district.

Since the special districts either raise or are awarded funds to carry out their purposes, politics enter the picture. A dispute over the allocation of funds between drainage and irrigation provoked opposition to the incumbents on that district's board in a recent election. A far more substantial conflict erupted over the Browns-ville Navigation District when the commissioners licensed a non-union stevedoring firm to operate at the port. The ensuing election saw a partially successful challenge to the incumbents from pro-union sympathizers. The conflict continued into the following election.

City and special district elections are non-partisan, but competition between Republicans and Democrats emerges at the county level. Until recently, that competition has meant little as a combination of the Texas tradition of Democratic dominance and the preference of the poor and minority population for Democratic policies and politicians has enabled that party to hold sway. Indeed, although the Republicans have achieved a few successes at the county level, and Cameron County has voted for Republican presidential candidates on occasion, the sole breakthrough for Brownsville was the election of Tony Garza as county judge in 1988.

When Judge Garza left to pursue his political career in the state government, the stage was set for State Appeals Court Judge Gil-berto Hinojosa to grasp the reins of power in the Cameron County

Commissioners Court. A graduate of Georgetown University Law Center and a former BISD board member, Hinojosa gave up a significantly larger paycheck to seek the county position and the political power it offered. Hinojosa easily crushed a Republican opponent in 1994. Commissioner Carlos Cascos attributes Hinojosa's decision to his love for politics and the opportunity to practice law. Hinojosa created an uproar in 1995 when a Clinton administration proposal for a border crossing fee inspired the judge to declare that "the administration is probably writing off Texas."

Legislative office holders are veterans who have survived intra-party warfare but have faced little serious opposition in this Democratic stronghold. Incumbent Governor Ann Richards carried Cameron County handily in her losing bid for reelection. Former teacher Eddie Lucio served two terms as Brownsville's state representative before successfully challenging Senator Hector Uribe. Rene Oliveira, upset earlier by Lucio, reclaimed his state representative seat when Lucio moved to the senate. Senator Lucio, a moderately conservative Democrat, has achieved success through a combination of support of tort reform and staying close to his constituency.

As in the case of Pat Ahumada, partisan office-seekers in the nineties are utilizing modern political techniques in Brownsville. Ahumada hired local pollster Dann Rivera in 1991, becoming the first client of Rivera's company, Victory Data, Inc. Rivera conducts polls and provides advice about creating a campaign image through advertising and issue-selection. But television, polls, and computers have not completely transformed local politics. At almost any precinct polling place on election day voters are likely to encounter a small forest of campaign signs, some being waved by hired workers, others by volunteers. Sample ballots are often handed out, some bearing the inscription, *"Jale la palanca numero uno"* (pull lever number one) in an effort to encourage straight-ticket voting.

One of the most enduring local political traditions is the use of *politiqueros,* which dates back to the last century. *Politiqueros* are *barrio* political activists who recruit voters for particular candidates and usually receive some form of remuneration. State law permits reimbursement of political expenses, but some *politiqueros* receive an average of $200 per week in "gas money." The motivation for *politiqueros* may go beyond money, however. Some seek respect or influence in the community by obtaining favors from those they helped elect. Others believe they have a mission to educate uninvolved citizens.

Politiqueros (or *politiqueras:* probably most are women) often have a negative image because some are prone to switching sides during a campaign. One influential *politiquera* sees herself as "honest" because she always tries to put "good" people in office and is neither *"chaquetera ni chueca"* (turncoat nor crook), refusing to change allegiance during the campaigns. Some are accused of rigging votes by preying on the elderly and infirm, forging signatures, and marking ballots.

Recent changes in election laws have practically guaranteed the survival of *politiqueros.* "Early voting" provides ample opportunity for organizers to recruit voters. In off-year, local races early and mail-in voting constitutes a sizable portion of the total, sometimes providing the margin of victory. *Politiqueros* are regarded as a "necessary evil," and consequently will remain, together with *pachangas,* a part of Brownsville politics regardless of the inroads made by technology.

Organized community activism has also affected Brownsville politics. In 1981 Ernesto Cortez of the Texas Industrial Areas Foundation came to the Valley at the invitation of Brownsville Catholic Bishop John Fitzpatrick. With the Bishop's support, Cortez organized Valley Interfaith, an association of lower income families for civic involvement as a political force. Initially viewed by many as radicals and potentially divisive, as well as a threat to the political status quo, Valley Interfaith leaders and members eventually demonstrated a focus on issues of general concern — education, health care, and conditions in the *colonias.* Their style, however, remained confrontational. Many an elected official felt the sting of Valley Interfaith's tightly-structured "accountability sessions," which coerced officials into directly responding to the organization's agenda. Valley Interfaith does not endorse or campaign for political candidates, but many officials and candidates have found it prudent to respond to the organization's concerns.

The county officials are particularly vulnerable to the wrath of Valley Interfaith's thousands of members because of the focus on primarily rural issues such as *colonia* infrastructure. Commissioners Carlos Cascos and Lucino Rosenbaum represent portions of

Brownsville and large rural areas, and County Judge Gilberto Hinojosa represents the entire county. In addition to attending meetings of the commissioner's court (a misnomer: the "court" performs legislative and administrative functions and no longer serves a judicial role), the commissioners are responsible for taking care of county roads in their respective precincts. Carlos Cascos advocates a consolidation of the road maintenance function. Then, Cascos argues, the $35,000 salary of commissioners should be reduced because their primary administrative duties would have ceased. Road consolidation has been opposed in the past by commissioners who see it as a threat to their ability to wield power in their precincts, a practice known as "caliche politics."

Like the city commission, the county commissioner's court has the power to set tax rates, adopt a budget, and appoint or hire personnel. Through its fiscal authority, the court is able to influence the sheriff's department and other agencies. The court's authority to supervise elections resulted in controversy when a secretary to the Democratic county chairman was appointed elections administrator and again when it was acknowledged that voting machines had been subjected to tampering. Additional problems emerged in the form of scandals in the district attorney's office resulting in the defeat of the incumbent in the Democratic primary.

Commissioner Cascos, a certified public accountant, has sought to avert even the appearance of impropriety (and graft scandals, like those in Hidalgo County) by initiating a committee purchasing system excluding elected officials. Cascos also points to the fiscal successes of the county: a low tax rate and an "A" rating on bonds. The challenge of funding county needs has led commissioners to seek innovative ways of obtaining and spending money. Cascos sees the county as the logical conduit for other local governments to find solutions to interrelated problems.

Despite the accomplishments listed by Cascos, the image of *compadre* (crony) politics throughout the county endures. Local analysts write of a "clique" that conspires to maintain control and acts to cover up improprieties committed by members of the clique. A more competitive two-party system would reduce the power of what *Herald* columnist Anthony Gray calls the Democratic Revolutionary Institution (a play on the name of the long-dominant Mexican party, the *Partido Revolucionario Institucional*). The Republicans, however, continue to appear as the party of Anglo matrons from Harlingen, despite efforts to recruit Mexican-Americans as candidates.

Politics and government in Brownsville exhibit the trappings of modernization, some degree of development, and much of Valley tradition. The tension between tradition and change makes this aspect of Brownsville life a premium source of entertainment — a major spectator sport.

A. K. K.

CHAPTER 13

A Survey of Brownsvillites

When this book was first conceived it was decided by the two authors that it would be worthwhile to poll Brownsville's citizenry to learn what ideas they might have for the possible improvement of the city. Initially, it was thought that a single poll of Brownsville's elite — its political, social, professional, and business leaders — would prove the most fruitful ground for producing these ideas and, accordingly, a list of 185 such leaders was carefully compiled after consulting with prominent individuals in each occupational area. These 185 individuals were mailed the polling instrument shown in Appendix A during the first week of January 1996. Exactly 100 of these persons completed and returned the survey. Because any response above 50% is considered very good for a mail survey, it was decided to forego a planned "follow-up" mailing. Besides, working with a round 100 eliminated any difficulties in converting absolute numbers to percentages.

At some point in the book's planning, it was decided that rendering a similar (although not identical) poll to Brownsville's general public would also be useful — useful in two respects: firstly, it, too, might be fruitful in eliciting ideas for Brownsville's improvement, and secondly, and perhaps more importantly, it would show if Brownsville's community leaders were "on the same track," so to speak, as the general public. Do the leaders and the public perceive the same problems? Or are the views and problems of the two groups so disparate as to defy any unified plan for the city's improvement?

This second survey was carried out in January and February of 1996 in the form of a random telephone survey conducted by Russell Adams, the twenty-six-year-old, bilingual son of one of the authors. The telephone book was sectioned and the 10th, 20th, 30th, 40th and 50th residential listings on each page were contacted on weekday evenings or Saturdays. Two hundred such telephone surveys were completed using the instrument shown in Appendix B, and the pollster's individual comments are contained in Appendix C. Of the 200 surveys completed, 133 were with adult females, 67 with adult males. The imbalance was largely because women are more likely to answer the phone in most Hispanic households.

In the community leaders' survey, the leaders were presented a list of eleven suggested problem areas and asked to rank-order the top three problem areas from that list, or to nominate other problems if they deemed them more serious. In assigning weights to responses, problems that were listed first were assigned a weight of three points, problems ranked second were given two points, and problems ranked third were given one point.

GREATEST PROBLEMS
CURRENTLY FACING BROWNSVILLE
COMMUNITY LEADERS SURVEY

		Points
1.	City Leadership	115
2.	State of the Economy	97
3.	Education System	62
4.	Appearance of the City	30
5.	Lawsuit Abuse	28
6.	Illegal Aliens	25
7.	State of Downtown Area	24
8.	Crime	20
9.	Environmental Issues	10
10.	Property Taxes	8
11.	Affordability of Housing	4

Other problems that community leaders identified included: the future of the city's water supply; the "welfare mentality" of much of the population; the burden the illegal aliens place on the city's educational and medical establishments; the one-party, Democratic control of politics; the "old boy syndrome" in city politics; the inability of many residents to speak English; the city's "disastrous" economic dependence on Mexico; the need to renovate the downtown area, but the lack of business leadership downtown — "All they do is complain"; low educational level of the population; teen pregnancy; the large number of single-parent families; the "irresponsible begetting of children"; the young people's "lack of respect for authority: God, parents, teachers"; the "disregard of public civility"; the "brutal" nature of local politics; the "me only" attitude of the community's leaders; the "irregularities" in county government; an educational system that "stinks"; illiterate high school graduates; the "roughness" of the Border Patrol and INS agents; the very low property tax base which is insufficient to meet the city's needs; the useless rivalry with Harlingen and McAllen when the city should be cooperating with them; the need "to engage the services of visionaries and not politicians on the city commission"; and, again and again, the criticism of citizen apathy and lack of a coherent plan to develop the city.

For their part, the general public responded as follows:

GREATEST PROBLEMS
CURRENTLY FACING BROWNSVILLE
GENERAL PUBLIC SURVEY

		RESPONSES
1.	Poor Economy	51
2.	Crime	31
3.	Illegal Aliens	30
4.	City Leadership	25
5.	Lawsuit Abuse	6
6.	School System	5
7.	Dirtiness of City	3
8.	Property Taxes	3
9.	Lack of Affordable Housing	2
10.	The Environment	1

Forty-three of the 200 general public respondents in the telephone survey nominated other problem areas, most frequently naming problems associated with unemployment, drugs, dropouts and juvenile delinquency. Several people mentioned the dearth of wholesome recreational opportunities for youths. Other problems named were: "too many people on welfare"; "parental lack of responsibility"; "inability of the city to keep pace with population growth"; "fraud"; and "corruption."

In contrasting the two lists — the problems as seen by the leadership and the general citizenry — it should be noticed how much more seriously the citizenry regards the problems of crime and illegals. Crime is much more likely to visit their neighborhoods than the neighborhoods of the elite, and, of course, it is the general public, not the elite, that suffers from job competition (and wage depression) as a result of illegals working in the community. Notable, too, is the public's evident complacency regarding the school system which the elite views as one of the city's three most acute problems. Nevertheless, there are some areas of congruence: both public and the elite see the economy and the city's leadership as important "problems."

Brownsville's community leaders were secondly given a list of twelve Brownsville institutions and asked to indicate the three institutions they felt were the most effective and efficient. Three points were assigned to first rankings, two to second rankings, one to third rankings. The results were:

BROWNSVILLE'S MOST EFFECTIVE
AND EFFICIENT INSTITUTIONS
COMMUNITY LEADERS SURVEY

		Votes
1.	Public Utilities Board	62
2.	University of Texas at Brownsville/TSC	56
3.	Brownsville Police Department	35
4.	Brownsville Navigation District	27
5.	Brownsville Medical Establishment	23
6.	Municipal/County/District Courts	12
7.	Sanitation	7
8.	Brownsville Airport	6
9.	Brownsville City Commission	5
10.	*Brownsville Herald*	5
11.	Brownsville Independent School District	5
12.	Sheriff's Department	2

Conversely, the leaders were asked to indicate the three institutions they felt were least effective and efficient.

BROWNSVILLE'S MOST INEFFECTIVE AND
INEFFICIENT INSTITUTIONS
COMMUNITY LEADERS SURVEY

		Votes
1.	*Brownsville Herald*	52
2.	Brownsville City Commission	49
3.	Brownsville School District	42
4.	Sheriff's Department	28
5.	Brownsville International Airport	21
6.	Municipal/County/District Courts	20
7.	Sanitation	12
8.	Brownsville's Medical Establishment	11
9.	Brownsville Navigation District	8
10.	University of Texas at Brownsville/TSC	7
11.	Brownsville Police Department	4
12.	Public Utilities Board	4

Obviously, the PUB, the University, the Police Department, and Port establishment are recognized as "excellent" by community leaders, and equally obvious is the fact that the city's newspaper, governance, school system, and the sheriff's organization are unesteemed. But how does this compare with the estimations of the general public?

BROWNSVILLE'S INSTITUTIONS EFFECTIVENESS
GENERAL PUBLIC SURVEY

	Good Job	Poor Job	No Opinion
1. Brownsville Police Department	154	35	11
2. University of Texas at Brownsville	152	25	23
3. Brownsville Medical Establishment	144	38	18
4. Brownsville ISD	135	54	11
5. *Brownsville Herald*	134	44	22
6. Public Utilities Board	127	59	14
7. Sanitation	120	59	21
8. Municipal/County/District Courts	119	37	44
9. Sheriff's Department	116	59	25
10. Brownsville International Airport	116	66	18
11. Port of Brownsville	108	45	47
12. Brownsville City Commission	85	71	44

In noting the general public's responses, attention should be paid to the high number of "no opinions" registered for the Courts, the Port, and the City Commission — this may reflect some of the public's relative infamiliarity with those institutions and their functions. At any rate, it adds a degree of "mushiness" to these statistics. Nevertheless, it is clear that the Police Department and University and, to a degree, the Medical Establishment, are highly regarded by all segments of the community — and the City Commission is not. In general, though, the public is much less critical of the city's institutions than is the elite, and even the City Commission, the most lowly-rated of the twelve institutions, was given slightly more "favorable" than "unfavorable" votes. Most surprising is the public's high marks for the local public school system and the *Brownsville Herald* newspaper — two of the least effective and efficient community institutions in the view of the community leaders.

This poll's results will, no doubt, be most welcome at the *Herald* — they apparently are much appreciated by the majority of their readers, the general public. But every thinking person in Brownsville should be troubled by the high marks given to BISD. Virtually every educated member of Brownsville society knows BISD is doing a woeful job in educating this city's youth, and yet, most Brownsville parents apparently think their children are receiving a good education. These parents are satisfied with the system as it is. Since the BISD board is popularly elected and, in turn, appoints the superintendent, there is little chance of a parents' revolt to force significant reform.

Another question in the polls asked the respondents to identify three projects and institutions they believed should be afforded more money and/or effort and three that should be given less. The community leaders gave these responses.

PROJECTS AND INSTITUTIONS THAT SHOULD BE GIVEN MORE MONEY/EFFORT
COMMUNITY LEADERS SURVEY

	Votes
1. Street Repair and Maintenance	38
2. International Bridges	31
3. Beautification of the City	28
4. Building a Convention Center	23
5. Brownsville Independent School District	21
6. Parks and Recreation	20
7. Railroad Relocation	19
8. Street Construction (Beltway)	19
9. Law Enforcement	18
10. Maintaining Air Passenger Service	17
11. Arts/Culture/Library	16
12. Expansion of University/College	15
13. Sanitation	12
14. Port Improvements	5
15. Public Housing	4
16. Provision for Homeless	4

PROJECTS AND INSTITUTIONS THAT SHOULD BE GIVEN LESS MONEY/EFFORT
COMMUNITY LEADERS SURVEY

		Votes
1.	Maintaining Air Passenger Service	36
2.	Building a Convention Center	27
3.	Public Housing	26
4.	Expansion of University/College	20
5.	Provision for Homeless	19
6.	Brownsville Independent School District	14
7.	Port Improvements	12
8.	Arts/Culture/Library	11
9.	Railroad Relocation	11
10.	International Bridges	7
11.	Beautification	5
12.	Parks and Recreation	3
13.	Street Construction (Beltway)	3
14.	Sanitation	2
15.	Law Enforcement	1
16.	Street Repair and Maintenance	1

Notice that these two survey results are in no way mirror images of one another, with results just reversed as some might expect. The building of a convention center and the maintenance of air passenger service are both hot-button issues in Brownsville and elicit strong support from some, stiff opposition from others, and hence, their top ranking as projects least deserving of money or effort. Incidentally, a number of survey respondents wrote in the margins that in voting for BISD as "needing more money/effort," they wished to indicate that more *effort* was needed and *not* more money.

In the survey of the general public, respondents were not confined to three votes and were asked to indicate all areas they felt needed more money and those which should receive less.

SHOULD BROWNSVILLE SPEND MORE OR LESS MONEY IN THESE AREAS?
GENERAL PUBLIC SURVEY

	More	Less	No Opinion
1. Repairing Old Streets	188	11	1
2. The City's Appearance	175	23	2
3. Expanding the University/College	166	23	11
4. Arts/Culture/ Library	165	29	6
5. Law Enforcement	161	33	6
6. Sanitation	159	32	9
7. Port of Brownsville	156	26	18
8. Moving Railroad Tracks Out of Town	152	40	8
9. Building New Streets	148	46	6
10. Parks and Recreation	143	48	9
11. Paying to Keep Air Passenger Service	141	49	10
12. Providing for Homeless	141	55	4
13. Building More Public Schools	140	48	9
14. Improving Public Housing	137	49	14
15. Adding More International Bridges	125	67	8
16. Building a Convention Center	122	69	9

Note, first of all, that the general public would, if possible, like to spend more money in all areas. . . on all projects. But in prioritizing the areas and the projects, there are noticeable similarities in how the elite and the general public would like to see money spent — repairing streets is the number one priority with both groups, and beautifying the city is also very important to both groups — whereas building a convention center is given little support by either group.

But there are some striking dissimilarities as well. For instance, the general public is less keen to build any more international bridges, while building bridges was the elite's second highest priority. In actual fact, there was a very high correlation among members of the general public who did not want more international bridges built and those who identified illegal aliens and crime as being Brownsville's greatest problems. Somewhat anomalous, too, is the general public's strong support for expanding the University — their third highest priority — whereas this project was given little priority by the community leaders. The difference might be, in part, explained by the leaders' greater awareness of other financial stratagems available to UTB/TSC to expand without further burdening community resources. That same explanation might also apply to the Port of Brownsville's disparate ranking on public and elite lists. One heartening aspect of the survey is the public's desire for money and effort to be devoted to improving arts, culture, and the library. It was the public's fourth highest priority, whereas the elite assigned it little importance.

One final, very controversial topic was broached in the surveys: the desirability of building an "alien wall" in the Brownsville area. The question was posed this way: "Some border cities and U.S. government officials favor constructing strong walls or fences at the main crossing points used by illegal aliens. Would you be in favor of building such walls or fences in the Brownsville area?"

SHOULD "ALIEN WALLS" BE BUILT IN THE BROWNSVILLE AREA?
COMMUNITY LEADERS SURVEY

YES	NO	NO OPINION
29	65	6

SHOULD "ALIEN WALLS" BE BUILT IN THE BROWNSVILLE AREA?
GENERAL PUBLIC SURVEY

YES	NO	NO OPINION
90	96	14

There is an important difference here, but the bottom line is that neither the elite nor the public favor a wall at this time. Nevertheless, with the general public it is very nearly a toss up. Perhaps the best explanation for the elite's and public's discrepant views on this issue is that it is the general public that is more susceptible to competition with the illegal aliens when it comes to jobs, public housing, even elbow room in crowded hospital emergency rooms. The community leaders need to be sensitive to this fact.

W.L.A. and A.K.K.

The Ten Most Powerful

In 1987 Russell Richardson and Anthony Knopp published *A Citizen's Guide to Government and Politics in Brownsville* — a brief "self-help manual," as Russell put it, for citizens seeking to know how the city worked and which individuals and bodies were responsible for the various organs of city government. The final chapter of that guide listed the results of a 1986 survey in which the community's elite were asked to identify the ten most powerful persons in the community. One hundred and twenty of the elite were polled — each being asked to rank-order the city's five most influential individuals. Sixty-eight responded (56.5%), and their votes rendered this result:

BROWNSVILLE'S MOST POWERFUL PERSONS—1986
COMMUNITY LEADERS SURVEY

1. Reynaldo G. Garza — Federal Appeals Court Judge
2. R. M. (Bobby) Duffy, Jr. — Chairman and CEO Texas Commerce Bank
3. Emilio Hernandez — Mayor
4. John J. Fitzpatrick — Bishop of Diocese of Brownsville
5. Raul A. Besteiro, Jr. — BISD Superintendent
6. Michael B. Putegnat — TSC Board Chairman
7. Juliet V. Garcia — TSC President
8. Ruben H. Edelstein — Businessman and former mayor
9. Juan Nicolau — Pastor, Christ the King Church
10. R. A. (Ray) Ramon — Businessman, former County Judge

A decade has passed since the 1986 poll and inevitably some of those individuals have passed from the scene or become less active in public affairs, while just as inevitably other individuals have accrued power and influence and risen to replace them.

Using a methodology similar to Richardson's 1986 poll, 185 community leaders were polled in 1996 — 100 of whom responded (54.1%). In tallying the results, as in 1986, a first-place vote was awarded five points, a second-place vote four points, a third-place vote three points, fourth-place two points, fifth-place one point. The poll rendered this list:

BROWNSVILLE'S MOST POWERFUL INDIVIDUALS — 1996 COMMUNITY LEADERS SURVEY

			Points
1.	Juliet Garcia	President of UTB/TSC	188
2.	Gilbert Hinojosa	Cameron County Judge	100
3.	Henry Gonzalez	Mayor of Brownsville	77
4.	Eddie Lucio	State Senator	74
5.	Reynaldo Garza	Federal Appeals Court Judge	73
6.	Mary Rose Cardenas	Businessman/Chairman of TSC Board	65
7.	Filemon Vela	Federal Judge	62
8.	Mary Yturria	Philanthropist	51
9.	Raul Besteiro	Port Consultant	43
10.	Wally Jackson	Superintendent BISD	40
11.	Reymundo Peña	Bishop of Diocese of Brownsville	37
12.	"Nacho" Garza	Commissioner Texas Dept. of Parks and Wildlife	32
13.	Bobby Duffy	Advisor/Director Texas Commerce Bank	32
14.	Fred Rusteberg	President, IBC Bank Brownsville	27
15.	Tony Garza	Texas Secretary of State	27
16.	Andy Vega	Brownsville City Manager	26
17.	Rene Oliveira	State Representative	25
18.	Frank Yturria	Rancher, businessman, philanthropist	20
19.	Juan Nicolau	Pastor, St. Luke Catholic Church	19
20.	Jackie Lockett	City Commissioner	16
21.	Dave Gelfer	Businessman	15
22.	Doug Hardee	Publisher of the *Brownsville Herald*	14
23.	Ben Reyna	Chief of Police	14
24.	Ray Cardenas	Businessman	13
25.	Michael Putegnat	Executive Director of TSC	10

Doubtless the community leaders polled to elicit the above list are in the best position to actually know who wields the greatest influence in Brownsville. Nevertheless, for comparison's sake, and for comparison's sake only, it was decided to also poll the 200 members of the general public who participated in the 1996 telephone survey. Their perceptions were far different from those of the community leaders. Indeed, the majority of the public surveyed could not name a single powerful person by name, and often not even by title. Typical responses being: "Well, I guess the mayor"; or "Maybe the police chief"; or "Whoever's in charge of the schools"; or "What's-her-name. That gal they've got down at the college."

BROWNSVILLE'S MOST POWERFUL INDIVIDUALS — 1996 GENERAL PUBLIC SURVEY

			Votes
1.	Henry Gonzalez	Mayor of Brownsville	47
2.	Ben Reyna	Chief of Police	28
3.	Alex Perez	Cameron County Sheriff	24
4.	Wally Jackson	Superintendent of BISD	16
5.	Reynaldo Garza	Federal Appeals Court Judge	14
6.	Juliet Garcia	President of UTB/TSC	13
7.	Luis Saenz	Cameron County District Attorney	7
8.	Andy Vega	Brownsville City Manager	6
9.	Tony Garza	Texas Secretary of State	5
10.	Eddie Lucio	State Senator	5

THE TEN MOST POWERFUL

(1) Juliet V. Garcia

Juliet Garcia, nee Villarreal, a native Brownsvillite, was born in 1949 as the second of three children and her parents' only daughter. She grew up on East Washington Street a couple of blocks from the old high school (now Central Middle School). Her father, a Mexican citizen, was a janitor at Pan American Airways and later became a customs broker for Pan American and Mexicana Airways. Juliet was just nine when her mother died, and Juliet prides herself on having been a "good daughter" to her father. [When asked what constituted being a "good" daughter to her father, Juliet replies with a glint of humor, "I nagged him."]

After graduating from high school, Juliet decided to forego college and set off for Houston where she started work as a PBX operator. Three months later, a wiser Juliet returned to Brownsville and enrolled at Texas Southmost College. She was just seventeen. Later she transferred to Southwest Texas State University in San Marcos where she enjoyed membership on the debate team. However, before she

— Courtesy Jose Duarte

could complete her baccalaureate, she met Oscar Garcia — her "Rock of Gibraltar" — who had returned to Brownsville after army service in Japan. The two married and moved to Houston where, at the University of Houston, Juliet pursued first a B.A. in speech and English, and then an M.A. in the esoteric discipline of classical rhetoric. Meanwhile, she was having babies: Oscar in 1970 and Paulita in 1971. "I was the pregnant Mexican at the U of H."

After securing her master's degree, Juliet taught briefly at Pan American University in Edinburg and then at Texas Southmost College in Brownsville. But in 1974 she won a Ford Foundation fellowship at The University of Texas at Austin and took a two-and-a-half year leave of absence to complete a Ph.D. in communications and linguistics. One year later, back at Texas Southmost College, and just twenty-seven years old, she applied for the TSC presidency. She was not successful, but, then again, she was not unsuccessful: she was a "finalist" for the position and, perhaps more importantly, she had put community leaders on notice that they had a bold and confident personality in their midst. Her rise was rapid. In 1981 she was appointed Dean of Arts and Sciences and five years later, in 1986, she was named president — the first Mexican-American woman in history to head an American college.

As the college metamorphized into The University of Texas at Brownsville-Texas Southmost College partnership, Dr. Garcia was made dual president of both institutions. In 1994 she was elected board chairman of the American Council on Education. By 1996 rumors were rife that a Clinton reelection might translate into a cabinet-level appointment for Dr. Garcia, most logically Secretary of Education. However, Dr. Garcia dismissed such rumors as groundless, and added, "I cannot imagine going to Washington . . . and I cannot understand the enticement it has for folks."

But clearly, Dr. Garcia feels her years at the helm of the university/college are drawing to a close. She puts it this way: "There is a time for a Churchill and a time for a Chamberlain [readers are at liberty to make their own assumptions as to whom Dr. Garcia is to be equated], and there must come a change for the institution's sake."

When asked what she regards as the greatest problem facing Brownsville, Dr. Garcia thinks for a few moments before commenting: "Responding to the urgent needs in this community: education, infrastructure, growth, leadership. There is an overwhelming imbalance in needs and resources. But we cannot give up . . . . Solving our problems will take very creative and innovative folks — an army of folks — marching in the same direction."

(2) Gilberto Hinojosa

Judge Hinojosa, born in 1952, was raised in Mission where his father was a radio station engineer and disc jockey. Gilberto has two brothers, one of whom is now Port Isabel's city manager. Gilberto graduated from Mission High School and received a B.A. in political science from Pan American University in Edinburg before going on to prestigious Georgetown University in Washington D.C., where he earned a law degree in 1978. There followed a period when he worked for migrant legal aid organizations in Washington D.C., Colorado and, eventually, Brownsville (Texas Rural Legal Aid). He served briefly on the BISD board in 1984, but resigned a year later when appointed judge of Cameron County Court-at-Law No. 2 to complete the unexpired term of Menton Murray, Jr. In 1986 Judge Hinojosa took over the 107th State District Court, and, finally, in 1990, was elected to the state's 13th Court of Appeals in Corpus

Christi. Upon completing his four-year term on the appeals court, Gilberto successfully ran for the office of Cameron County Judge — a non-judicial, purely administrative post — a post vacated by popular Republican Tony Garza whom Governor George Bush Jr. had appointed Texas Secretary of State.

As chief administrative officer of Cameron County, Judge Hinojosa hopes to run the county "the way a business is run" and "to promote the necessary infrastructure to make us economically strong" and stresses that this

— Courtesy Jose Duarte

includes not only roads, highways, and international bridges, but also human infrastructure. He feels fostering a "well-educated, well-trained workforce" capable of attracting industries that "offer good pay, good benefits, and are environmentally friendly" is his top priority. He is optimistic that the county's large, young workforce is a great asset and will attract the desired industries if those industries can also be sure "that they have a well-trained work force to meet their present and future needs."

Gilberto is very optimistic of Brownsville's prospects and thinks the city is "right on the verge of big changes," and that "people won't recognize this city five years after the Los Tomates Bridge is built." Moving the levee back in preparation for bridge construction will free up 950 prime acres for commercial development at the edge of downtown and that, along with the growth of South Padre Island and the Port of Brownsville, will be a further sign that "everything is moving in the right direction." Gilberto concludes: "People might not believe this now, but Brownsville could become a San Diego over time."

(3) Henry Gonzalez

Mayor Henry Gonzalez was born to humble circumstances in San Benito in 1935. He was one of eight children fathered by a Los Fresnos ISD cafeteria worker and bus driver. The family moved to Brownsville in 1943, and Henry eventually graduated from St. Joseph Academy before going on to Texas A&M where he secured a bachelor's degree in marketing and business. Further study at Pan American University earned him teacher certification. For three years he was a Browns-

— Courtesy Jose Duarte

ville fourth grade and junior high history teacher, and then became BISD's Director of Transportation and Supplies.

In 1971 Henry and his brother-in-law opened Oyster Bar Restaurant #2 in Brownsville. (Henry's father-in-law, Justo Barrientes, Sr., had founded the original Oyster Bar Restaurant on Levee Street back in 1950.) And today various members of the Barrientes family, including Mayor Gonzalez, own and operate five Oyster Bar Restaurants strung out across the Valley from Brownsville to Laredo. In 1974 Henry was elected to the BISD school board and served eight years, part of the time as board president. During that time he also helped his nephew, Rene Oliveira, in a successful campaign for state representative. For a decade, from 1981 to 1991, Henry remained politically dormant before re-emerging to defeat Dan Morales for city commissioner. When Pat Ahumada resigned the mayoralty in mid-term, Henry challenged and defeated Ernie Hernandez for the position, and was re-elected in 1995. Asked if he has any higher political aspirations, Henry replies, "No." Asked if he is sure of that, he replies, "Yes. I'm very, very sure of that." When asked to describe his mayorial "style," he responds: "Well, I'll tell you one thing: I don't do anyone any 'favors'; and I never make any 'promises.'"

To the question of whether one of Brownsville's main problems might be its frequently changing mayors — unable to deliver the continuity of perennial mayors Bill Card in Harlingen and Othal Brand in McAllen, Henry is unsure. He does know that Brownsville mayors tend to "get tired," and that to take the unpaid position "you have to want to give." Henry views it this way: "If this city prospers, my business prospers."

In Henry's estimation the city's biggest problem is the exceedingly low tax base: "We have a lot of poor people. We just don't have the tax base to meet infrastructure needs . . . but we're going to have to grow. There are no two ways about it."

(4) Eduardo "Eddie" Lucio, Jr.

— Courtesy Jose Duarte

Senator Lucio, born in 1946, was the second of ten children and grew up in West Brownsville. His father was a Cameron County deputy sheriff. Eddie attended Brownsville public schools and then, in succession, Texas Southmost College, Texas A&I in Kingsville (on a golf scholarship), and finally Pan American University from which he graduated. In 1966 at age twenty, he was hired as a physical education teacher and coach by BISD. Four years later, at the tender age of twenty-four, he launched his political career with a successful run for county treasurer, a post he held for eight years. In 1978 he was elected a county commissioner, but failed in his re-election bid in 1982. At that time he returned to teaching and coaching, but the following year he branched out into business with his "Rio Shelters, Inc." — an imaginative venture whereby Eddie offered to build the

City of Brownsville cost-free public bus shelters in return for exclusive advertising rights to the shelters' walls. It was an offer the city could not refuse, and "Rio Shelters, Inc." soon grew into "Rio Consultants," a business which he still runs and which provides him with the financial wherewithal to pursue politics in a state that pays its legislators only $7,200 a year. In 1986 he defeated Rene Oliveira to gain a seat in the Texas House of Representatives, and in 1990 defeated incumbent Hector Uribe to secure a seat in the Texas Senate. Eddie describes himself as a "moderate to conservative Democrat," and his rigorous efforts to stem lawsuit abuse have earned him the ire of the state's trial lawyers. In just six years Eddie has risen to 13th in seniority in the 31-member senate, and, partly because of the clout that seniority affords him as a Valley advocate, he decided in 1996 to forego contesting retiring Kika de la Garza's seat in the U.S. House of Representatives.

The senator — congenial, unpretentious, and an inveterate hand-shaker and baby-kisser — believes the greatest single problem facing Brownsville revolves around education and youth, and cites the need for "better infrastructure in the school system, modern technology, and well-trained educational personnel." He feels that illegal children in the schools "pose a tremendous challenge" and that drugs are "rampant" in the public schools. He thinks parents need to be held more accountable for their disruly and delinquent children, and favors creating "boot camps" for these youths — boot camps that would be financially supported, not by the taxpayers, but by the parents of the camp inmates.

(5) Reynaldo G. Garza

Native Brownsvillite Judge Reynaldo Garza was born in 1915, the sixth of eight children. His parents had moved to Brownsville from Matamoros in 1901, two weeks after their marriage in the Matamoros cathedral. The father worked at the Yturria Bank and, although not "wealthy," the family "didn't lack for anything." Reynaldo and his three brothers attended Brownsville public schools so that the family could afford to send the four sisters to the private convent school. At the age of seven Reynaldo settled on his life's occupation. Listening with his mother at Mass to the gospel story of the adulteress whom Christ succeeded in sparing with the words: "Let he who is without sin cast the first stone," Reynaldo told his mother, "Jesus was a good lawyer, and that's what I want to be."

In time Reynaldo worked his way through Brownsville Junior College (now Texas Southmost College) by serving as an assistant coach at Brownsville High School. He then went on to The University of Texas at Austin where he received a law degree in 1939. In 1939 he started his own law practice on Washington Street, and

— Courtesy Jose Duarte

shortly thereafter, with the help of *Brownsville Herald* owner Mose Stein, he was elected to the school board in order to push for the revocation of a board decision requiring all teachers over age seventy to retire. In 1942 Reynaldo joined the Army Air Corps and spent most of the war teaching aerial gunnery at the Harlingen air base. At war's end he resumed his Brownsville law practice and won election to the city commission in 1947 — an experience he "did not choose to repeat" when his term expired. Never again would he run for public office.

In the years that followed, his law practice prospered, now as a partner in the firm Sharpe, Cunningham & Garza. He was surprised — but not stunned — when President John Kennedy appointed him a federal judge for the Southern District of Texas. (The appointment came at the prompting of Vice President Lyndon B. Johnson, whom Reynaldo had known since his law school days in Austin. Reynaldo had proven himself useful in a tight 1937 congressional race by introducing LBJ to Catholic and Hispanic voters in Austin.) The decision to accept the appointment was not an easy one for Reynaldo, as it meant exchanging an annual income in excess of $100,000 for a $22,000 salary — "a terrific adjustment." However, he did accept, and he served for eighteen years, when again a president called him. This time it was newly elected Jimmy Carter asking Reynaldo to become his attorney general and, incidentally, the first Mexican-American cabinet member in U.S. history. Despite the unprecedented honor, after conferring with his family, Judge Garza elected to decline. The Judge's eldest son, Reynaldo Jr., himself an attorney with some acquaintance of Washington, proved persuasive. He warned his father that, "Washington's a rat race. You'll die." However, Judge Garza did recommend Judge Griffith Bell of Atlanta for the position and, indeed, that is who President Carter appointed. Not long after that, President Carter phoned Judge Garza again and asked the Judge to join the U.S. Fifth Circuit Court of Appeals in New Orleans. The Judge did so. He explains: "How could you turn a president down twice?"

Since 1981 Judge Garza has held the status of "senior judge" at the Court of Appeals, meaning that in recognition of his advancing age he is granted a much-reduced workload. Nevertheless, when he is not in New Orleans or on the circuit, nearly every day finds him in his handsome chambers on the fourth floor of Brownsville's Federal Building. Now in his eighties, this deeply religious man — a daily Mass-goer — is a figure of immense gravitas. He "wears" power about as gracefully as it can be worn.

As for problems confronting Brownsville, one is that "a lot of people are satisfied with the status quo — especially the chamber of commerce in the not too distant past." But, be that as it may, the Judge thinks: "We're going to boom. I see a bright future if we can ever get our immigration problems solved and our welfare problems solved. . . . I don't want people coming here because they want to get welfare; I only want them if they've come to work . . . like my parents did."

(6) Mary Rose Cardenas

Mary Rose Cardenas, nee Arzamendia, was born in Mercedes in 1932, the oldest of four children. Her father, a second-generation Spaniard, managed a hardware store and sold insurance in Brownsville, where he raised his family. The family had no luxuries but "managed all right," even during the Depression years, thanks in part to Mary Rose's mother's relatives who owned farms in the mid-Valley and who helped provide the family with farm produce and rabbits, fish, and venison. Mary Rose graduated from Brownsville High in 1948 and started attending Brownsville Junior College (now Texas Southmost College), but was made to withdraw by a "very old-fashioned" father alarmed by the large infusion of ex-servicemen who began attending the college on the G.I. Bill. Another blow to Mary Rose's prospects came shortly after: her father became irreparably ill, had to leave his job, and the family was forced to move into pub-

— Courtesy Jose Duarte

lic housing — the Bougainvillea housing project on East Tyler Street. Mary Rose, seventeen, and the family's oldest child, had to become the breadwinner. Her first job was as an office worker and book-keeper at Cisneros Oil Company, but soon she moved on to El Centro Supermarket at Four Corners. In 1950 she was hired by Claire Key of the Credit Bureau of Brownsville, a firm she would stay with for the next sixteen years. She started as a collector of bad debts, but gradually branched into counseling debtors and luring them away from loan sharks, many of whom gouged their clients with 100% interest on short term loans. In the meantime, she married Renato (Ray) Cardenas in 1955. Ray owned a Texaco filling station at Third and East Elizabeth, and began selling used cars off the station lot — this eventually evolved into Ray's Auto Sales. Working side by side, the couple's business prospered and in 1971 they secured the city's Buick franchise. Today Cardenas Motors is recognized as one of the nation's largest Hispanic-owned enterprises, with three dealerships in Brownsville and Harlingen. When asked which of them actually heads the enterprise, as the public is unclear, Mary Rose explains, "The buck stops with him. But I was always an equal with him, even though he's a Mexican from Mexico."

In 1984 Mary Rose was considering a run for mayor, but was persuaded by her friend, TSC board member Jean Eckhoff, that she could better benefit the community by joining the college board. The college was at a crucial stage in its development. Entrepreneur Michael Putegnat was also running and if their elections were successful the threesome could form a "critical mass" in shaping the college's future. The only problem was that either Michael or Mary Rose would have to take on powerful board member Eddie Hernandez in the election. Mary Rose did not think Michael, an Anglo, had much chance of unseating an Hispanic incumbent, so she decided that task would have to fall to her, leaving Michael the easier competition of running for an open seat. When Eddie Hernandez learned that Mary Rose had challenged for his seat, he approached her and pledged he would not fight a "dirty" campaign against her. Blunt-spoken Mary Rose, never one to mince her words, responded: "How could you fight a 'dirty' campaign against me? What's dirty? You could say that I'm fat, but then I could say that you're ugly." In the end Mary Rose's strategy paid off, and Jean Eckhoff, Michael Putegnat, and Mary Rose Cardenas coalesced into a nucleus on the TSC board that forged The University of Texas at Brownsville-Texas Southmost College partnership, surely one of the city's great gains of the past decade and, for Mary Rose, "the most rewarding experience of [her] life."

Asked if now, having served the board for twelve years, the last six as chairman, she might revive her old desire to run for mayor, Mary Rose says, "No, I don't think so." She cites two reasons: for one thing, her health is not as good as it once was; and, for another, she is much more satisfied with, and confident in, the community's present leadership, in particular the Inter-Agency Task Force that has been formed to cooperate in the city's development.

As for the single most important problem facing the city? "Education. Making higher education accessible and improving the products of our school districts, and our UTB/TSC product as well, because we are turning out the teachers. We cannot put all the blame on BISD. We are in this together."

(7) Filemon B. Vela

Judge Vela was born in Harlingen in 1935, the eighth of nine children. His father was a bookkeeper, an occupation that afforded few luxuries for such a large family during the Depression. In his early years Filemon shared a bed with five brothers in the family's non-electrified home on Harlingen's Hispanic west side.

At the age of nine, while listening to an attorney speak at a political rally, Filemon was so inspired as to decide then and there that he would dedicate himself to a legal career. After graduating from Harlingen High, where one of his teachers predicted he would "never amount to anything," Filemon attended

— Courtesy Jose Duarte

Texas Southmost College and The University of Texas at Austin. From 1957 to 1959 he was enlisted in the army, spending much of that time at Ft. Leonard Wood, Missouri — "a genuine hell hole, but a fantastic experience." Upon leaving the army Filemon entered San Antonio's St. Mary's University and completed his law degree in 1962. A year later he opened his own Brownsville law office on Madison Street, opposite the old courthouse. Filemon was elected a city commissioner in 1971, and 107th State District Judge in 1974 and again in 1978. Two years later, at the prompting of Texas' senior senator, Lloyd Bentsen, President Jimmy Carter appointed Vela a U.S. District Judge for the Southern District of Texas. In his sixteen years as a federal judge since then, Judge Vela has tried to demonstrate his "strong commitment to the work ethic" and considers his service "an incredible privilege."

Asked if it hurts him, depresses him, to go home at night, having spent the day sentencing men to long terms in prison and watching them shuffling off in shackles, Judge Vela replies: "Of course it hurts me. Of course it hurts me . . . and the day it stops hurting me is the day I stop being a judge. Anyone who would enjoy sentencing a man to a penitentiary shouldn't be a judge." Judge

Vela estimates he has meted out sentences to between 7,000 to 10,000 individuals, and although he is "not enthusiastic about capital punishment," he currently has a case before the U.S. Supreme Court of an individual he did sentence to die.

As for the greatest problem that faces Brownsville, Judge Vela says it is "the same problem that faces all of our communities in the Valley: education, completing high school. There is one underlying problem in society: not enough people are finishing high school and going on to college. Every major problem that faces this society — crime, welfare, single mothers — is caused mainly by people who don't finish high school."

Another problem the judge sees is that we, as a society, are too critical of each other, we are "not finding the greatness and uniqueness in each person that really exists." And we extend this cynicism to our leaders when it is "unwarranted and unfair to criticize politicians as is being done in this community . . . implying that they're not good individuals. It's very damaging."

(8) Mary Yturria

Philanthropist Mary Yturria, nee Altman, was born in York, Alabama, in 1925, the first of four children. Her precocious father, who had commenced college at the age of thirteen, was a lawyer and a plantation owner. Mary clearly remembers the Depression years when each weekend the family would leave the town of York where they lived and drive out to the family's cotton and peanut plantation to collect the meat, vegetables, eggs, and other foods that would sustain them in town during the week. When she was twelve, Mary's parents

— Courtesy Mary Yturria

divorced, and she moved with her mother to New Orleans. There she attended a private girls' school before going on to Louisiana State University in Baton Rouge — a poor substitute, in her mind, for her childhood dream of studying fashion design in New York City. At any rate, she grew restless at LSU, partly because World War II was at its height and Mary, always a stalwart patriot (her mother claims she was born with a flag in her hand and to this day Mary's most characteristic accoutrement, aside from her outsize glasses, is an outsize brooch of the American flag depicted in rubies, diamonds and sapphires), felt she was not doing enough for the war effort. She decided that her best course was to serve as a stewardess with Pan American Airways — at that time a quasi-official arm of the government that carried only war priority passengers: high military officers, diplomats, and foreign service personnel. Mary was employed on the New Orleans-Latin America run in which the planes hop-scotched through Houston, Brownsville, Mexico City, and down into Central and South America and back. She recalls a wartime routine in which passenger documentation was scrupulous, gold bullion was constantly loaded and unloaded for arcane purposes, and the cabin curtains had to be closed for security reasons when going into such places as the Panama Canal Zone.

When, during the course of the war, Pan Am's New Orleans base of operations was closed, Mary was offered transfers to a number of U.S. cities, including Brownsville. Despite the warnings of locally based stewardesses — "Oh Mary, Brownsville is the worst city in the world . . . you simply can't believe it's part of the United States" — Mary chose Brownsville. She lasted one day . . . and one sleepless night in a Brownsville motel with "roaches that big [her right thumb and forefinger are spanned to indicate a typical Brownsville whopper] running around in all directions."

Fleeing Brownsville, Mary opted to base herself in Guatemala and join Pan Am's U.S.-Latin America flights there. On one flight back to the U.S. she encountered the name Yturria on the passenger manifest and concluded they had a Japanese on board. Only in flight did she meet South Texas rancher and lawyer Fausto Yturria. Fausto pressed Mary to meet his son Frank — truly a kind, fatherly deed as Mary is a handsome woman even in her seventh decade and, as photographs reveal, in those days she was sinfully attractive. But Mary, being engaged to a young man in Houston, was not interested and it was not until some months later when she retransferred to Brownsville that she met Fausto and Frank walking one day on Palm Boulevard near her apartment. Seeing that Frank was "harmless" and "had a cute personality," she agreed to go dining and dancing with Frank (and a chaperone) to Matamoros' famous, elegant, incomprehensibly-named Drive-In Restaurant. They were married in 1947 on Mary's twenty-second birthday and are now approaching their golden wedding anniversary.

It has been a half century of famous friends, travel, and philanthropy for Mary. Frank has become a South Texas Republican powerbroker. [A few hours after this interview Governor George Bush, Jr. was to be their guest at a political fundraiser they were hosting.] The walls of the couple's lovely French colonial-style Brownsville home are studded with the photographs of their famous friends — Nelson Rockefeller, Phil Gramm, the Reagans, Barbara Bush, President Sukarno, Charles Rangel, Imelda Marcos . . . Charles Rangel! What's he doing there hiding amongst all those conservatives? But Mary explains, she occasionally visits the liberal Harlem congressman and his wife in their Washington home to share ideas on the poor — Harlem's poor, Brownsville's poor.

Mary's philanthropic activities include co-founding the "Villa Bethany" home for homeless girls (now Esperanza House), founding and providing the seed money for the Historic Brownsville Museum, acting as a "guardian" of the Texas Historical Trust Fund, and serving as a board member of the Gulf of Mexico Foundation, the Brownsville Health and Education Foundation, the Literacy Center of Brownsville and others. More recently, she has joined the Bi-National Board of Philanthropy — an organization whereby wealthy American corporations "introduce wealthy Mexican corporations to philanthropy . . . something the Mexicans don't have much experience with." Mary adds, wealthy Mexicans need to do this "or else the lid is going to blow off."

Mary believes Brownsville's most pressing problem is education: "Education is a tremendous problem. Our people are ill-equipped to hold down any job of consequence. If we woke up in the morning and not another illegal alien came in, we would still be playing catch-up. We are so splintered. We have a little group over here trying to do something, and another little group over here trying to do something. We all have to get together on this — improve the quality of life in Brownsville so that everyone wins."

(9) Raul A. Besteiro, Jr.

Raul Besteiro, or "Mr. B." as he has been known to countless students and teachers, was born in 1935 a block from Brownsville's Immaculate Conception Cathedral. He was an only child, and his father was in charge of purchasing and stockrooms for Pan American Airways in Brownsville. Raul attended Texas Southmost College, The University of Texas at Austin, and Texas A&I in Kingsville. He majored in zoology and chemistry and hoped to enter medical

— Courtesy Jose Duarte

school, but an illness of his wife intervened. As a result, he needed to find work right away and so hired on in 1958 with BISD as a teacher — a temporary solution to a temporary financial problem. Or so he thought. He stayed with BISD for the next thirty-two years, rising steadily through the ranks: teacher, department head, assistant principal, deputy superintendent of schools, and, finally, from 1976 to 1990, superintendent of a school district that had become the Valley's largest employer.

Since retiring from BISD in 1990, Raul has become the Port of Brownsville's resident consultant. (The Port has another consultant based in Washington, D.C.) He is intimately involved in the railroad relocation project, the planned Port Bridge to Mexico, and the prospective channel dam project. He also feels Brownsville needs to consider now acquiring a desalination plant on Port property to meet the future water needs of the community. In an effort to attract manufacturing lessees (and jobs) to the Port, Raul has traveled to Costa Rica, Honduras, Germany, Japan, Taiwan, and South Korea. For a time it looked as though the Port was to get a Mercedes-Benz assembly plant, but ultimately an unbeatable $250 million incentive package lured the auto manufacturer to Alabama instead. Nevertheless, Raul is very optimistic of the Port's prospects and future expansion, one reason being that the Port's 40,000-acre tract represents "the largest port area in the nation."

Aside from his work at the Port, Raul, along with his wife, owns and operates B's Hobbies, Toys and Collectibles in downtown Brownsville. Also, he is board chairman of IBC Banks of Cameron County, president of the Historic Brownsville Museum, vice president of the South Texas Independent School District, board member of the Texas Turnpike Authority, board member of the Brownsville & Rio Grande Railway, and U.S. Congressman Solomon Ortiz's "lay representative" to the Hispanic Caucus. In 1996 Raul was elected president of the Southern Association of Colleges and Schools — the main educational accrediting agency for the eleven states of the South.

Raul loves Brownsville: "There is no better place to live in the world, and I've been everywhere." He does not believe the city has any insurmountable obstacles, so long as "we make sure all entities unite together as one voice to promote Brownsville."

(10) Wally Jackson

Brownsville's new school superintendent, Wally Jackson, was born in Chickasha, Oklahoma, in 1945, the oldest of three children. He was raised in the army town of Lawton, Oklahoma, adjacent to Fort Sill, where Wally's father found work as a civil servant after leaving the army. Wally finished high school in Lawton and went on to Bethany Nazarene College outside Oklahoma City where he completed a B.A. in social studies and physical education. He taught at Putnam City's Western Oaks

— Courtesy Jose Duarte

Junior High from 1968 to 1971 while simultaneously working on a

master's in educational administration, which he received from Central Oklahoma State University in 1971. Afterwards, he moved to Harlingen, Texas, and began a career as a school administrator, holding a variety of assistant and associate principalships over the next decade and, ultimately, serving as principal of Harlingen High School (2,700 students). In 1982 Wally left education to become a partner in, and general manager of, the Valley-wide Hurricane Fence Company, but returned to educational administration in 1990 and joined BISD in 1994 as an "area administrator" for student services, health, special education, and counseling. In May 1995, upon the resignation of Superintendent Esperanza Zendejas, Wally was appointed interim superintendent and, in January 1996, was named superintendent by the BISD board, under the board's new chairman, John Weber.

Wally believes the city of Brownsville's main problem is the economy — especially the low property tax base concomitant with the city's poverty — and the "tremendous burden" it places on the school district . . . "especially with the number of children we have to educate." Wally "guesstimates" that of BISD's 40,000-plus students, probably between 4,000 to 6,000 are illegal aliens. Asked if BISD didn't have employees whose jobs it was to follow suspect children crossing the international bridges each day to see if they were going to our schools, Wally responds to the negative: "That was the practice some years ago, but it is no longer the case." BISD now studies students' residency documents.

When asked about complaints that BISD students don't seem to get much homework, Wally responds that he doesn't want "homework just for homework's sake." If it is assigned it should be "meaningful homework," and he understands that the teachers often become frustrated because students just won't do the homework.

As to suggestions that "social promotions" ought to be ended, but that many teachers claim there is an unwritten rule at BISD that any teacher who fails more than ten percent of a class will find themselves "in trouble," Wally responds, "I would discount that." There is no such rule, there is no such percentage, and Wally is himself opposed to social promotions. However, if large numbers of students do fail, Superintendent Jackson believes the causes of those failures have to be investigated: "We may have to explore different modalities in the way instruction is provided."

W. L. A.

CHAPTER 14

With the Curandera

The chupacabra *(goat-sucker) was in the vicinity . . . and on every newscast, the front pages of the newspapers, and even t-shirts. Supposedly, a vampire demon that drains blood from goats, the* chupacabra *was the latest manifestation of the mysterious, spiritist side of Mexican folk culture. The time seemed propitious for my foray into this aspect of life in Brownsville. I had no intention, however, of seeking out vampires of any persuasion; my goal was an encounter with a* curandera, *a Mexican faith healer.*

Knowledge of curanderas *is largely a matter of word-of-mouth, but the* Bargain Book, *a local shopping guide, conveniently listed several advertisements for "consultations." Believing arrangements would go more smoothly if made in Spanish, I had Alma, my fianceé, call "Señora Rosita" (not her real name) for directions. The purpose of my visit would be to seek relief for chronic back pain and the consequent minor depression . . . all of which was true.*

Alma joins me at 4:00, and we drive to a brick home in a middle-class northside neighborhood. Señora Rosita greets us, after much doorbell ringing and knocking, and indicates that we should go to the garage door, which she opens from the inside. A clothesline and sheets divide the two-car garage — one side was set up for consultations. Señora Rosita, blond, late thirties, wear-

ing a white pullover and pants, invites us to be seated in front of her desk. A medallion on a chain around her neck shows an inscribed pentagram identical to one on the wall behind her desk. On the desk is a can of "Bless This House" aerosol spray. To our left an eclectic shrine displays images of Christ, several saints, at least two Buddhas, a statue of stacked elephants, an elephant tusk, a death's head statue, and several candles. One of the candles memorializes Pancho Villa, while another bears the inscription "muerte contra mis enemigos" (death to my enemies). I hope I don't become one.

After listening to my tale of woe, Señora Rosita suggests a limpieza *(cleansing), to which I readily agree. She begins by applying scented oils and holy water to a brown egg, then adds three spoonsfuls of salt to a glass of water, all the while offering prayers for a* hermano *(brother) — me. Having prepared a charcoal brazier for burning incense, Señora Rosita places the smoking brazier behind us in the middle of a six-pointed star outlined on the floor and indicates that I should join her. A honking car in the driveway disrupts the ritual — a teenager looking for Señora Rosita's son.*

The curandera *lights a gigantic candle and approaches me to apply oil to my head, chest, and hands. She then hands me the egg to hold between my hands while she reads prayers from a sheet of paper calling on God to drive away any negative forces. Taking the egg in her hands, she thanks God for allowing her to use it to sweep away evil influences, then moves the egg across my body, finally cracking the egg open and into the glass of salt and water. Moving the still-smoking brazier in front of me, she stands on the opposite side and with raised voice orders Satan to depart.*

The denouement of my limpieza *begins with* Siete Machos *liquid pouring into my hands and the* curandera *splashing some on my head, arms, and legs, brushing away the negative energy. After lighting a votive candle on the floor, she returns to her desk and I to my chair. Examining the egg yolk in the glass, she covers it with a cloth, only to remove it for a second examination a few minutes later. She informs me that she could see no physical ailments, but she does find emotional stresses based on worry about the problems of others, who show little gratitude. I couldn't have put it better myself, since her diagnosis confirmed what I'm sure many of us feel.*

Alma discreetly brings up the question of payment. Señora Rosita suggests a ten dollar donation and blessses the money as I hold it in my hand. She observes that if people were closer to God and religion they wouldn't need her services, but many get caught up in the challenges of day-to-day living. Reeking of oil, smoke, and incense, we take our leave. When I relate our adventures to my colleagues the following morning, several suggest other aspects of my psyche that could benefit from treatment.

To complete my research into the spiritist milieu of the local Mexican folk culture, I decided to visit the sources of the oils, incense, powders, and liquids utilized by the curandera. *These are available from a dozen or more outlets in Brownsville (and many more in Matamoros) known as* yerberias. *Yerberia La Azteca is located on Elizabeth Street in the heart of downtown. As I enter the store I am immediately struck by the uncluttered, upscale lay-out and appearance. To the left are shelves of candles bearing labels denoting their dedication or purpose. Directly ahead are glass cases containing hundreds of holy cards,* oraciones *(prayers), and novenas. To my right are cases of incense and shelves of herbal teas, vitamins, and other items typically found in nutrition and health food stores. Ruben, the owner, greets me in Spanish but quickly shifts to English after I fumble an initial question. He claims that Mexican-Americans rarely buy the candles, almost all sales going to Mexicans. He also notes that his store no longer sells the folkloric teas and powders associated with* curanderismo. *In response to my question about* una de gato *(cat's claw), a popular imported herb with reputed healing powers, Ruben produces a scholarly tract in both English and Spanish. He explains that he provides information but finds it risky to make recommendations in this era of excessive litigation. He suggests that I visit another* yerberia *to check out the folkloric teas.*

A few blocks away is the more traditional and cluttered Yerberia La Esmeralda. The owner and several clerks are well-occupied as I enter. Candles are everywhere: "Bingo Luck," Pancho Villa, "La anima sola" (the lonely soul), and El Nino Fidencio (a famous Mexican faith healer). There is a profusion of incenses, perfumes, teas, and a shelf of aerosol cans: "Money House Blessing," Gato Negro de la Suerte *(black cat of luck), and "Love Spray." Though tempted by the latter, I depart before*

*my note-taking makes the clerks and clientele too nervous. The
ready availability of yerberias, several having opened only recently, assures me that this aspect of Mexican folk culture is not
likely to disappear any time soon.*

A. K. K.

The Flavor of Brownsville

Americans driving south from the mainstream United States
to the Lower Rio Grande Valley and Brownsville — to "Occupied
America" — are in for an experience. As they proceed south from,
say, Dallas or Houston, they will get their first inkling of what they
are in for at about San Antonio or Corpus Christi — cities in which
the population scale is already tipping in favor of the Hispanics.
And with every mile southward, aside from the same rural pockets
of Anglos, the weight of the Hispanic preponderance grows relentlessly. By the time Brownsville is reached, one is clearly in another
culture. Brownsville's population is about 93% Hispanic, and that
percentage is apparently increasing: 97% of the Brownsville Independent School District's 40,000 students are Hispanics. Anglos are
downright scarce, while blacks are genuine rarities.

And yet while almost every newcomer's first comment about
the area is "I can't believe this is America!" the second comment is
often, "I can't believe how friendly the people are." These words, so
often a cliché elsewhere, are in this case quite true. The ethnic ten-
sions we hear about in southern California and Florida are happily
absent in Brownsville. Perhaps it has something to do with the
sheer numbers. In California and Florida Hispanics, blacks, and
Anglos are sufficiently strong in numbers to actually challenge for
cultural dominance. Not in Brownsville. There is no struggle. There
is no contest. The culture is Hispanic, and non-Hispanics just have
to deal with that. Once accepted, tension evaporates. Certainly,
there appears to be very little ill will between Anglos and Hispanics:
no name calling; no taunts; no fear of physical violence erupting out
of prejudice. In fact, anyone, Anglo or Hispanic, can walk in any
part of the city at any hour without fear of harassment, and almost
free of danger. (The levee embankments beside the river where the
border bandits operate would be an important exception.) Indis-

criminate violent crime in Brownsville is unusual. There are violent crimes and there are murders, but they are almost always drug related, with both victim and perpetrator being involved in the drug sub-culture, or romance related, with someone "fooling around" with someone else's wife or girlfriend — a suicidally dangerous undertaking in this *machismo* society. But innocent Brownsville residents and visitors do not have to fear physical harm, although they do have to look out for theft: theft of their vehicles, house break-ins, purse snatchings.

Another feature of Brownsville that strikes visitors and new-comers is the poverty — seeing the visible translation of the phrase, "America's poorest city." The evidence is immediate and pervasive. One notices, first of all, that the average age of the cars on city roads is much older than "up north." ("Up north" for Brownsvillites being anywhere else in the country.) There are lots of junkers on the road; lots of vehicles eaten through with rust; lots of patchwork cars with mismatched doors and fenders salvaged from scrapyards. All day long auto-transport trucks can be seen unramping exhausted look-ing cars from "up north" at the used car lots that line the Express-way's Frontage Road. These unwanted discards are purchased at auctions in Dallas, Houston, and further afield and rushed south to the border to be snapped up by a poorer clientele — often first gen-eration Mexican-American families eager for their first car, families taking a big step forward on their way toward the American dream. And these people are partial to big cars — big old Cadillacs, Conti-nentals, and Mercurys — cars capable of handling large families, cars capable of hauling lots of folks. And then there are the people on bikes, not yuppies out for aerobic jaunts on ten-speeds, but poor people and older people without cars or who never learned to drive pumping along on ungeared, wide-treaded, ancient Schwins.

Homes, too, are indicative of the poverty. They are, on the average, much smaller than elsewhere in the nation and usually sim-ple wood framed. A typical Brownsville home will have a living room, two bedrooms, kitchen, and bath. Many are even tinier. Often these homes are very brightly painted in what the unkind might refer to as "peasant" colors: turquoise, pink, yellow, even orange. But regardless of what sophisticates might say, these homes and tones do lend many neighborhoods a festive air, as do the flower gardens that grace many yards. And this is an important point. There are very few what might be called "slums" in Brownsville. Yes, the people are for the most part poor; half live below the poverty line. But in no way should Brownsville's poor neighborhoods be equated to the sullen, burnt-out slums found up north.

Poverty is both relative and a state of mind. It is one thing to feel yourself a member of a despised minority marooned in an urban ghetto surrounded by suburban plenty and quite another to be part of an emotionally intact majority living pretty much as well as everyone else around you. There is no sense of hopelessness or abandonment. Quite the contrary. Poor as many of Brownsville's residents are, many can remember far leaner times in Mexico and can measure how far they've come: they have jobs (even if at minimum wage); they have homes; they have cars; and they are, after a fashion, getting their kids educated. Surely, this represents real success for most, and while, sadly, this success breeds a certain degree of complacency in many city residents, and they may be content to stay on minimum wage (frequently supplemented by Lone Star food cards and public assistance), for many others the taste of success has merely whetted the appetite. Many Brownsville families are living out the classic immigrant story: the first generation struggling to establish a working-class beachhead, making it possible for the second and third generations to forge ahead into new territory — college educations, middle class careers. This is occurring in Brownsville, and that is why this is a city of optimism.

Nor will newcomers to Brownsville only "see" the difference of the border culture. They will hear it also. Spanish is spoken in most of the stores, although shop assistants are usually bilingual and address customers in the appropriate language according to their "look." Seldom do they make a mistake. The Spanish language also permeates the airwaves in Brownsville. Matamoros radio stations pump out *ranchera, tropical,* and Mexican "pop" styles, while their American-side counterparts offer *Tejano* interspersed with disc-jockey patter that flip-flops between English and Spanish — often in the same sentence. Meanwhile, Matamoros and Reynosa television stations, coupled with cable network U.S. channels, enable Spanish speakers to enjoy movies, soaps, variety shows, and news without ever venturing into the English domain.

Mexican culture pervades other aspects of local entertainment. Brownsville's most important civic celebration is Charro Days (a salute to the Mexican cowboy or *"charro,"* as well as the binational community culture). Both Mexican and American holidays are greeted with school celebrations and various gatherings, while sporting victories by either the Dallas Cowboys or the Mexican national soccer team will prompt spontaneous motorcades of honking, decorated cars along Boca Chica Boulevard. Fireworks explode in all parts of the city, not only on the Fourth of July, but also on Christmas Eve and New Year's Eve. The explosions are not limited to fireworks — a steady rat-a-tat-tat betrays the involvement of semi-automatic weapons. The falling bullets dent car roofs and citizens' heads on occasion.

Less raucous entertainment is provided by family celebrations of weddings and *quinceañeras* (a coming-of-age, fifteenth birthday party for young women). Both weddings and *quinceañeras* begin with formal church ceremonies followed by a dinner and a *baile* (dance) for friends and family. Often guests at *bailes* are expected to bring their own alcoholic refreshments, and ice chests are brought by the guests for that purpose. Music for the *bailes* is provided by local bands and depends on the preference of the celebrants for *Tejano, ranchero,* or *tropical.* The cost of these celebrations is often far too much for a single family to bear, but that problem is alleviated by the tradition of the *padrino* (literally "godfather," but here meaning sponsor). An often large number of *padrinos* provide money or specific services for the event: there may be a *padrino* of the cake, a *padrino* of the music, etc. Thus, the community shares the burden of supporting its own celebrations and entertainment.

The Mexican culture also dominates the culinary and gastronomic environment of Brownsville, although American fast-food restaurants have made strong inroads. *Tortilla* factories are found in all parts of the city; many of these also serve the Brownsville Sunday morning tradition of *barbacoa* (barbecued meat from cows' heads). Children especially favor the many *raspa* (snow-cone) stands which offer an incredible variety of flavors such as *leche* (literally "milk," but here a cream). Local H.E.B. supermarkets feature stands where *gorditas* (thick corn *tortillas*) are prepared "while you wait." Meat counters abound with such delicacies as *mollejas* (beef saliva glands) and tripe, which comes in two forms — *tripas* and tripe of *menudo* (a popular soup-like dish). The Mexican poor make a virtue of the necessity of utilizing the unpopular parts of animals.

Fajitas were grilled on Brownsville barbecues long before they crossed yuppie palates in expensive Dallas restaurants.

Not surprisingly, Mexican restaurants abound in the city, and many others find it advisable to include Mexican items on their menus. While some restaurants seek a mixed middle-class and tourist clientele, others presume the ability of customers to order in Spanish and limit their menu to items under $5. Wow-wee Burgers in an obscure location serves the biggest flour tortilla in town, filled with *carne guisada* (beef stew) or other ingredients. Seating is at picnic tables on the porch. Many restaurants open for breakfast and lunch only, offering daily specials such as *chiles rellenos* and *bistec ranchero*. Small Mexican restaurants appear and often disappear with great rapidity.

To those willing to experience more of the local culture than is offered by a casual foray into Mexican restaurants and cantinas, a visit to an *yerberia* or a *curandero* would be instructive. *Yerberias* and *curanderos* form an integral part of a pattern of superstition that is widely accepted, in varying degrees, in Brownsville *barrios*. These beliefs are not limited to the poor and ignorant, however. A notorious murder case in Brownsville a few years ago involved a mother, a member of the city's wealthy and educated Hispanic elite, who consulted and paid a *curandera* to act as a go-between in arranging a "hit" on an Anglo boy who had jilted her daughter.

Curanderos are not witches *(brujos)*, but *brujos* of both black and white witchcraft can be found in the vicinity. *Curanderos* may be used to lift "spells" cast by *brujos* as well as curses resulting from the *"ojo"* (evil eye). Mexican-American children are raised with folktales such as *La Llorona* (the weeper), which invokes the lamentations of a tormented spirit roaming the countryside in search of her lost children. The *cucuy* is a widely recognized Mexican version of the bogeyman.

Much of the pattern of spiritualist belief is associated with organized religion — specifically, Catholicism. Many local Mexican-Americans see no conflict between the two, and often consider their spiritualist beliefs to be an extension of their Catholic faith. There is a particulary strong belief in miraculous intervention and the efficacy of appeals to saints. A few years ago someone noticed that a peculiar formation on the trunk of a tree in the heart of downtown bore a resemblance to the Virgin Mary. Almost immediately, crowds began to gather and police had to be called in to direct traffic. Candles, flowers, and forms of religious memorabilia appeared at or on the tree, vendors dispensed soft drinks, while the delighted owners of the property slapped together a stall and sold photos of the Virgin.

Mexican culture (and its Tex-Mex variant) has such a pervasive influence on the Brownsville community that Anglos moving into the city often experience "culture shock," overwhelmed by finding themselves an ethnic, linguistic, and cultural minority. Their response to this condition varies with the individual: some, like journalist Gerry McHale, embrace Mexican culture wholeheartedly, while others reject it and tend to isolate themselves to the extent that is possible. Most "rejectionists" remain only a year or two, but some Anglos remain for years to enjoy the superficial aspects of the culture while disparaging the values of Mexican society. "Native" Brownsville Anglos have come to terms with the culture, some enthusiastically, others reluctantly. It's entirely possible to weave an Anglo cultural cocoon so as to minimize the intrusion of Mexican influence, but then there would be little point to living in Brownsville.

It is the local version of Mexican culture that provides the unique flavor of life in Brownsville while the charm of the community lies in the ethnic cultural coexistence, the mutual tolerance and, in many cases, the mutual admiration that have evolved here.

W. L. A. and A. K. K.

Appendices

Appendix A

1996 SURVEY OF BROWNSVILLE
COMMUNITY LEADERS

A. WHAT DO YOU THINK ARE THE THREE GREATEST PROBLEMS CURRENTLY FACING BROWNSVILLE? (YOU MAY, FOR INSTANCE, WISH TO CONSIDER ILLEGAL ALIENS, CRIME, CITY LEADERSHIP, THE STATE OF THE ECONOMY, THE STATE OF THE DOWNTOWN AREA, ENVIRONMENTAL ISSUES, THE EDUCATION SYSTEM, AF-FORDABILITY OF HOUSING, PROPERTY TAXES, LAWSUIT ABUSE, GENERAL APPEARANCE OF THE CITY.) HOWEVER, PLEASE DO NOT BE UNDULY LED BY THESE SUGGESTIONS—FULLY EXERCISE YOUR INDEPENDENT JUDGMENT.

1. ____
2. ____
3. ____

B. WHICH, IF ANY, OF THESE BROWNSVILLE INSTITUTIONS DO YOU SEE AS ESPECIALLY EFFECTIVE AND EFFICIENT? CHECK (X) NO MORE THAN THREE.

____ City Commission

____ Municipal/County/District Court Systems

____ Police Department

____ Sanitation Department

____ BISD

____ UTB/TSC

____ Brownsville Navigation District

____ Brownsville Airport

____ Sheriff's Department

____ PUB

____ Brownsville's Medical Establishment

____ *Brownsville Herald*

C. WHICH, IF ANY, OF THESE BROWNSVILLE INSTITUTIONS DO YOU SEE AS ESPECIALLY INEFFECTIVE AND INEFFICIENT? CHECK (X) NO MORE THAN THREE.

_____ City Commission	_____ Brownsville Navigation District
_____ Municipal/County/District Court Systems	_____ Brownsville Airport
_____ Police Department	_____ Sheriff's Department
_____ Sanitation Department	_____ PUB
_____ BISD	_____ Brownsville's Medical Establishment
_____ UTB/TSC	_____ *Brownsville Herald*

D. IN WHICH OF THESE AREAS, IF ANY, DOES BROWNSVILLE NEED TO EXPEND MORE EFFORT AND/OR MONEY. CHECK (X) NO MORE THAN THREE.

_____ Street construction (Beltway)	_____ BISD
_____ Street Repair and Maintenance	_____ Parks and Recreation
_____ Railroad Relocation	_____ Arts/Culture/Library
_____ International Bridges	_____ Law Enforcement
_____ Convention Center	_____ Public Housing
_____ Sanitation	_____ Provision for Homeless
_____ Beautification	_____ Port Improvements
_____ Expansion of UTB/TSC	_____ Maintaining Air Passenger Service

E. IN WHICH OF THESE AREAS, IF ANY, SHOULD BROWNSVILLE EXPEND LESS EFFORT AND/OR MONEY. CHECK (X) NO MORE THAN THREE.

_____ Street construction (Beltway)	_____ BISD
_____ Street Repair and Maintenance	_____ Parks and Recreation
_____ Railroad Relocation	_____ Arts/Culture/Library
_____ International Bridges	_____ Law Enforcement
_____ Convention Center	_____ Public Housing
_____ Sanitation	_____ Provision for Homeless
_____ Beautification	_____ Port Improvements
_____ Expansion of UTB/TSC	_____ Maintaining Air Passenger Service

F. SOME U.S. BORDER CITIES AND SOME U.S. GOVERNMENT OFFICIALS FAVOR CONSTRUCTING VIRTUALLY IMPENETRABLE WALLS OR FENCES AT THE MOST COMMON CROSSING POINTS USED BY ILLEGAL ALIENS. WOULD YOU FAVOR SUCH BARRIERS IN THE BROWNSVILLE AREA? CHECK (X) ONE.

_____ YES   _____ NO   _____ NO OPINION

G. LIST BY NAME AND/OR POSITION THE FIVE PEOPLE IN BROWNSVILLE WHOM YOU BELIEVE TO HAVE THE GREATEST POWER AND INFLUENCE IN THE COMMUNITY.

PERSON   POSITION OR FIELD OF
                                              ENDEAVOR

1. ____________________________   ____________________________
2. ____________________________   ____________________________
3. ____________________________   ____________________________
4. ____________________________   ____________________________
5. ____________________________   ____________________________

Appendix B

1996 SURVEY OF BROWNSVILLE GENERAL PUBLIC

GOOD MORNING/AFTERNOON/EVENING.
MY NAME IS ______________________ AND I'M CALLING ON BEHALF OF THE UNIVERSITY OF TEXAS AT BROWNSVILLE'S SOCIAL SCIENCE DEPARTMENT. WE ARE CONDUCTING AN OPINION SURVEY IN THE HOPE OF IMPROVING THE LOCAL BROWNSVILLE COMMUNITY. WOULD YOU HELP BY GIVING ME YOUR OPINION ON A FEW QUES-TIONS. THIS WILL ONLY TAKE 2 OR 3 MINUTES? THANK YOU.

FIRST, DO YOU THINK BROWNSVILLE SHOULD SPEND MORE MONEY OR LESS MONEY IN THESE AREAS? (MARK + IF THEY ANSWER "MORE"; MARK 0 IF THEY ANSWER "LESS," LEAVE BLANK ITEMS WHERE THEY HAVE NO OPINION.)

___ BUILDING NEW STREETS	___ BUILDING MORE PUBLIC SCHOOLS
___ REPAIRING OLD STREETS	___ PARKS AND RECREATION
___ MOVING RAILROAD TRACKS OUT OF TOWN	___ IMPROVING ARTS/CULTURE AND THE LIBRARY
___ ADDING MORE INTERNATIONAL BRIDGES	___ LAW ENFORCEMENT
___ BUILDING A CONVENTION CENTER	___ IMPROVING PUBLIC HOUSING
___ SANITATION	___ PROVIDING FOR THE HOMELESS
___ IMPROVING CITY'S APPEARANCE	___ IMPROVING THE PORT OF BROWNSVILLE
___ EXPANDING THE UNIVERSITY	___ PAYING TO KEEP AIR PASSENGER SERVICE IN BROWNSVILLE

NEXT, I'M GOING TO READ YOU A LIST OF BROWNSVILLE ORGANI-ZATIONS. PLEASE TELL ME IF YOU THINK THEY ARE DOING A GOOD JOB OR A POOR JOB. (MARK + IF THE ANSWER IS "GOOD," MARK 0 IF THE ANSWER IS "POOR," LEAVE ITEM BLANK IF THEY HAVE NO OPINION.)

______ THE CITY COMMISSIONERS	______ THE PORT OF BROWNSVILLE
______ THE MUNICIPAL, COUNTY & DISTRICT COURTS	______ THE BROWNSVILLE AIRPORT
______ THE POLICE DEPARTMENT	______ THE SHERIFF'S DEPARTMENT
______ THE SANITATION DEPARTMENT	______ THE PUBLIC UTILITIES BOARD (PUB)
______ BROWNSVILLE INDEPENDENT SCHOOL DISTRICT	______ THE BROWNSVILLE MEDICAL ESTABLISHMENT
______ THE UNIVERSITY OF TEXAS AT BROWNSVILLE/TEXAS SOUTHMOST COLLEGE	______ THE *BROWNSVILLE HERALD* NEWSPAPER

NEXT, SOME BORDER CITIES AND U.S. GOVERNMENT OFFICIALS
FAVOR CONSTRUCTING TALL, STRONG WALLS OR FENCES AT THE
MAIN CROSSING POINTS USED BY ILLEGAL ALIENS. WOULD YOU
BE IN FAVOR OF BUILDING SUCH WALLS OR FENCES IN THE
BROWNSVILLE AREA? (CHECK ONE.)
_____ YES   _____ NO   _____ NO OPINION

NEXT, AND WE'RE ALMOST DONE. WHAT DO YOU THINK IS THE
BIGGEST PROBLEM FACING BROWNSVILLE? FOR INSTANCE CRIME,
ILLEGALS, THE SCHOOL SYSTEM, THE POOR ECONOMY, THE DIRT-
INESS OF THE CITY, THE CITY'S LEADERSHIP, THE ENVIRONMENT,
PROPERTY TAXES, LACK OF AFFORDABLE HOUSING, LAWSUIT
ABUSE, ANYTHING YOU THINK OF.   (CHECK ONE OR FILL IN
BLANK FOR "OTHER.")

_____ CRIME   _____ THE CITY'S LEADERSHIP
_____ ILLEGALS   _____ THE ENVIRONMENT
_____ SCHOOL SYSTEM   _____ PROPERTY TAXES
_____ POOR ECONOMY   _____ LACK OF AFFORDABLE HOUSING
_____ DIRTINESS OF CITY   _____ LAWSUIT ABUSE
                                     _____ OTHER:_______________________
                                     ____

LAST QUESTION. IF YOU COULD NAME 3 PEOPLE IN THE
COMMUNITY THAT SEEM TO HAVE THE MOST POWER OR
INFLUENCE, WHO WOULD THEY BE? YOU CAN GIVE EITHER THEIR
NAME, IF YOU KNOW IT, OR THE POSITION THEY HOLD. (DO NOT
PROMPT THEM!)

PERSON   POSITION OR FIELD OF ENDEAVOR
1 ._________________________   _________________________________
2 __________________________   _________________________________
3. _________________________   _________________________________

THANK YOU VERY MUCH FOR YOUR HELP. IT IS APPRECIATED.
GOODBYE.

Appendix C

The Pollster's Report on the 1996 Telephone Survey of Brownsville General Public

General Comments:
What surprised and disheartened me most doing this survey was the apathy and general lack of knowledge demonstrated by a majority of the public with regards to Brownsville. Only a small number employed analytical thinking when it came to spending money: setting priorities and not just giving a blanket response of "yes" to any and all money spending. Only two people asked from where this money was going to come. Surprisingly, not many people hung up, and I got the impression that many people appreciated the opportunity of having their opinion heard. (Some people would get carried away and speak for about half an hour.)

About 60% of the respondents spoke Spanish.

Q. Do you think Brownsville should spend more or less money in these areas?

Comments:
The question that sparked most comment was the one regarding the building of more schools. Many people responded that we need to build for the simple fact of the huge influx of students from Mexico. They felt that increased spending was necessary so as not to diminish the facilities for Brownsville residents. The feeling conveyed was that increased building would not be necessary if only Brownsville residents attended and if the facilities now available were used more efficiently.

Some people commented that improving the city's appearance should rely more on the residents themselves rather than on city efforts.

When asked if more money should be spent on improving Brownsville's arts and culture, large numbers of people couldn't help replying: "What arts and culture?"

Q. Brownsville institutions; good or poor job?

Comments:
City Commissioners — Many citizens were not aware of their function. One comment was that they spend too much time in-fighting.

Courts — Some commented that there were good and bad members of the system; but, overall, generally a good opinion.

Police Department — Doing the best they can with what they have. People with family members arrested did not like the police, and there were some complaints about slow response to calls.

Brownsville Independent School District — Doing well with what they have, a common response. One lady complained that most of the teachers were not educated themselves, let alone able to teach others. Many complained of the strains put on the system by illegal students.

University of Texas at Brownsville/Texas Southmost College —Most people were very positive about the school, although lack of parking was a complaint made by students.

Port of Brownsville — Many people are surprised that the port does not get more attention, believing it is Brownsville's greatest asset and should be our main source of industry. Some believe the tourist potential should be enhanced, and one lady suggested that the place should be turned into a place like the Riverwalk in San Antonio.

Brownsville Airport — This was definitely a controversial topic. Comments ranged from making it a true international airport with flights to Central America to the idea that it should stick to cargo flights. One man commented that he did not feel safe flying out of Brownsville. Many commented that we need more than one carrier in order to have competition.

The Sheriff's Department — Some felt it was bad. Many felt that the department was good, but that the sheriff needed to go.

Public Utilities Board — Common comment: "They must be doing a good job; the rates keep going up." Many people complained about the quality of the city's tap water.

Brownsville Medical Establishment — Many felt that they have improved a lot over the years.

Brownsville Herald *Newspaper* — Generally people like it — good coverage of local news. Those who didn't like it mentioned its lack of quality control. Comments: "If they can get it wrong they will"; "Sometimes they put the wrong date on the paper"; "The most horrid thing I have ever read"; "More news about Matamoros than the Valley."

Q. Yes or No to a Border Fence?

Comments:
Many replied "no" for the fact they felt it would make no difference, the illegals would get in anyway. A number said "yes" because they believed it would reduce crime, but most "yes" respondents gave as their reasoning the need to stop the drain on the welfare system. Those who said "no" usually commented that everyone has the right to seek a better life. (Spanish speakers were more likely to respond in this manner.) One interesting response was to build the wall so that people will stop drowning when they cross the river. The only extreme response was: "Build a six-foot, barbed wire fence from here to California and put machine guns behind it."

Q. What is the biggest problem facing Brownsville?

Comments:
Crime with regards to drugs and youth seemed to be the primary response. Many felt that juvenile delinquency was a big problem. Illegals and the poor economy (especially unemployment) were also real concerns.

Q. Three most influential or powerful people in Brownsville?

Comments:
The ability of the public to answer this question was dismally lacking. Fewer than half the public were able to offer a single name or even cite a powerful office. Of the minority who could name names, Judge Reynaldo Garza was quite popular — one lady commenting that he is "an inspiration to the youth of Brownsville."

Russell Paul Adams
February 16, 1996

Bibliography

Personal Interviews

Agular, David. (Patrol Agent-in-Charge, Brownsville Border Patrol Office.) Interview with W. L. Adams. Brownsville, November 16, 1995.

Alcocer, Manuel. (Staff Manager of Eaton Corporation.) Interview with W. L. Adams and A. K. Knopp. Matamoros, Mexico, July 4, 1995.

Beckwith, Sidney. (Director of Environmental Planning and Safety, Port of Brownsville.) Interview with W. L. Adams. Brownsville, March 4, 1996.

Besteiro, Raul. (Consultant, Port of Brownsville.) Interview with W. L. Adams. Brownsville, April 30, 1996.

Brown, Drue. (Director of Public Relations, Brownsville Independent School District.) Interview with A. K. Knopp. Brownsville, November 17, 1995.

Calapa, Joe. (Owner of J&O Men's Wear.) Interview with A. K. Knopp. Brownsville, September 22, 1995.

Carballido, Raul. (Resident Agent-in-Charge, Brownsville Office of the Federal Bureau of Investigation.) Interview with W. L. Adams. Brownsville, December 18, 1995.

Cardenas, Mary Rose. (Board Chairman, Texas Southmost College.) Interview with W. L. Adams. Brownsville, April 25, 1996.

Cascos, Carlos. (Cameron County Commissioner.) Interview with A. K. Knopp. Brownsville, April 19, 1996.

Cervantes, Robert. (Supervisory Deputy U.S. Marshal, Federal District Court in Brownsville.) Interview with W. L. Adams. Brownsville, December 19, 1995.

Dominguez, Dolores. (Shrimper.) Interview with W. L. Adams. Port Isabel, Texas, September 9, 1995.

Flores, Arnold R. (Lieutenant, Cameron County Sheriff's Department.) Interview with W. L. Adams. Brownsville, December 18, 1995.

Franceschi, James. (Brazos Santiago Pass Pilots Association.) Interview with W. L. Adams. Aboard the *Hai Wang Xing* at sea, March 5-6, 1996.

Galvan, Albert. (District Manager, Brownsville Office of the Social Security Administration.) Interview with W. L. Adams. Brownsville, January 23, 1996.

Galvan, Jose. (International Bridge System Director, Cameron County.) Interview with W. L. Adams. Brownsville, March 7, 1996.

Gonzalez, Henry. (Mayor of Brownsville.) Interview with W. L. Adams. Brownsville, April 22, 1996.

Garcia, Juliet. (President, University of Texas at Brownsville and Texas Southmost College.) Interview with A. K. Knopp. Brownsville, January 11, 1996.

———. Interview with W. L. Adams. Brownsville, May 8, 1996.

Garza, Reynaldo. (U.S. Fifth Circuit Court of Appeals Senior Judge.) Interview with W. L. Adams. Brownsville, April 22, 1996.

Gonzalez, Wally. (Trainmaster, Southern Pacific Railroad in Brownsville.) Interview with W. L. Adams. Brownsville, March 28, 1996.

Greene, Paula. (Chief Inspector, Brownsville Office of the U.S. Customs Bureau.) Interview with W. L. Adams. Brownsville, December 18, 1995.

Guerra, Sonia. (*Ropa Usada* Store Manager.) Interview with A. K. Knopp. Brownsville, September 19, 1995.

Hinojosa, Gilberto. (Cameron County Judge.) Interview with W. L. Adams. Brownsville, April 19, 1996.

Hostetler, Thomas. (Accounts Manager of General Motors Delco Electronics of Matamoros.) Interview with W. L. Adams. Brownsville, September 10, 1995.

Jackson, Wally. (Superintendent, Brownsville Independent School District.) Interview with A. K. Knopp. Brownsville, January 11, 1996.

———. Interview with W. L. Adams. Brownsville, April 24, 1996.

Johnson, Jim. (*Ropas Usadas* Owner.) Interview with A. K. Knopp. Brownsville, September 7, 1995.

Kennedy, Martin. (Vice President of TRICO Corporation.) Interview with A. K. Knopp. Brownsville, August 25, 1995.

Lackner, Bobby. (President of Brownsville Downtown Development Corporation.) Interview with A. K. Knopp. Brownsville, September 22, 1995.

Lard, Ron. (Agent-in-Charge, Brownsville Office of the U.S. Drug Enforcement Agency.) Interview with W. L. Adams. Brownsville, December 19, 1995.

Light, Gere. (Sportsman.) Interview with W. L. Adams. Brownsville, October 17, 1995.

Lopez, Mike. (President of Lopez Super Markets.) Interview with A. K. Knopp. Brownsville, April 11, 1996.

Lucio, Eduardo. (Texas State Senator.) Interview with W. L. Adams. Brownsville, April 18, 1996.

Lund, Mark. (Transportation Planner, City of Brownsville.) Interview with W. L. Adams. Brownsville, March 28, 1996.

Martinez, Jerry. (Jailer, Cameron County Sheriff's Department.) Interview with W. L. Adams. Brownsville, October 20, 1995.

Mena, Arturo. (Patrolman, Brownsville Police Department.) Interview with W. L. Adams. Brownsville, November 11, 1995.

Nieto, Robert. (Patrolman, Brownsville Police Department.) Interview with W. L. Adams. Brownsville, November 10, 1995.

Nunez, David. (Lieutenant, Brownsville Border Patrol Office.) Interview with W. L. Adams. Brownsville, December 23, 1995.

Ocker, Donald. (Meteorologist with National Weather Service in Brownsville.) Telephone interview with W. L. Adams. Brownsville, June 28, 1995.

Parker, Richard. (Program Director, Good Neighbor Settlement House.) Interview with W. L. Adams. Brownsville, January 11, 1996.

Parks, Leslie. (Director, Criminal Justice Institute at the University of Texas at Brownsville.) Interview with W. L. Adams. Brownsville, November 14, 1995.

Paul, Gene. (Geography Professor with University of Texas at Brownsville.) Interview with W. L. Adams. Brownsville, April 19, 1996.

Pena, Ernesto. (Executive Director, Brownsville Housing Authority.) Interview with W. L. Adams. Brownsville, January 24, 1996.

Pena, Minerva. (Corporal, Brownsville Office of Texas Department of Public Safety.) Interview with W. L. Adams. Brownsville, December 18, 1995.

Perez, Fred. (Purchasing Director of Duro Paper Bag Company.) Interview with W. L. Adams. Brownsville, August 22, 1995.

Ramirez, Ray. (Harbor Master, Port of Brownsville.) Interview with W. L. Adams. Brownsville, March 14, 1996.

Ratcliff, Cicely. (Founder and Director, Live Now Ministries, Inc.) Interview with W. L. Adams. Brownsville, January 11, 1996.

Resinger, Tony. (Cameron County Marine Extension Agent.) Telephone interview with W. L. Adams. Brownsville, September, 12, 1995.

Reyna, Ben (Chief of Brownsville Police Department.) Interview with W. L. Adams. Brownsville, November 9, 1995.

Reyna, Nick. (Director of Brownsville Convention and Visitors Bureau.) Interview with W. L. Adams. Brownsville, October 17, 1995.

Rios, Ruben. (Lieutenant, Brownsville Police Department.) Interview with W. L. Adams. Brownsville, November 10, 1995.

Rivas, Dora. (Director of Food Services, Brownsville Independent School District.) Telephone interview with W. L. Adams. Brownsville, January 31, 1996.

Rodriguez, Beatriz. (Nutritionist and Field Supervisor, Food Services, Brownsville Independent School District.) Interview with W. L. Adams. Brownsville, January 30, 1996.

Rodriguez, Lorelli. (Residence Manager, Brownsville Family Center.) Telephone interview with W. L. Adams. Brownsville, January 29, 1996.

Salinger, Leland. (Project Manager of AMFELS Corporation.) Interview with W. L. Adams. Brownsville, August 22, 1995.

Sanchez, Robert. (Production Manager, Tex-Mex Cold Storage, Inc.) Interview with W. L. Adams. Brownsville, September 7, 1995.

Santiago, Sister Fatima M. (Bishop Enrique San Pedro Ozanam Center.) Interview with W. L. Adams. Brownsville, December 24, 1995.

Selby, Paul. (Pilot Instructor with Southwind Aviation Corporation.) Interview with W. L. Adams. Brownsville, August 15, 1995.

Uhrbrock, Michael. (Public Information Director, Texas Department of Human Services, Edinburg Office.) Telephone interview with W. L. Adams. Brownsville, January 16, 17, 29, 1996.

Vega, Andy. (Brownsville City Manager.) Interview with A. K. Knopp. Brownsville, April 18, 1996.

Vela, Filemon. (Federal Judge, Southern District of Texas.) Interview with W. L. Adams. Brownsville, April 19, 1996.

Velazquez, John. (Air Traffic Controller, Brownsville-South Padre Island International Airport.) Interview with W. L. Adams. Brownsville, March 16, 1996.

Villarreal, Jose. (Assistant Director, Brownsville Office of the Social Security Administration.) Interview with W. L. Adams. Brownsville, January 23, 1996.

Walker, John. (Brownsville City Engineer.) Telephone interview with W. L. Adams. Brownsville, June 28, 1995.

Wang, Yu. (Captain of the *Hai Wang Xing*.) Interview with W. L. Adams. Aboard the *Hai Wang Xing* at sea, March 5-6, 1996.

Weaver, Roy. (Manager, Union Pacific Railroad in Brownsville.) Interview with W. L. Adams. Brownsville, March 15, 1996.

Weber, Dan. (Director of Brownsville-South Padre Island International Airport.) Interview with W. L. Adams. Brownsville, March 16, 1996.

Williams, Gordon. (Owner of shrimp boats and Gordon's Bait & Tackle.) Interview with W. L. Adams. Brownsville, September 7, 1995.

Yturria, Mary. (Philanthropist.) Interview with W. L. Adams. Brownsville, April 23, 1996.

Printed Sources

Andres, Evan. *Boss Rule in South Texas: The Progressive Era*. Austin: University of Texas Press, 1982.

Automotive Hall of Fame. "The Story of TRICO." *Automotive Hall of Fame News*. Vol. 25, No. 2, April-June 1991.

Brownsville Chamber of Commerce. *Guide to Historic Brownsville*. Brownsville: Brownsville Chamber of Commerce, 1995.

Brownsville Convention and Visitors Bureau. *Birder's Guide*. Brownsville: Brownsville Convention and Visitors Bureau, no date.

———. *Brownsville and Matamoros*. Brownsville: Brownsville Convention and Visitors Bureau, no date.

———. *Brownsville: 1995 Visitors Guide*. Brownsville: Brownsville Convention and Visitors Bureau, 1995.

———. *Fishing Guide*. Brownsville: Brownsville Convention and Visitors Bureau, no date.

———. *Guide to Historic Brownsville*. Brownsville: Brownsville Convention and Visitors Bureau, 1993.

———. *Marketing Plan Fiscal Year 1994-1995*. Brownsville: Brownsville Convention and Visitors Bureau, 1995.

Brownsville Economic Development Council. *Brownsville, Texas*. Brownsville: Brownsville Economic Development Council, 1995.

———. *Economic Overview of Brownsville/Matamoros*. Brownsville: Brownsville Economic Development Council, February 1995.

———. *Brownsville Visitors Guide*. Brownsville: Brownsville Economic Development Council, no date.

Brownsville Herald. January 1, 1994-May 20, 1996.

Brownsville Housing Authority. *Admissions and Occupancy*. Brownsville: Brownsville Housing Authority, 1995.

———. *Section 8 Administrative Plan*. Brownsville: Brownsville Housing Authority, 1995.

Brownsville Independent School District. *Profile & Initiatives From A-Z 1995-1996*. Brownsville: Brownsville Independent School District, 1995.

Brownsville Metropolitan Planning Organization. *1995-2015 Brownsville Urban*

Transportation Plan. Brownsville: City of Brownsville, 1995.

Brownsville Navigation District. *Directory of Lessees*. Brownsville: Brownsville Navigation District, 1995.

———. *Directory of Port Facilities and Port Services*. Brownsville: Brownsville Navigation District, 1995.

———. *Full Steam Ahead*. Brownsville: Brownsville Navigation District, January 1994 - January 1996.

———. *Port of Brownsville: Your Doorway to the U.S., Mexico and the World*. Brownsville: Brownsville Navigation District, 1995.

———. *The Most Important FTZ on the U.S./Mexico Border*. Brownsville: Brownsville Navigation District, 1995.

Chipman, Donald E. "Alonso Alvarez de Pineda and the Rio de las Palmas: Scholars and the Mislocation of a River." *Southwestern Historical Quarterly*. January 1995.

Cortinas, Miguel P., Jr., Editor. *The Creation of Cameron County*. Brownsville: Cameron County Commissioners Court, 1990.

Crossroads. January 1994 - May 1996.

Curtis, Gregory. "What Does 'Jolt' Mean?" *Texas Monthly*. December 1995: 9, 12, 14.

El Rocinante. January 1994 - May 1996.

Fehrenbach, T. R. *Lone Star: A History of Texas and the Texans*. New York: American Legacy Press, 1968.

Galvan, Jose. *Report on Cameron County International Bridge System*. Brownsville: Cameron County International Bridge System, January 26, 1996.

Kearney, Milo; Alfonso Gomez Arguelles; Yolanda Z. Gonzalez. *A Brief History of Education in Brownsville and Matamoros*. Brownsville: The University of Texas-Pan American in Brownsville, 1989.

Kearney, Milo; Anthony K. Knopp. *Boom and Bust: The Historical Cycles of Matamoros and Brownsville*. Austin: Eakin Press, 1991.

———. *Border Cuates: A History of the U.S.-Mexican Twin Cities*. Austin: Eakin Press, 1995.

"Maquila Scoreboard." *Twin Plant News*. February 1995.

Maril, Robert Lee. *Texas Shrimpers: Community, Capitalism and the Sea*. College Station: Texas A&M University Press, 1983.

Matamoros Economic Development Committee. "Labor" *Matamoros*. Spring 1995.

"Mexico." *Maquila Magazine*. January - February 1994.

MGT of America, Inc. *Brownsville ISD School Performance Review*. Austin: Comptroller of Public Accounts, 1994.

Resinger, Tony. "Aquaculture in Cameron County, Texas for 1994." Cameron County Marine Extension Agency Report, November 14, 1994.

Richardson, Russell C. and Anthony K. Knopp. *A Citizen's Guide to Government and Politics in Brownsville*. Valencia, California: Blue Moon Publishing Co., 1987.

Rio Grande Valley Business. Vol. 3, No. 25. August 29, 1995.

Social Security Administration. *Understanding SSI*. (SSA Publication No. 17-008.) Washington D.C.: Government Printing Office, 1994.

———. *1995 Social Security Handbook.* (SSA Publication No. 65-008.) Washington, D.C.: Government Printing Office, 1995.

Texas Department of Human Services. *DHS At A Glance.* Austin: Texas Department of Human Services, May 1995.

Texas Parks and Wildlife Department. *Texas Commercial Fishing Guide 1995-1996.* Austin: Texas Parks and Wildlife Department, 1995.

Tovar, Joel G. "De Politica y Cosas Peores." Unpublished paper, University of Texas at Brownsville, 1996.

U.S. Department of Commerce. "Local Climatological Data for Brownsville, Texas." Washington, D.C.: U.S. Department of Commerce, 1993.

Vela, Rafael. "An Analysis of the History of the Port of Brownsville." Unpublished graduate paper, University of Texas at Brownsville, 1995.

Walls, Jerry G., editor. "Order Decapoda." *Encyclopedia of Marine Invertebrates.* Neptune, New Jersey: TFH Publications, Inc., 1982.

Zamora, Ronnie. *All About B.I.S.D. 1987-1988.* Brownsville: Brownsville Independent School District, 1988.

Index